Savv

Tips and Tricks for
Winning the Travel Game

Savvy Business Flying

Tips and Tricks for Winning the Travel Game

Colin Haynes

Scott, Foresman and Company
Glenview, Illinois   London

*To Emma, Thomas, James, Robert, and Rebecca—may they
always experience the joy of traveling hopefully.*

The Hyatt Travel Futures Project Report on Business Travelers
(© 1988 Hyatt Hotels Corporation) is the source of certain information
contained in this book and is used with Hyatt's permission. "Hyatt" and
"Travel Futures" are registered trademarks of Hyatt Corporation. The
categories of business travelers, "Eagle," "Family Tied," "Tightrope
Walker," and "Road Warrior," are proprietary to Hyatt Corporation.

Thanks to John McAfee for advice on computer viruses.
Thanks to Dr. Roy Forest and Dr. Mark Gillman for advice on coping
with stress.
Thanks to Michael Whelan, Farad Azima, Ken Skier, William Liu,
Lance Miller, Mark Eppley, and Dave Thomas for input on portable
computers.
Reference to the P.C. Flight Guide by permission from Edward J.
Kligman.
The Foreign Voltage Guide on page 66 is reprinted courtesy of
Hybrinetics, Inc.
Thanks to Captain Tom Bunn and Fran Grant for their comments on
fear of flying.

Photograph on page 274 courtesy of Eastman Kodak Co.

Library of Congress Cataloging-in-Publication Data

Haynes, Colin.
    Savvy business flying : tips and tricks for winning the travel
game / Colin Haynes.
      p.   cm.
    ISBN 0-673-38801-8
    1. Air travel.   2. Business travel.   I. Title.
HE9776.H39   1990   89-28415
387.7'42—dc20   CIP

1 2 3 4 5 6 KPF 95 94 93 92 91 90

ISBN 0-673-38801-8

Scott, Foresman professional books are available for bulk sales at
quantity discounts. For information, please contact Marketing Manager,
Professional Books Group, Scott, Foresman and Company, 1900 East
Lake Avenue, Glenview, IL 60025.

Contents

Baggage   19

The Fear Factor 133

The Health Factor 151

The Efficiency Factor   235

Introduction
Bring back the joy of travel

Travel should be an ongoing passion, a love affair that never loses its novelty and declines into boring routine. The anticipation of a journey, the rising excitement, and the climax of arrival in a place with new experiences to savor should make travel a treasured element of the complete human experience.

Just over a century ago, Robert Louis Stevenson went wandering through Europe and was moved to write that "I travel not to go anywhere, but to go. I travel for travel's sake. The great affair is to move."

Mark Twain also extolled the virtues of travel. "To forget pain is to be painless; to forget care is to be rid of it; to go abroad is to accomplish both." The Bible, in *Daniel 12:4*, emphasizes the benefits of traveling as "many shall run to and fro, and knowledge shall be increased."

We still rhapsodize over leisure or adventure travel. An endless stream of television documentaries, books, Sunday newspaper supplements, and other media stimuli fuel our dreams of journeys to exotic places for fresh experiences. One of the blessings of contemporary business life should be that so many of us not only have ample opportunity to experience the joy of travel, but that our employers will pick up the cost of it.

"The world is his who has money to go over it," said the essayist Emerson, pointing to the major frustration of most travel dreams—lack of finance. The traditional English proverb that "the heaviest baggage for a traveler is an empty purse" underlines the blessings inherent in the business travel expense account.

The magic of travel, however, seems to figure little, if any, in contemporary perceptions of work-related travel, which not only is financed by someone else but comes also with a gift even more precious than money—time. The company pays the airfare, accommodation, and other costs, and also provides the time in which to indulge in the travel adventure. Yet the typical businessperson, who should feel the most privileged of all travelers of all times, seems to be missing the joy of this most fundamentally rewarding human experience.

When I research a book, one of the first steps is to gather previously published data on a subject by sitting down at a computer terminal, accessing a database, and typing in key words to produce relevant references. When I linked *business travel* with such positive associative words as *adventure*, *joy*, *reward*, and *pleasure*, I found very few published references. Just tap in instructions for a key-word search of *business travel* related to such negative associations as *stress*, *frustration*, *hassles*, and *problems* and the electronic circuits buzz with frenzied activity. Hundreds of articles and news reports relating to business travel cover the negative aspects and help to destroy the balanced attitude we should have towards one of the potentially most rewarding aspects of our working lives.

As a young journalist in the 1950s and 1960s, I marveled at my good fortune in choosing an occupation in which I was actually paid to go traveling. Since then, business travel has become a privilege in many occupations, and a large proportion of the population can now participate in what was previously restricted to an elite few. Americans make over a billion trips away from home every year; 36 million of us take 150 million business journeys of more than one hundred miles each way.

We no longer have to wait until age and seniority make us eligible for business travel. The majority of those who travel farthest and most frequently on business are in the prime of their lives, typically between the ages of twenty-five and forty-four. The typical business traveler not only is at an age most suited to extract full enjoyment from travel but has all the other advantages that come from belonging to the most privileged sectors of our society. The business traveler is usually in good health, thus able to cope with the physical demands of journeys. He or she is in regular employment with an income of $40,000 or more. Being comparatively free from financial restraint and with discretionary income enables business travelers to get the most out of the typical trip. It is no problem to afford tickets to a show or museums, art exhibits, and other cultural or purely pleasurable experiences to be found in new places.

In addition, because today's business travelers are typically well-educated—college level or higher—they are well equipped to make the most of the many opportunities for self-improvement and pleasure that travel offers.

Travel can always be beneficial to the individual. It is, said Francis Bacon 300 years ago, "part of education for a young man, part of experience for an elder." In 1778 Samuel Johnson advised that "the use of travelling is to regulate imagination by reality and, instead of thinking how things may be, to see them as they are."

Self-development is an important human motivation to which travel can contribute a great deal. "How much a dunce that has been sent to roam, excels a dunce that has been kept at home!" wrote William Cowper. Thomas Fuller believed "he that travels much, knows much," but warned that "if an ass goes travelling, he'll not come home a horse."

It seems to me that to concentrate on the negative aspects of business travel is to waste marvelous opportunities. Such a mindset prevents us from extracting the joy inherent in travel of all kinds and keeps us from exploiting business travel as a learning experience.

In the corporate world, it has become commonplace to consider travel in negative terms. "Why do we travel so *#!?! much?" proclaimed a headline in *Fortune.*

Business Week commissioned Louis Harris & Associates to poll more than a thousand air travelers in December 1988. Although most respondents still regarded flying as a pleasant experience, over one-third considered a flight as something they "just have to tolerate."

Contrast that attitude with the upbeat approach to flying that I encountered when I interviewed much-traveled jewelry designer Kate Drew-Wilkinson.

"Flying is fabulous," she said. "It is a unique experience that I always feel privileged to be enjoying. Every trip is another opportunity to get different perspectives on the wonderful world in which we live. At lower altitudes you can check out the health of the planet close to, see the impact we are having on it and reflect on our world on a human scale.

"Then, at higher altitudes, a jet airliner gives you completely different perspectives, similar to those we have seen in photographs from space, in which we can sense the unity of the planet and relate our world to the universe. Not only do we get these visual perspectives, but we have also, when flying, the time and the environment in which to relax and think. Flying is a marvelous place in which to develop one's ecological outlook and psychological balance. It is an experience that somebody who has never flown cannot properly understand by trying to imagine it or by watching movies. I feel privileged every time that I experience the joy of flying, whether it is on business or simply for pleasure."

Yet many frequent fliers do not even look out of the window at the incredible wide-screen, full-color, three-dimensional views laid out before them. Others deliberately isolate themselves from one of the most rewarding aspects of travel, the opportunity to meet interesting people.

In a *Wall Street Journal* series on executive travel, some leading businesspeople advised on how to minimize such perceived negative aspects of travel as, horror of horrors, being seated next to other passengers who actually wanted to talk!

"I do not engage in conversations on airplanes," said Jack Valenti, president of the Motion Picture Association of America. "I'm polite but firm, and make it clear I want to work."

"I try to just nod when I take my seat, and not even say hello," Barbara Block, assistant treasurer for an Oregon electronics company told the *Journal.* "Unfortunately, if you say hello to some people, they become very chatty."

Winthrop C. Nielson, senior vice president of a Wall Street investor relations firm, puts off such fellow travelers by wearing casette tape recorder headphones "whether I'm listening or not."

Many travelers pay large sums from their own pockets to upgrade their tickets to get the additional seclusion that first and business class sections provide. Access to the sanctuaries of airline club lounges is a treasured privilege to keep us away from the mass of fellow travelers.

The irritation many suffer from their fellow travelers is slight compared with the annoyances caused by the inadequacies so many business travelers perceive in the service, punctuality, and cost of flying. The celebrated Victorian explorer Sir Richard Burton believed that "travellers, like poets, are mostly an angry race," but he could have had no idea, in this age of comparatively easy, economical, and efficient travel, just how much anger is generated among the nearly half-a-billion passengers who now board commercial airliners in the United States annually.

A passenger plane lifts into the air about every five seconds in the United States, and the pool of anger so many feel about contemporary travel increases, fostering hostility and resentment; this, of course, affects other travelers, colleagues, families, and the many others with whom frequent fliers come into contact. Some of us have developed a rage about flying that burns up a lot of corporate energy better deployed on more constructive matters.

The level of complaints about various aspects of air

travel has risen faster than the frequency of flying, yet I can find little hard evidence that service has really deteriorated to that extent. Business travelers, like most other people, make subjective judgments, and their perceptions are greatly influenced by the prevailing negative attitudes to business travel. In some months the Department of Transportation gets over five thousand complaints on its hot line, and the airlines probably receive at least 10 complaints for every one referred to the DTA.

So we are complaining vociferously about travel hassles and letting the inevitable shortcomings in such a complicated operation develop into major causes of stress and hostility.

There are many stimulating, positive aspects of business travel that should encourage more of us to find the joy and adventure in flying. At the same time, one must be realistic and admit that there are many real problems in business travel. However, they can be minimized by adopting the defensive travel strategies I have distilled from my own experiences as a business traveler for over thirty years and from those that others have generously shared with me.

In the following pages, you will find strategies to help you ease the frustration and practical complications posed by the nearly four hundred thousand flight delays occurring in the United States every year. Being *airport smart* means knowing some insider tips on how airports function and developing a new perspective on them as stimulating places of entertainment. Airports can be fun, and business travelers can enjoy time in them, despite occasional frustrations, such as spending more time waiting to fly than actually flying.

Of course, there is a lot of genuine bad news around about frequent flying. The Air Traffic Controllers' Association has decried "the collapse of public confidence in air travel," and there is some justification in calls for the return of federal regulation. Tough postderegulation competition has tempted some carriers to let maintenance standards slip, and the battle to woo business fliers has become so fierce that some airlines may not be able to deliver on their frequent flier bonus programs.

Postderegulation hub and spoke flight networks have become the unpleasant hub and choke. There is now more aluminum than concrete—a crisis in airport capacity as the number of planes exceeds the ability of many airports to handle them. The shortage of aircrews has led the FAA to warn airlines not to pair inexperienced pilots.

Even the aircrew personnel, for whom delays have become part of the job, find that getting paid to wait around can be as frustrating as it is for their passengers. One Eastern pilot ended a long career by taxiing back to the terminal after a series of delays and walking off the plane—with eighty surprised passengers—into an early retirement.

There are growing concerns about safety as the planes in which we fly get steadily older and their maintenance becomes increasingly suspect. The airlines paid a record $12 million in fines for bad maintenance in 1987. A 1989 Congressional study revealed that air traffic control computer systems are so overloaded that critical information about aircraft speed, direction and altitude can disappear off controllers' screens for as long as 16 minutes. The terrorist threat causes fear and inconvenience, creating further anguish for the estimated 25 million Americans who find flying itself a fearful experience, even without the possibility of a hijack or a bomb in the luggage bay.

Passengers have good cause to worry about health risks also. Air quality suffers when fuel-saving measures cut down on air conditioning and purification. The issue of cigarette smoking raises such passion that there have been near-riots on some flights. Even the water on many planes is not fit to drink because tanks have been topped up from contaminated supplies. Canny aircrew and cabin attendants fly with their own drinking water in bottles.

Baggage is a hot issue too; there are new regulations about what you can carry on and tighter enforcement of allowances. Bags are being lost in disturbing numbers.

As the globalization of business increases and the economic climate boosts export activities, more American businessmen and businesswomen are flying long distances. Jet lag is an expensive consequence, costing millions in lost productivity and impaired performance.

The joy of travel is countered by the physiological and psychological problems associated with business travel, including the symptoms of jet lag and other health consequences of long-distance flight. We must pay more attention to the psychological consequences of prolonged absences away from home and office support systems.

Women—who are now responsible for the majority of new business starts—are flying more frequently, and they often get a raw deal from hotels, airline personnel, and male business travelers.

Bumping is back with a vengeance as the profits squeeze encourages overbooking. Some nine hundred thousand passengers are bumped annually in the United States alone. They all grumble, but few know their rights to substantial compensation for being bumped on a flight or delayed in reaching their destination. The ethical standards of some airlines, particularly as reflected in their advertising, have become so bad that more than forty states are taking the unusual step of initiating tough action to make airlines treat consumers better. Congress is drafting an airline consumer protection bill.

Put the negatives of frequent flying into proportion, however, treat them as challenges rather than problems, and travel can become a joyous adventure again.

Business Travel—The Love-Hate Relationship

Are You an Eagle, a Family Tied, a Tightrope Walker, or a Road Warrior?

"Business travel is both a high-pressure path toward achievement and career advancement as well as an experience wherein the individual can recapture and reestablish feelings of excitement, enjoyment and fulfillment."

Think about that next time your flight has been delayed for the third time at O'Hare, or you arrive in New York but your luggage has gone to Hawaii, or the hotel has lost your reservation and a convention has filled every room in town!

That definition of contemporary business travel comes in the conclusion to the most detailed investigation of the attitudes and problems of frequent travelers—and what should be done to make travel a better experience. Called the Hyatt Travel Futures Project Report on Business Travelers, it involved hundreds of interviews in hotels, airports, and even those frustrating queues that form at rental car counters. Further input came from tape-recorded diaries kept by business travelers while they were actually experiencing the joys and frustrations and from follow-up interviews with both business travelers and the spouses they left at home. The findings from this research were further validated by a telephone survey of 601 frequent business travelers.

WHEN IS TRAVEL FREQUENT?

The definition of a frequent traveler is subjective. Surprisingly, 39 percent of those in the sample said that just one trip a month qualified for the title, while 12 percent thought it should be a trip or more a week. In fact, all the respondents in the Hyatt sample traveled on business at least fifteen times a year, and 53 percent had taken more than thirty overnight business trips in the past year. The report did not quantify the length of flights and number of time zones crossed, which can be important influences on attitudes and stress factors in frequent business travel. For instance, at one point in my career I was making sometimes two or three international business trips a month within Europe. I was chalking up comparatively few air miles compared with those required to qualify for the major American frequent-flier benefits but was spending one-third of my working life traveling to and from airports, waiting in them for flights and baggage, and being subjected to extensive travel-related stress, even though I spent much less time actually airborne than I spent later in my career commuting only occasionally between Africa and the United States.

Changing time zones, which we look at in detail in the chapters on jet lag and international travel, is another important factor not reflected in the first Hyatt report, and it should also be considered when evaluating the stresses and other problems associated with frequent flying. Travelers can go up and down longitudes frequently without experiencing the health problems and other consequences of crossing them east to west and west to east, which severely disrupts circadian rhythms. I find, for example, that I sleep soundly on a night flight between, say, London's Heathrow and Johannesburg's Jan Smuts airports, and I get off in either city ready and raring to go into a productive business day. But go from Heathrow west across the Atlantic to JFK in New York, or worse still across the pole to LAX or San Francisco International, and I stagger down the ramp looking gray and listless, with my mouth feeling like the bottom of a bird cage and probably my head aching and digestion upset.

We have known of the effects of jet lag for a long time,

but when the results of the unique Hyatt project were released in 1989, we got the first really comprehensive picture of the main positive and negative aspects of frequent business flying within the United States, including the associated experiences of ground travel, staying in hotels, and functioning away from office and home. We also learned much about the *cumulative effects* of frequent travel—on the travelers themselves and on their families and companies.

STRESS AFFECTS PERFORMANCE

One of the most startling findings was confirmation that the stress of travel has a marked effect on work performance and family life. Most travelers can maintain their effectiveness only for a few days away, and such absences can have serious repercussions on the family, especially if there are young children.

The Hyatt report showed that women, particularly young women, have far more extreme attitudes to travel than do men. They seem to feel more of the positive benefits, such as career advancement and excitement, but they also suffer more from the stress.

Everybody feels the stress of travel, but surprisingly, the report found that we do not necessarily cope better with it as we get more experienced. The most difficult form of stress is the feeling of being out of control. At the same time, many of us find a wide range of emotional gratifications in frequent business travel, regarding it as a peak experience that offers excitement, opportunities for personal growth, and enhanced feelings of importance.

WHICH CATEGORY OF TRAVELER ARE YOU?

If you are a frequent traveler, then the experience is having a major impact on your life—and the lives of those

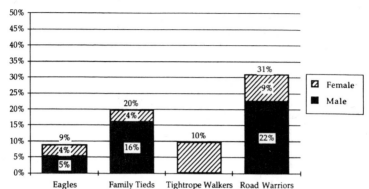

The four types of frequent travelers. This is how the sample of frequent business flyers in the Hyatt study broke down by category. The increasing importance of women as business travelers comes across clearly. This trend will continue as more women become Tightrope Walkers and others move from this category to become Road Warriors or Family Tieds. *Source*: Hyatt Travel Futures Project Report on Business Travelers (1988).

near and dear to you. The negative and positive effects on your mental and physical well-being are important to you and are covered in detail in this book. To understand them better, determine whether you are an *Eagle*, a *Family Tied*, a *Tightrope Walker*, or a *Road Warrior*. Those are the four main travel types who emerged from the Hyatt project. This checklist will show which category is most applicable to you. If you agree with all the points in a particular category, or disagree with only one, then that is your typical travel type.

EAGLES

You enjoy frequent business travel. ☐

You have very positive feelings about business travel. ☐

You enjoy meeting new people and seeing new places. ☐

You feel business travel is important to your
career and personal growth. □

You are probably young and unmarried or
married without children; you travel a lot
and find being on the road stressful even if
it does give you a psychological lift. □

FAMILY TIEDS

You are married, probably with young
children. □

You find that frequent business travel is
stressful, causing conflict with your home
life. □

You do not consider business travel a
positive aspect of your work. □

You rarely feel a sense of accomplishment
after a business trip. □

You would really prefer to be at home with
familiar surroundings and people than in
unfamiliar places mixing with strangers. □

TIGHTROPE WALKERS (Women only)

You are a woman under thirty-five years of
age who has only recently begun to travel
frequently. □

You have difficulty coping with the physical
stresses of travel. □

You feel more powerful when you are on the
road. □

You feel tense and harassed while traveling
and particularly concerned about your loss of
control. ☐

You seek out security and comfort, for
example by staying on the concierge floor in
your hotel and taking a taxi rather than
public transport to and from the airport. ☐

ROAD WARRIORS

You are a veteran business traveler. ☐
You do not feel particularly stressed,
pressured, or nervous when traveling. ☐
You feel heroic when you travel. ☐
You regard travel as an important element in
your work and for your career advancement. ☐
You can cope quite easily with being in
strange places and away from home and
family. ☐
You can function efficiently away from home
for a week or more. ☐

As business trends make work-related travel such an
important element in deciding what occupations or particular jobs to pursue and as a way of achieving promotion, it
is worth assessing which category is most appropriate to
you. Many of the Eagles, who made up 9 percent of the
report's sample, have not been traveling frequently for
very long, and while they may enjoy the experience for its
novelty and challenges, many will change these attitudes
as they get older or acquire more demanding family responsibilities. Some will develop into the veteran Road
Warriors; others will become Family Tieds. There could be

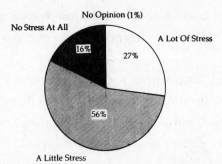

Travelers' perceptions of how much stress travel imposes on their spouses. Business travelers have widely ranging perceptions of the stress that their spouses and other family members suffer because of their absence. *Source*: Hyatt Travel Futures Project Report on Business Travelers (1988).

points in many careers at which value judgments should be made about the impact frequent travel will have on individual life-style aspirations.

Incomes

Certainly temptations in the form of material advantages can come from being a typical frequent business traveler. The sample yielded an average household income of over $60,000, more than three times the income of the average American family. The Road Warriors were the highest paid of all, with the most influential corporate positions in terms of employees controlled.

The Road Warriors include a high proportion of successful managers and executives with positions and life-styles to which many of the younger Eagles and Tightrope Walkers aspire. But there may well be a degree of self-delusion among those who define themselves as Warriors yet are not actually the seasoned travelers who really have adapted well to the stresses of the experience and are more able than the average to sustain high levels of performance efficiency during extended periods on the road.

The Warriors also include a high proportion of the travelholics we look at in detail later in the book—those for whom business travel is a compensation for unsatisfactory home or work circumstances, meeting particular personal emotional needs and undertaken more frequently than strictly necessary to carry out their work.

Gender Differences

The Tightrope Walkers highlight the important gender differences between men and women business travelers, a particularly valuable result of the travel research which the sponsor, Hyatt, says will influence its planning of hotel services and is likely to have an effect throughout the travel industry.

The data collected give a clear indication that women are far more sensitive than are men to the details, both positive and negative, of business travel. As women represent a major growth consumer sector for travel and travel-related services, their impact will be felt increasingly. A precedent is the impact of women on another male-dominated transport area—trucking. Women truckers used their influence to produce significant improvements in many of the facilities offered at truck stops and in the comforts and conveniences of sleeper cabs in the trucks themselves. The report found that no detail was too small to go unnoticed by the typical woman traveler—from cab drivers who drive dangerously to the color of a hotel room, to portion size and the preparation of hotel restaurant food.

The travel experience has significantly different effects according to age, with younger people of both sexes suffering the most stress. Fifty-four percent of those under age 35 who were surveyed said they found business travel stressful, but only 35 percent of those 45 and over felt the same way.

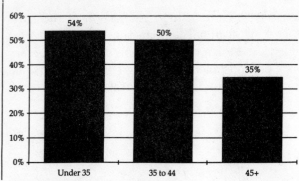

The percentage of those who find business travel stressful varies with age. *Source*: Hyatt Travel Futures Project Report on Business Travelers (1988).

The report concluded that business travel is a heightened and charged experience for most people of both sexes and all ages. Every pitfall is magnified and every small inconvenience is perceived as a threat, both to the business mission on which the traveler is engaged and to the individual's own sense of personal mastery and control of the situation. But, however stressful and frustrating the journey, a business trip is rarely regarded as a completely negative experience. It usually represents progress in work and career, while on a personal level "it rekindles a sense of freedom, offers the lure of adventure, excitement, sophistication and a temporary escape from the more routine worlds of work and family."

Travelholism: Addiction to Frequent Flying and Compulsive Travel

Is your journey really necessary? Or are you an addict to travelholism?

It is impossible to estimate the cost of travelholism because the extent of the problem has never been quantified—and probably never can be accurately. However, clearly it merits concern by budget controllers; travel and associated entertaining expenses are among the largest controllable operating expenses in many enterprises, often surpassed only by payroll and data processing costs.

Corporate budget controllers have been noticeably unsuccessful in trying to trim the billions of dollars spent every year on business travel, despite the added incentive that only 80 percent of meals and entertainment is deductible under the new U.S. tax regulations and average ticket prices are expected to increase by about 10 percent annually. The alternatives to face-to-face meetings created by new technology have not made as big a dent on business travel as was expected. Video and telephone conferencing, for example, are growing only comparatively slowly, as we seem reluctant to curb the extent of our travel despite all the complaints we have about it.

The usual justification for any trip is that the cost in cash and time will be more than compensated for by the greater efficiency achieved by an on-the-spot interface with the problem, or challenge, or exchange of information that is required. Novelist John le Carré's advice on successful spying—"a desk is a dangerous place from which to watch the world"—is adapted to the business environment to justify travel when, in theory at least,

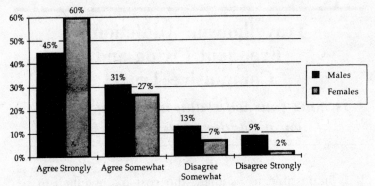

"Business travel is important to my career advancement." The graph of responses to this statement shows that we travel on business so much in part because we believe that it is important to our careers.

technology offers efficient alternatives that do not involve leaving the desk.

This justification is prompting research—still in its early stages—into the extent to which many business travel decisions are not based on a rational assessment of the cost-benefit aspects of making the trip, but stem from emotional and psychological needs that have never been properly examined or quantified before.

Dr. Mark Gillman, one of the world's leading researchers into addiction and the human brain, told me that a very high proportion of business travel could be attributed to these factors and not to a real need to make the journey to perform a task more efficiently.

Expensive Problem

"Travelholism could be a very expensive problem for the international business community, totaling billions of dollars a year—which might add several millions to the operating costs of a single large corporation," he said. "Travel stimulates both chemical and electrical changes in the brain and central nervous system which can have an enervating effect similar to the runner's high that vigorous exercise creates.

"Much of this may result from the series of adrenaline hits that occur before and during any travel experience. Before leaving there is the anticipation and apprehension of new places and new challenges. Our ancestors got the adrenaline hit before they left the cave to go out into a dangerous world to battle or hunt for food. It is an essential function of the body's internal stress system to release this chemical to make us more alert, sharpen our reflexes, and generally equip our minds and our bodies to cope with the threat of physical danger."

Adrenaline Kick

"The typical business traveler, like our ancestors," Dr. Gillman continued, "faces some physical danger on the journey, but his or her real adrenaline kick comes from the intellectual and emotional stresses involved. Instead of leaving a cave, he has temporarily to abandon similar supportive, comfortable and familiar environments at the home and office and go off to strange places to meet unknown foes and do battle for sales or other competitive business objectives. Much may be at stake—promotion, earning the commissions necessary to meet pressing personal commitments, recognition by colleagues, personal self-esteem—a whole host of complex emotional demands that get the adrenaline flowing.

"The frequent flier repeats these stresses and the adrenaline reaction so often that a physical dependency—an addiction—to adrenaline may result. Sportsmen, people in the entertainment world, police and military personnel and others have been found to unconsciously create situations which will stimulate their adrenal glands and give them this high, which can be very pleasurable. Many businesspeople do this to a marked degree in their travel activities without realizing it."

Equating travelholism with workaholism is a mistake that occurs frequently in the business community, positioning both patterns of behavior as being praiseworthy traits reflecting loyalty and dedication to the organization. A West Coast airline even built a whole advertising campaign around a character who never appears because he is whizzing from one place to another on the airline doing deals while back at head office he is the object of much praise and admiration. In fact, however, the executive, manager, salesperson or other employee traveling more frequently than is strictly necessary can be an expensive liability.

Psychological Problems

The urge to travel excessively can reflect psychological problems both at home and at work. It may be a way of manifesting excessive aggression or a subconscious desire to escape from the home or work environments to avoid responsibilities or unsatisfactory relationships. Business travelers' tales often take on heroic proportions in their descriptions of the rigors and challenges that were faced. This can reflect a lack of self-esteem and a subconscious attempt to distract attention from poor performance at the job by elevating minor "conquests" while traveling to being an end in themselves.

A particular aspect of travel that may have addictive properties is the anonymity that results from being away from the symbols of status and identity associated with the workplace, particularly for those who are part of a management hierarchy. It has been assumed in some research that this loss of identity is a negative, stressful consequence of travel, but for some who are dissatisfied with their work situation, it can be a refuge, an opportunity to hide in the crowd and relinquish many responsibilities to the supportive nurturing provided by airline and hotel staff. There are many parallels to the flight attendant in the role played by the Japanese geisha as a reassuring, attentive, and—especially—nonthreatening female.

Boost to Self-Esteem

Indeed, many businesspeople enjoy greatly enhanced status while traveling, their self-esteem being given a boost by the elevation to a superior stratum of society, that is, business or first class, and admission to an exclusive prestige group as a member of one of the airline status clubs with their cozy lounges away from the crowd of "ordinary" travelers. These privileges extend to the hotel, where simply being a regular customer can result in substantially enhanced status in the form of better rooms or admission to special floors. Business travel has many ego-boosting features, which can become disproportionately important for certain types of people or those going through some kind of life crisis. One clear indication of this is that using frequent-flier points to upgrade from coach to higher classes, even on short flights, is so popular that some airlines have been forced to impose severe restrictions on this practice.

So the compulsive traveler is a reality. A vicious circle can occur in which too-frequent absences can result in dysfunction at home and at work, in turn providing an incentive to get away and travel again whenever the opportunity arises or can be created. Some businesspeople even seem to develop a kind of cabin fever, a form of claustrophobia, when travel is denied to them for a period. These are clearly travelholics, and you will find them in most organizations. I know a small start-up company that failed very quickly, largely because the CEO was so dependent on the status and emotional escape that frequent flying gave him that he traveled excessively, endlessly seeking new information and input in the guise of extended test-marketing or "networking," when he should have stuck at his desk and got on with the far more difficult job of creating products and services.

Corporate Budget Losses

"Does the urge to roam lead people to travel more than business really requires?" asked *Fortune* in an examination of the travelholism issue. "The health of corporate budgets, not to mention family relationships, often hangs in the balance."

The airlines' frequent-flier programs must have aggravated this problem considerably. There have been remarkable instances of program members who obsessively pile up miles in ways that make no sense for their employers or even for themselves. Passenger miles have increased dramatically during triple-mileage promotions, despite higher fares and no rational explanation to justify the greater amount of traveling at that time. The corporate community loses thousands—probably millions—of hours annually because travelholics take circuitous routes, make lay-overs, and accept other time-wasting arrangements just to collect additional mileage coupons.

Travelholism is a yuppie-generation problem with symptoms that can be identified readily in some individuals but that are more obscure, often very well hidden, in others. The consequences can be damaging for the individual, for the employer, and for the family, and they represent a challenge that the human resources specialists are not tackling effectively.

Examine Alternatives to Travel

One way of assessing the extent of the problem in an individual—or in an organization as a whole—is to measure attitudes to valid alternatives to travel. These include telephone conferences, exchange of written information and comments, for example by fax, and other means of communicating across space. An employee whose travel activity is high but whose level of long-distance telephone and other communications traffic is low may well be a travelholic. The valid business trip usually generates rather than reduces such communications if it really represents progress on a project. The efficient business traveler seeking to make the trip highly cost- and time-efficient will use advance communications to set up the face-to-face meetings and on return will communicate again to advance the results of those distant meetings. The travelholic will tend not to have so much communication related to his trips because the traveling has to at least some extent become an activity in its own right, not a means to an end.

One of the most promising technological developments to reduce unnecessary travel is the electronic work group. This is an extension of electronic mail in which communications are passed directly between computer terminals. You use a network of electronic mailboxes to send and receive messages. Work group computing takes this into a whole range of cooperative activities linking people through their computer terminals rather than bringing them together physically for a meeting. The big difference between the electronic work group and those participating in an e-mail service is that members of the work group interact through their computers to make collective decisions. A typical application could be a task force to solve a particular problem: perhaps a manufacturing glitch at a distant plant requires input from research and development specialists, manufacturing engineers, and suppliers, all far apart.

Effective work group computing can increase the speed of tackling such a problem by eliminating the need for time-consuming travel. Experience also indicates that among computer literates, the quality of decision taking can be enhanced by such electronic networking, with each specialist able to use the resources available at his or her home base and communicating with less inhibition via a keyboard.

However, there must remain many situations in which

it is beneficial to be on the spot, particularly when human issues are involved.

While travel may become an addiction in itself, it is now being used also as a treatment for a whole range of addictions, from chemical dependency on alcohol and drugs to breaking behavior patterns among chronic gamblers and workaholics. There is now a wide selection of trips customized for groups trying to break themselves of addictions. Apart from the support of a group with a similar problem, this travel experience is considered therapeutic because it breaks behavior patterns during the crucial withdrawal phase.

IDEAL PRESENT FOR THE TRAVELHOLIC

Jet planes have prompted a unique art form that can generate particularly appropriate gifts for the travelholic.

Remarkable paintings are created by Germany's Prince Juergen von Anhalt, who stands behind an engine and throws buckets of paints into the airflow. The paint globules hit the canvas in various abstract forms.

Baggage

Beating Baggage Hassles to Reduce Stress and Increase Safety

Frequent fliers are being obliged to learn a whole new set of rules about the baggage they take with them. We must travel both lighter and smarter, or the commercial air transport system may seize up and we will continue to burden business travel with unnecessary stress and create unnecessary risks.

The writing was on the wall even before the electronic timer in a radio-cassette player detonated a bomb made of plastic explosive and blew Pan American World Airways Flight 103 out of the leaden winter sky over Scotland on December 21, 1988. It did not take the tragic deaths of 271 people on that flight to tell us that air luggage can be fatal, but it was a turning point in passenger attitudes toward security.

Except for regular passengers on especially politically vulnerable air carriers such as El Al, Air India, and South African Airways—which strictly impose baggage control rules—most of us frequent fliers have been playing ducks and drakes with our safety by ignoring luggage regulations. This has been the case particularly on domestic flights in the United States, the world's busiest air routes, where the security procedures for passenger baggage have been woefully inadequate and the intense competition for business since deregulation has led to a relaxation of both the written regulations and the plain unwritten common-sense rules about luggage and safety.

A BILLION BAGS

We check in about 500 million pieces of luggage on U.S. airlines every year and have been carrying on probably a billion pieces more, which we have tried to pack into every nook and cranny on the aircraft. We seem to have developed a neurosis that anything we check in is quite likely to be lost forever as it disappears down the conveyor belt into the bowels of the airport's baggage handling area. As a result there has been a tendency to take as much into the cabin as possible, creating a totally illogical situation unless the flier really cannot spare the usually comparatively short additional time required to collect checked baggage, or has fragile, valuable, or irreplaceable items, which it makes good sense not to relinquish. It would, for example, display too much trust in even the best baggage handling system to check in the only copy of a hundred-thousand-word book manuscript. An author did that—and the airline lost it!

In most situations passengers add unnecessarily to the stress of travel—and impose additional risks to their own health and welfare—by refusing to make effective use of the baggage handling services offered by the airlines and for which they have paid in the ticket price. Instead of handing over our luggage with a sigh of relief and walking onto the plane encumbered only with the things we will need on the flight, we stagger through security checks, around airport shops and restaurants, along endless corridors, and up loading ramps weighed down by heavy, awkward baggage.

When we get on the plane we battle with our own and our fellow passengers' excessive baggage. Congestion and friction result as we try to squeeze our loads into lumbar-disk-displacing overhead bins out of the comfortable reach of all but those of professional basketball players' dimensions or in spaces under seats designed to accommodate feet, not bags. One airline ordered new planes with seat modifications that would accommodate oversized carry-on bags, only to be forced to replace them after complaints from other passengers who were smaller than the average and whose feet could no longer reach the floor when they were seated.

Often flights are delayed by carry-on bags, the plane waiting on the tarmac unable to taxi away from the departure gate because passengers are scrambling in the aisles for the few remaining cubic inches of space in the overhead bins or under the seats.

DELAYS AND STRESS

We add to the discomfort and stress of the journey by having our personal space, already restricted on any aircraft, further limited by the carry-on baggage, which makes it more difficult to relax, eat meals, watch the movie, or stretch out and sleep. Just one example of the consequences is being forced to bend your legs at the knee at an uncomfortable angle, which, with leg and foot movement restricted because of bags, can substantially increase the risk in some people of thrombosis or an embolism.

If you suffer from varicose veins, are a middle-aged smoker, a woman who is pregnant or taking birth control pills, or have phlebitis or some other blood disorder, then you are among the many passengers with a special health interest in the carry-on luggage problem. You have a real need to move your legs around during a flight and get up out of your seat easily and frequently. Your ability to do that can be greatly inhibited by carry-on bags.

Carry-on baggage adds other physical danger to those inherent in flying. We take into the cabin potentially lethal items that in an emergency could become missiles. A bowling ball can roll out of an overhead rack, even in normal flight, and brain an innocent passenger underneath. Other hazards include television sets, golf clubs, auto spare parts, and other miscellaneous bits of machinery and impedimenta. All of these can be transformed into 500 mph missiles in a crash or emergency landing or even just when encountering air turbulence in flight.

Even if you are not hit by a piece of luggage in an emergency, the fact that it is there may kill you. When two Boeing 747s collided on the airport runway in the Canary Islands in 1977, a significant number of the 541 people who lost their lives did so because baggage in the cabin blocked routes to the escape doors. They burned to death because of their bags.

DIABOLICAL GARMENT BAGS

The passion for carry-on baggage led to invention of what many chiropractors with frequent fliers among their patients regard as a really diabolical device—the carry-on garment bag.

"One of the worst things you can do for your back and neck is to fly frequently with a fully loaded garment bag," warns California chiropractor Dr. Roy Forest. "You suspend all this weight from one shoulder, walk considerable distances with it when you are already in a stressed state with muscles tense, and then spend hours in aircraft seats which may cost thousands of dollars each but which are almost always ergonomically awful. Carrying any heavy shoulder bag or briefcase adds to the medical problems associated with air travel. No wonder so many frequent fliers suffer from lower back pain, headaches, and problems with their necks, shoulders, and arms. So much suffering could be saved if passengers just checked in more of their luggage, certainly anything heavy."

There are details later of simple in-flight exercises that Dr. Forest recommends to ease stress and aches and pains, but there is not much point doing them if you are not prepared to eliminate the most common self-inflicted hazard to your joints and muscles. Check in all your heavy baggage, for your own health's sake at least.

The option not to do so is fast running out anyway. The first positive moves to end the nonsense of the sky being the limit for carry-on bags was begun by the more than twenty-thousand members of the Association of Flight Attendants in 1984, when they asked the FAA to bring in new carry-on regulations. Action was slow at first but later gathered momentum.

TOUGHER OVERSEAS

The deregulated airlines in the United States initially resisted doing anything much because of their fierce competition for passenger goodwill and fears that tougher rules would cause additional delays in getting flights away promptly. Now domestic carriers are more strongly motivated to follow the example set by overseas airlines, which because of their perceived greater vulnerability to terrorism, among other reasons, have been far tougher on cabin luggage for a long time. Those that have virtual monopolies on some routes can more easily impose unpopular rules. Airport traffic density overseas tends not to be so great as in the U.S., so the possibility of delays while pretakeoff baggage regulations are strictly enforced is not such a concern. There has been much greater awareness in some countries of the security risks resulting from lax carry-on controls. Particularly on long flights, the increased fuel consumption caused by the weight of excessive cabin baggage can be critical. South African Airways, for example, is banned from landing in many countries, so it has to cover exceptionally long legs without refueling on some of its international routes. Arrive for such a flight with the baggage you are accustomed to take on a typical U.S. domestic flight, and you are in for a rude shock. Everything will be weighed, you are likely to be charged heavily for amounts over your allowance, and what you take into the cabin with you will be restricted. In Hong Kong and Japanese airports, you are quite likely to be turned away at the gate if you have got that far with more than one carry-on bag. Similar policies are now becoming far more widespread around the world.

The FAA regulations that came into force in 1988 limit carry-on baggage to two pieces, but just how big they can be and the flexibility with which the rules are enforced vary considerably from airline to airline, from airport to airport, and even from day to day.

STOW SECURELY

These bags must fit either under the seat or in an overhead bin, the key factor being that it must be possible to secure them during a flight so that they will not move around and become a hazard. In fact, a heavy bag partially under the seat or in an overhead bin with a lid quite likely to pop open in a crash will never be properly secure. But that is the stated object of the rules, and it is in every passenger's interest that they be followed more carefully.

To fit under a typical airline seat, a bag must be no more than nine inches by fourteen inches by twenty-two inches. Even if it is of legal dimensions, such a bag can add substantially to discomfort, stress, and restriction of a passenger's movement during a flight.

The bag to go in the overhead rack must be no more than four inches by thirty-two inches by forty-five inches, which embraces most garment bags if they are not stuffed full of clothes and other items. That size and possible weight slung from one shoulder, picked up and put down several times in the airport, then lifted up and down into the rack or maneuvered into the special hanging section provided on many planes can be very stressful, even do actual physical damage to muscles and joints and send your chiropractor bills soaring. Far better to check it in.

THE GARMENT BAG PROBLEM

The garment bag—especially one that is really well designed and can be put on wheels—is a great piece of luggage, but its widespread use and growth in size have made it a problematical carry-on item posing particular stowage problems. It by no means becomes redundant if it cannot be taken into the cabin, although many garment bags—especially those designed to impress and made of fancy materials that lack the requisite scuff-resistance and other physical qualities—can be damaged easily when entrusted to the baggage handling facilities. One solution is that most airlines in the United States now offer special cardboard containers into which you can slip your garment bag and turn it into a boxed, protected piece of check-in freight.

If a flight is not more than 70 percent full, you may be permitted to have a third carry-on bag. Airlines have been fairly lax about whether a small handbag or briefcase is actually counted in your allowance. According to the rules, a bag is a bag is a bag, whatever you call it or however small it may be, although common sense usually prevails. We are not likely to get to the ridiculous situation in which airline ground staff will measure the dimensions of every piece, but we can expect to see more of the simple gauges found near departure gates in some airports that enable passengers to check if their carry-ons fall within the stipulated dimensions.

The uncertainty of just how strictly the rules will apply is a major hassle for frequent fliers. I've gone past these gauges scores of times with bags that would never fit into them, then one night running late to catch a red-eye special out of LAX was stopped by an airline official and made to go through the routine. There was no way my soft-sided case would fit into the gauge and he sent me back. In a restroom nearby I had to go through the farcical procedure of taking out camera, reading material and other bits and pieces, putting what would fit into my raincoat pockets and draping the rest over me so that the bag could be squashed to fit in the gauge. Then I put everything back in again once on board.

"FREE" ITEMS

Such items as cameras; a "reasonable" amount of reading material; umbrellas; walking sticks and other aids for the handicapped; and infant seats, diaper bags, and other requirements for a young child are not counted, so you can take a lot of junk into the cabin with you if you must. However, every separate loose item is a hassle, adding to the stress and inconvenience of moving around the airport and in and out of the plane.

When I need to travel with lots of carry-on items, my most useful bag is a conventional one, well within the legal limits and with soft sides so that it can be flexible in what it will hold. This flexibility is enhanced by a section that can be unzipped to allow the bag to extend vertically by several inches. The bag has a rigid bottom with four small caster wheels and a clip-on extension strap.

I check in with it in the normal way, keeping out my briefcase, books, umbrella, camera, and other loose items if it is necessary to do so to get past controls. Then, at an opportune moment while waiting for the flight, I unzip the extension and pour everything into the bag, together with any airport shop purchases, snap on the extension strap, and pull the now-heavy bag around after me. This is a particularly useful bag when the climate requires me to carry a topcoat and umbrella, which become a nuisance in the plane or airport building, or on a foreign flight when I have different currencies, passport, ticket and other documentation to add to all the bits and pieces I am trying to control. All these small oddments go securely into a pocket on the side of my wheelie bag.

EXCESS WEIGHT

My wheelie bag has paid for itself many times over in countries and on flights where the weight of checked-in baggage is monitored strictly. I have put lots of high-mass things into my tough carry-on bag, which thanks to its wheels is not stressful or tiring to move around however heavy it gets. It will swallow a sweatsuit and soft shoes with no problem, enabling me to check into a long flight with just the one bag and to change out of my business clothes after takeoff and put on the sweatsuit to be comfortable during the trip.

Incidentally, it's worth emphasizing how much a loose, comfortable garment like a sweatsuit can reduce the stress of a flight. Tight clothes, a girdle, garters, braces, a close-fitting bra, tight pantyhose, even socks with strong elastic to keep them up—all can aggravate in-flight blood circulation problems. It's better to let it all hang out on a long flight, either changing into suitable garments in the airport or cabin or ideally going all the way from home or office at your departure to your hotel or other arrival destination dressed in the most practical frequent-flier garments.

THE IN-FLIGHT ESSENTIALS

The sweatsuit with a T-shirt beneath it gives flexibility in keeping comfortably warm or cool despite the considerable variations that can take place in cabin temperature. Otherwise you need to carry on a sweater, which may be undesirably bulky and difficult to fit into a small bag or briefcase. The only other things that most of us really *need* in the cabin are reading materials, something to write with, any medications, perhaps the personal stereo with a tape or two, an eyeshade or earplugs, eyeglasses or contact lens supplies, nasal decongestant, wallet with travel documents, and a toothbrush and toothpaste.

As far as mouth freshness and hygiene are concerned, you can usually get toothbrush and toothpaste supplied on board long flights, especially in business or first class. I sometimes substitute sugar-free chewing gum, which can be a quick fix for a sour mouth. Chewing gum also helps to reduce the effects of pressure changes in the ears when going up and down, although excessive chewing may aggravate bloating and the muscle tension that causes headaches, stiff necks, and other frequent-flier maladies.

Smart packing for a trip actually starts with the decision whether or not to check in bags, and it is to be hoped that after reading the last few pages, you are far more strongly motivated to do so. Anyway, your choice to do so will inevitably become more limited because of the critical need for greater attention to carry-on baggage rules for security, if no other reason. For example, the electronic equipment that many passengers like to carry with them is becoming increasingly unpopular with both airlines and airport security people and will be subjected increasingly to restrictions, careful inspection, and other hassles that will provide a strong incentive to leave these items at home whenever possible.

BAN ELECTRONIC GADGETS?

Some security experts would like radios, cassette players and recorders, laptop computers, and other electronic devices banned completely from commercial flights— whether in checked baggage or carried into the cabin. As the Pan Am tragedy over Scotland demonstrated, it is too easy for them to be used to disguise bombs. If you take such equipment with you in future, you must expect it to be examined more carefully, causing inconvenience and delays. You may also be asked on occasions to check it instead of taking it into the cabin, which presents packing problems to reduce the risk of damage; we will get to that subject in a moment.

Checking in bags really isn't as big a worry as we often think. The actuarial risks of the airline losing your bags are quite small, and it need not be a disaster if it happens. Let's look at some facts. At times during the postderegulation period, problems with lost bags have become a genuine cause for frequent fliers' concern. The introduction of hub-and-spoke operations, which have required more changes of planes and more complex routing, often resulted in mislaid bags. Even the mergers and other corporate realignments among the airlines had their effects in the baggage handling area, especially when severe cost-cutting measures were introduced and there were serious airline human resource problems, ranging from demotivated, frustrated employees to open strikes such as that against Eastern in 1989.

NINETY-NINE PERCENT SAFE

The performance of the airlines in handling our bags accurately and efficiently has tended to get better since late 1987, when they began to release records of their efficiency in this sphere in addition to revealing how well or badly they were doing in getting the planes off the ground and to their destinations on time. Altogether, the airlines do lose or delay about three million items of checked baggage every year, but it is a minute proportion of what they handle, and many of these mishaps are the fault of the passenger, not the airline. *You have a better than 99 percent chance of being reunited promptly with your checked luggage when you reach your destination if you take a few simple precautions.*

CURBSIDE CHECK-IN CAN BE RISKY

If you go for the convenience of curbside check-in, you considerably increase the risks to your luggage. At major airports the curbside chaos is so great that it sometimes seems miraculous that a bag even gets as far as any plane, let alone the correct one. A common problem is that sky-caps, agents, airline personnel, or the passengers them-selves put inadequate or incorrect tags onto the luggage—or the tags come off.

So before you leave for the airport, remove all the old tags from your bags and label your luggage clearly with your name, business, and destination addresses, plus tele-phone numbers and details of your itinerary. You need to describe the itinerary in case your bags are misdirected and the airline needs to work out the fastest way of getting them to you.

Put the same information inside each bag. Do not put your home address on the outside of your luggage. Thieves have taken address details off the suitcases of de-parting passengers as a way of identifying homes to rob while the owners are away.

If you travel a lot, it may be worthwhile formatting the labels and other information on a computer so that the data can be changed easily from trip to trip and printed out legibly. You could include in your travel database credit card, driving license, passport, and other important numbers, adding details of traveler's checks and other currency on foreign trips. You can even computerize—any word processor will do it—the list of contents that should be inside each bag, printing one copy to put inside the bag and another copy to be kept with you. That's a tough discipline for a frequent flier to maintain, but the contents list helps to reduce the risk of forgetting some-thing important and really pays off if you lose your bag and need to make a claim. *Important note:* In some situations, particularly where being kidnapped or taken hostage is a risk, security considerations should take priority in deciding what information to put on bags.

IDENTIFICATION MARKS

It is also a help to mark each bag with special identification that you can see at a distance and so distinguish it when one of a hundred thousand clones from the same manufacturer arrive on the same luggage carousel, as is probable unless you have exclusive, customized bags—which probably aren't ideal for air travel anyway!

A distinctive mark will also help the airline find your bag if it does get lost. A large bright sticker is a good choice—auto bumper stickers have good adhesive and long distance visibility qualities, but it is difficult finding one that doesn't tend to downgrade the status of your luggage. The words or graphics you can live with on the back of your car to raise a smile or send a message to fellow motorists pose a potential embarrassment as your bags are unloaded under the haughty eyes of the doorman or bellhop at a five-star hotel. A safe choice is something apolitical and environmentally sound—like save the whales or the rain forests. You can even buy fake labels for well-known prestige hotels and cruise ships to give your luggage instant but transparently phony veteran traveler status and a unique appearance. I often stick on a corporate logo appropriate to the client I am representing on a business trip, which also helps to identify me if my client has sent someone to meet me at the airport. Really distinctive luggage labeling—indeed, anything that makes your luggage stand out—makes it riskier for a thief to take and reduces the chance of another passenger picking it up by mistake. However, expensive-looking luggage attracts thieves, and corporate identification may not be wise in high-risk places. (See section on personal safety.)

CHECK THE TAGS

Always—that's *always*—check immediately before parting with your bags that the printed information on your claim check has the same destination code and flight number as your ticket. Even the best-intentioned skycap might have thought you said you were going to Washington, D.C., when you were actually heading for Washington state, or to Paris, France, instead of Paris, Texas. You may get a novice baggage handler unfamiliar with the three-letter airport codes. Or you may inadvertently cause confusion by saying, for example, that you are going to Atlanta, which is true but only as an intermediate stop on the way to San Francisco. You know you have to get on another plane in Atlanta to reach the West Coast, but your bag is not so smart. It will not be able to complete its journey and so will remain in Georgia unless it is tagged correctly all the way through.

Accurate tagging is particularly important if you and your bags are to benefit from the bar codes and laser readers being installed at many airports. This high-tech reading of routing information on the tags reduces much human error, but it is meaningless if the tag is wrong in the first place.

Changing airlines or leaving too short a time between connections, even if successive legs of a flight are with the same carrier, increases the risks of your bags being delayed or lost.

TO LOCK OR NOT?

Should you lock your bags? It makes sense, although most suitcase locks and the small padlocks used on zippers can be either picked or broken open in a few seconds. But locking is a deterrent, especially when your bags pass through airports where theft is a problem. Stealing from bags is easier for handlers than taking away the whole bag and trying to get it past the security screens around baggage handling areas. At London's Heathrow there was once a wave of thefts from passengers' baggage; handlers opened up suitcases and tried on clothes to decide which items to steal. Heathrow was also the scene of the cheekiest airport crime of all—a passenger who left his car in the car park had the good engine removed during his absence and a worn-out one installed in its place.

Heathrow looks after passengers' possessions well these days, but in Third World countries theft from baggage can be a persistent risk; a locked suitcase may well be passed over and reach you intact because thieves will concentrate on easier targets. If you are neurotic about your possessions or have good reason to believe that your bags may be tampered with, it is far more convenient to check that a locked suitcase is still locked than to run a detailed examination of the contents of an unlocked bag.

Also, your bags may be out of your sight on a number of occasions during a trip and be at far more risk of pilfering than when they are checked into the airline's care. The locks will not foil a determined thief, who can force them; slash open the bag with a knife, a favorite trick in some countries; or steal the whole bag. However, a lock does improve your odds somewhat, and it is a precaution against your bag opening accidentally and spilling everything out.

Soft-sided bags and suitcases are more vulnerable to both theft and damage en route than well-built rigid-sided ones, but you get more flexibility in how much you can get into them. It's not a serious trade-off because most bags that sustain damage suffer as a direct consequence of being overloaded by the passenger. This causes the handles, locks, seams, or zips to break, especially when, as inevitably happens sometimes, the bag undergoes rough handling. You increase the chances of your bag being mistreated if it is overweight or has features like awkward handles or loose flaps. These make it more difficult for the humans and the machines behind the scenes processing hundreds of items of passenger luggage every minute.

SYMPATHETIC HANDLES

Select bags with strong, easily grasped handles that are sympathetic to human hands. Bags should have no dangling straps, protruding wheels, hooks, or other appendages that can get caught up in conveyors. Your luggage should have a really tough outer covering. It is no longer a status symbol to have expensive leather luggage, which may look great as you bring it out of the trunk of a Merc or BMW but will soon scuff and tear from the rigors of frequent flying. Anyway, such traditional status materials for luggage as leather usually make for heavy bags—even when they are empty—and unnecessary weight is the last thing you want. Besides, expensive-looking bags are more likely to be stolen on the thieves' reasonable assumption that the contents are probably valuable also.

Although an increasing proportion of frequent flying is done on large jets with containerized freight handling, there is still considerable potential for damage when the luggage is being moved manually outside the containers. Of course, the risk is even greater on smaller planes without containerized facilities, where bags have to be packed in tightly by hand.

At your destination, with a reasonably timed schedule to reduce stress, you should not need to rush to the baggage claim area and wait with increasing frustration if you get there before the luggage from your flight starts tumbling onto the carousel. However, delaying too long can substantially increase the risk of your luggage being stolen.

Many airports—indeed, the majority—have woefully

inadequate security in baggage claim areas. Often the only defense your bag has against a thief picking it off the conveyor and walking out of the airport with it is your own observation. There are not usually sufficient on-the-spot guards, video monitoring, or other precautions. Sometimes strict security is introduced for a time after an epidemic of thefts but then falls away again. In most places there is no official confirmation as you leave the baggage claim area that you have the claim checks corresponding with the tags on the bags you are removing, so innocent mistakes occur as well as outright thefts.

DON'T BECOME A PAWOB

One of the worst moments for any frequent flier is to watch all your fellow passengers depart with their possessions and be left alone with an empty carousel. If you do become a PAWOB—passenger arriving without baggage—all is not lost. Most lost bags are recovered, especially if they have been properly labeled.

Nevertheless, the experience of being separated from your possessions on top of the other hassles of travel can be very stressful. The Hyatt report highlighted how frequent fliers tend to develop routines to give them reassurance on trips. If anything happens to thwart the completion of these familiar routines, there can be a real sense of incompleteness and heightened frustration.

"One traveler who lost her luggage complained to airline personnel, not so much for the inconvenience as for her subsequent inability to 'end the trip,'" the researchers reported. "She felt incapable of reentering the routine world of home and work without taking her clothes to the laundry, finishing up paperwork, and so on. One traveler made it a point to go through his mail before even taking off his coat."

Do not leave the claim area without doing all the right

things either to get your bag back or to ensure that you are properly compensated for its loss. The first thing is to report the problem to the airline's baggage service representatives. Of course, that's also the first action if you observe that your bags have been tampered with in any way or damaged en route. The airline should compensate you promptly for any damage to the bags and consequent injury to the contents which can reasonably be attributed as being the airline's fault. You should either get paid for the necessary repairs or negotiate an acceptable figure for the depreciated value. You will have problems getting any compensation for damage that is demonstrably your fault, such as that caused by careless packing, or for cameras, radios, and other high-value, fragile, or easily stolen items.

DON'T FORGET THE PAPERWORK

Do not even think about leaving the airport until your claim has been properly documented. Your baggage check tabs are the only documentary confirmation you have that you ever entrusted your bags to the airline, so they should not be given up unless details are recorded on an official form, which should state specifically that you have surrendered the tags. Also provide as much information as you can from the copies of your labeling and list of contents. You should receive a file reference number, which will be important when making enquiries about the progress of your claim.

Airlines do take lost luggage seriously and have good systems established to locate items that get mislaid. Indeed, the increased concerns about security against terrorist attack should substantially reduce further the already very small proportion of checked bags that get lost. It is a prime security requirement that luggage put on a plane should have a matching passenger to go with it, on the assumption that most terrorists tempted to plant bombs are not out to commit suicide as well. That is one of the reasons why flights these days are delayed if passengers who have checked in fail to board. There have been numerous occasions when, the missing person failing to turn up, the passengers and all the luggage are unloaded and matched up again.

GETTING COMPENSATION

You have a 98 percent or better chance that your missing bags will turn up—but it may take time. If they missed your flight, the airline will try hard to get them on the next one and reunite you with your possessions after only a short delay. You do not need to hang around the airport waiting, but expect the airline to take reasonable steps to deliver your bags to your hotel or wherever you are staying or working.

If your bags have gone to the other side of the country—or the world—on the wrong plane, there will inevitably be a longer delay, which may be very inconvenient. If you are away from home and will need emergency replacements, the airport staff have the discretion to advance you money. About $30 a day is typical, but guidelines vary considerably; some carriers are much better than others.

Even with the most generous, you cannot expect a voucher for $1,000 to get a temporary replacement for the Dior gown or Saville Row tuxedo you were planning to wear that evening. But you should at least be helped to rent clothes or even buy some essentials to tide you over. These arrangements are intended to be limited to necessities, and whether you get a cash advance or an agreement—in writing—that you will be reimbursed for emergency expenses, you should keep all receipts.

INVALUABLE CONTENTS LIST

The contents lists for the missing bags will be invaluable and should state if any of the items are new. The airlines are not keen to compensate you to replace old lost clothes with new ones. On other items they will probably encourge you to rent where possible rather than buy replacements because there is such a good chance that the lost bags will be found. You have little if any recourse if you have checked in goods that will be spoiled by delay, even if the airline is at fault.

You may have difficulty getting your bag officially listed as lost for some time. Certainly it will not be listed for several days as the search for it continues. It may take as long as a year before the airline finally accepts that your bag is lost for good, not just strayed, but that is unreasonable and you should complain vociferously if there are excessive delays in processing your claim. When your bag is officially listed as lost, the search for it may well go on and the bag still be found, so don't give up all hope.

If you cannot live without what you have lost, or it is another only copy of a hundred-thousand-word manuscript representing a lifetime's work, you can always go to Alabama. Permanently lost luggage doesn't finish up at some great eternally revolving carousel in the sky. Most unclaimed baggage in the United States goes to Scottsboro, Alabama, where contractors buy it from the airlines to retail again. But to find any one item among the thousands that pour into the little town is worse than looking for a needle in a haystack.

KEEP RECEIPTS

You may be required to complete further documentation before your claim for compensation is processed, and you will probably have to produce evidence, such as receipts or credit card records, about the age and value of more expensive missing items. The airlines get a substantial number of fraudulent claims, so they are naturally suspicious, but if yours is genuine, you should get paid within three months or so. You may have to do some haggling, and you cannot expect more than the legal limit of $1250 per person on U.S. domestic flights. You can increase this by paying extra for a higher valuation of your luggage when you check it in, but the airline may refuse to increase its liability if it considers the risk too great, for example, for fragile items or for valuables that could be stolen easily.

INTERNATIONAL LIMITS

The maximum liability for bags lost on international flights is set by the Warsaw Convention in a formula that limits value, calculated in gold French francs, to checked-in weight. This worked out to just over $9 per pound at the time of writing. To be able to make a claim, you need the weight of checked-in bags recorded on your ticket, which should happen automatically. However, many airlines have a policy, detailed on the ticket, of assuming a certain weight—usually 70 pounds or 32 kilos—for each checked bag. This may well limit your claim even more and make baggage insurance purchased before the flight a wise investment. However, check first whether your homeowner's policy provides sufficient coverage.

HAZARDOUS BAGGAGE

Don't claim if you have packed any of the long list of hazardous prohibited items—indeed, don't ever try to buck the rules about what you may take on commerical aircraft.

The physical risk to yourself and other passengers can be high—as are the punishments, up to $25,000 in fines and five years in jail in the United States, sometimes more overseas.

Employers may be liable to the same penalties if employees traveling on business break the hazardous items rules.

The main banned items are those that can cause damage—and that includes pressurized aerosols as well as explosives. Aerosols just do not belong on a frequent flier's packing list, nor do any corrosive or inflammable substances. Even a tube of adhesive or a bottle of cleaning fluid can be extremely dangerous, and you should carry book or boxed safety matches with you, not put them in your checked luggage.

Explosives of all kinds are banned, although there are exceptions for personal and sporting ammunition, which must be properly packed and checked in, not carried into the cabin with you. Radioactive materials and compressed gases are out also, although you may be able to make advance arrangements for them to accompany you on the flight in a special freight area of the aircraft.

DISGUISED BOMBS

The ease with which plastic explosive can be concealed in electronic gadgets means that these items may well be scrutinized very carefully, so you should keep them readily accessible, not at the bottom of a carefully packed suitcase. Radios, recorders, video equipment, and the like should be marked with your name and address. You may be required to operate them to verify that they have not been converted into bombs, so batteries should be fresh or charged up.

It may well become the practice on some airlines and in some countries not to allow electronic devices in

checked baggage at all because conventional security
equipment—notably x-rays and sniffing devices—have
great difficulty identifying new types of plastic. Electronic
devices may increasingly have to be carried by passengers
so that they are available for detailed hand examination—
another incentive to leave them behind wherever possible. Indeed, the persistent message throughout any discussion of the frequent flier's baggage arrangement is the
need to travel light.

Seven-Step Frequent Flier's Low-Stress Baggage Plan

THE ART OF LEAVING THINGS BEHIND

Traveling light starts with the initial planning of a trip. The more experienced the traveler, the more skilled he or she is at leaving things behind. Some Road Warriors have got it down to a fine art, and I am indebted to those frequent flier veterans who shared their packing expertise with me.

This list is distilled from that expertise—ranging from multinational corporation executives to salespeople, from foreign correspondents to flight attendants.

Step 1. To Carry On, or Not to Carry On— That Is the Question

Your whole baggage strategy hinges on whether you are going to check your bags or will carry everything with you into the cabin. That will be dictated largely by the clothes you take, which in turn will be influenced by such factors as

- *Length of the trip*
- *The type of business you are conducting*
- *The climate at your destination*

Once having decided whether the luggage needs and other circumstances make it appropriate to go for minimal carry-on baggage or more generous checked bags, you can start refining your list of what to take and what to leave behind.

Step 2. Eliminate the Unnecessary

You now have to compromise between what you want to take and what you are able to put into your baggage. It is far more difficult if you are going the carry-on route, in which case all but the essentials must be left behind.

The length of the trip, your activities on it, and the climate will have the most impact on the type and quantity of clothing needed, influenced by your personal preferences about changing. Even when I was a wire service war correspondent, I always managed to plan with reasonable success for at least a daily change of underclothes and socks, twice daily in the tropics or hot summer weather. It's good for personal morale, quite apart from combating such undesirable consequences of overused undergarments as offensive body odor and jock itch! Some passengers find being in unfresh clothes, even if they appear to be clean and presentable, a significant cause of stress and discomfort.

Some veteran travelers favor a policy of pack less and take more cash, using hotel laundry services extensively. However, as far as underwear is concerned, I support the philosophy of taking enough for the trip of a type that I can, if necessary, launder myself in the hotel bathroom overnight. Light cotton pants and the open-weave type of undervest both pack compactly and wash and dry easily. The vest—a refinement of the string vests that those working in very cold conditions favor—provides next-to-the-skin insulation, which makes it practical for both warm and cold weather. The insulating air pockets in the fabric's weave have the ability to adjust thermal values to keep you comfortable in a wide range of ambient temperatures, which reduces somewhat your need to pack in anticipation of environmental extremes. Anyway, insulation close to the body is by far the most effective, and with a good-quality open-weave vest I can get by in most places with a summer-weight business suit and a raincoat, without a bulky overcoat or heavy jacket and trousers.

Shoes are among the heaviest and bulkiest clothing items, and the consensus of my travel light experts is that two pairs are a minimum on all but very short trips because of the strange need to rest shoes, not wear the same ones day after day, especially if you do much walking. Most business trips—except to California, where you may get away with sneakers all the time!—require a reasonably formal pair of shoes for both work during the day and going out to restaurants and shows in the evening. I used to take a pair of all-leather shoes with me for the more formal occasions and either jogging shoes or slip-on casuals according to my needs for other times during the trip. Now there are some great universal shoes, ideal for the business traveler, with dressy leather uppers in brown or black and lightweight flexible synthetic soles, which make them both smart and suitable for extended walking or other leisure activities. They tend to be lighter than conventional shoes also—I take a massive size 12, and these new shoes weigh only 12 ounces, about the same as my jogging shoes.

Because shoes are so awkward to pack, you should try to take the minimum number; that means color coordinating with your main business clothes—black shoes with dark suits, for example. If I am taking a gray or dark business suit, I also take gray slacks so that the same shoes go well with either. The frequent flier's sock drawer tends to be color-conservative so that socks readily adapt to the clothes taken on business trips.

Shirts or blouses, ties, and other accessories should be as compatible as possible also, which is easier to do with light, subtle colors. Heavy patterns or bold colors may look great in one combination and horrible with something else. Because I have traveled extensively doing business in hot climates, I have a selection of lightweight, conservatively colored and patterned cotton shirts with short sleeves and collars suitable for buttoning up with a tie or wearing open-necked. They look formal under a business suit, while also being comfortable on their own for leisure.

Both businessmen and businesswomen can dispense with the formal suit altogether and take a smart blazer or jacket with two pairs of slacks to be worn with it or separately. Upper garments always seem to have a much longer life span than trousers or skirts, and their differing durabilities apply on business trips also, so mix-and-match outfits prove very flexible and practical. Packing a second jacket takes space and weight, so if an extra upper garment is required, I put in a lightweight waterproof windcheater, which combines smartness with functionality for semiformal, leisure, and sporting situations.

If the climate at the destination is likely to require added protection from the cold or wet, veteran travelers add thermal values from the skin out by taking extra underwear. You can keep warmer by wearing two undervests than by putting on an overcoat. You also get more thermal flexibility by having other open-weave or knitted garments in a basic travel wardrobe—woolen or composite heavier knits for cold weather, cotton knits for warm or temperate conditions. All the clothing should be in wrinkle-resistant fabrics that will overcome creasing readily. You can help them to keep smelling fresh by putting scented fabric softener sheets or cedar wood chips in the case with them.

A really careful evaluation of your clothing needs and how they can be most efficiently met will give you a strong indication of whether you can take one carry-on bag or will need to check-in luggage.

Step 3. Zone Packing

Zone packing is a technique developed by backpackers to keep the center of gravity of the pack as close to the body as possible, reducing strain on muscles and joints. If you have walked any distance carrying a badly loaded pack that pulls out on your shoulders and forces you to lean forward, you will know how effective proper packing can be in making even a very heavy load far less stressful. The technique also groups objects so that they are much easier to locate within the bag and your possessions stay better organized. Both advantages can benefit the frequent flier.

(Backpacks are not very practical for flying, mainly because of the frequency with which you need to pick your bags up and put them down. A pack really only comes into its own when you can leave it on your shoulders for extended periods. However, a lightweight small nylon backpack without a frame, folded up to next to nothing and slipped in a corner of your flight bag, can be a real boon for leisure excursions while on the road. You can put camera, wallet, folding umbrella, sweater and other things in it and go off exploring shops, flea markets, museums, and so on with both arms free, in the greatest comfort and reducing the risk of theft in public places. The hunter's or photographer's vest is useful in the same way.)

To zone-pack into any kind of bag, lay out everything on a bed, large table or the floor. Have a plentiful supply of clear plastic bags—preferably the kind with resealable openings—and perhaps a few light plastic boxes with tops. These come in a variety of shapes and sizes for storing food in the fridge or freezer.

Combine what you are taking with you into logical groups, or zones. Create a small filing system for your clothing just as you have separated and classified the business papers you take with you. Socks go together, as do handkerchiefs, underwear, shirts, ties, medications, toilet gear, and so on. (An alternative is to pack by outfit, putting items that are to be worn together into the same bag.) Put crushable items into the plastic bags and anything fragile needing protection into the boxes. Medications and toilet gear can go into a box, as can anything susceptible to crushing or other damage, such as a tape player or spare pair of glasses.

Then pack your bag in zones so that you can most easily get at what you will need during the journey and on arrival at your destination. Although the positioning of the center of gravity is not so critical for a carry bag or suitcase as it is for a backpack, it is an advantage to try to get your bag or suitcase reasonably well balanced, with heavy objects at the bottom. Placing clothes and other light things at the top with heavy objects underneath also reduces creasing of the clothes.

Getting the weight low down really pays off when you are pulling a bag on wheels, like my own which I described earlier. Properly packed, my bag on its leash follows me easily like a well-trained dog, with no fuss. If it is badly balanced and topheavy, it drags, falls over, collides with things, and generally behaves like a demented pit bull.

Zone packing really saves time and hassle if you are making a number of short one-night stops and it is tempting not to unpack but just live out of the suitcase. With normal packing, by the time you arrive at the second hotel, everything in your bag can be crumpled up and in a real mess. Using zone packing, grouping things into transparent plastic containers, it takes but a few seconds to lift out the bags or boxes to get at items you need, and then they all go back into the bag just as easily. Even if you still do not want to unpack, taking what you need as you need it straight out of the case goes far more smoothly if you have zone packed on the principle of first in, last out.

You can buy travel accessories that make zone packing easier. Called suitcase organizers, they come in various types. One model is in the form of an air-cushioned inflatable plastic ring that fits around the inside of a suitcase and has pockets for toiletries, jewelry, cosmetics, etc. I find kitchen plastic bags and boxes work just as well and are more versatile and cheaper. However, running belts around the inside circumference of a case is an effective way to pack them.

Another packing technique is called interpacking. Instead of packing each garment separately, you lay each one out over the open suitcase and fold others into it. For example, a jacket is laid in the suitcase with the collar up against the interior of the hinged side and the bottom and sleeves spread out and hanging over the other edges of the case. Then you might lay a pair of trousers horizontally across the suitcase and fold the legs of the trousers and the arms and bottom of the jacket in among each other, interleaving different garments and filling up gaps with underwear and socks or stockings.

Interpacking really does reduce creases and wrinkles, but unless you plan to unpack completely on arrival, it is time wasting, it makes it difficult to get at individual items quickly, and it turns both packing and unpacking into a kind of Chinese puzzle that can fail to entertain when you are tired after a long flight or in a hurry to get changed to make an appointment. You can combat creasing as effectively by interleaving clothes with tissue paper, plastic bubble pack, or the large dry cleaning plastic bags left doubled so that they trap an air cushion between layers of clothing.

Step 4. Choose the Best Bag for You

A good garment or other carry-on bag may have pockets that help you to zone pack more efficiently. Some are very well designed; others—including some of the most expensive—are awful. The best garment bags take a lot of clothes, protect them from creasing, and make them easily accessible. The bag should be easy to pack and unload and should offer the option to suspend it from the hotel room door and live out of it comfortably. Key points to look for:

- *Plenty of pockets of appropriate size. Some garment bags have only two or three, the better ones a dozen.*

- *The ability to use normal coat hangers, not just special folding ones, which get mislaid and are inconvenient. If the bag will take ordinary hangers, you can load it straight from your wardrobe and unpack it the same way. A nice refinement on some bags is a hanging bar that will extend so that you can get to clothes underneath without removing those on top.*

- *A waterproof section, preferably removable. You may think you will never need it, but one day it will be invaluable when you are in a rush to pack something wet or soiled, perhaps the favorite shirt or skirt on which you spilled the breakfast coffee.*

- *Reinforced pockets—those with stiffening around them and usually in the top corners. In theory these are for shoes. In practice I find it easier to put shoes separately into bags and fit them in anywhere they will go, depending on the other contents. Then the reinforced pockets come in useful for items that really need protecting. Of course, shoes also make good, virtually unbreakable storage containers themselves. I have a 35 mm camera and strobe that travel very securely inside a pair of my shoes.*

- *A top-quality hook with a secure place to stow it. The hook should be in wide, flat metal, angled and on a chain so that it will go right over the top of a door without damaging the wood or preventing the door from opening and closing. In this way you suspend the opened bag so that you can get at everything inside easily. It is vital when you are traveling that the hook stow away securely. If it*

comes loose and dangles, it will catch in everything, including luggage conveyor belts, taxi doors,
your clothes, the wire mesh of luggage carts, and
so forth.

- *A strong, comfortable handle and adjustable shoulder strap.* A luggage manufacturer should have no
difficulty in obtaining strong handles, but anchor-
ing them properly to the bag is far more challeng-
ing, and an examination of how well this work is
done will give an indication of the thought and
quality that have gone into any piece you are considering buying.

- *Tough, washable, scuffproof exterior finish and interior materials that will clean easily with a wipe
from a sponge.* I brought a garment bag back from
a trip into the Kalahari Desert and just could not
get out the sand and dirt that had worked its way
into the woven fabric used in the interior. In frustration I took it outside and sluiced it down with
the garden hose, which resulted in the interior
coming unglued, shrinking, and making the bag
useless. You may not be going to the desert often,
but dirt is a problem everywhere, and your luggage must be able to resist it, or at least be on
your side when you try to clean up.

- *Good-quality nonjamming self-healing zippers.*
However good the rest of the bag is, a bad zipper
will make you hate it.

- *Internal frame or straps that are easy to use and
efficiently help to minimize the creasing of large
clothes items—trousers, jackets, skirts, and the
like.*

- *A practical way of opening.* There are various
ways of getting into a garment bag, and before

buying it pays to give careful attention to how successfully the designer has tackled this challenge. Some bags open up like books and can be very accessible and convenient if the interior layout is done well. Others have zippers and pockets inside and out that require you constantly to be turning the bag over to get at different items.

● *External pockets that meet your particular needs. If flying with just the one carry-on garment bag, I usually take a soft leather document case instead of a briefcase, so my garment bag must have one large pocket that will accommodate the document case and other papers. I also like to have at least two other smaller pockets on the outside that will hold a book, toilet gear, tape player, compact camera and other in-flight impedimenta. Other travelers have different needs and will prefer maximum inside space without all these pockets on the outside.*

There are a number of other carry-on alternatives. Many frequent fliers got excited at the introduction of one of the few really novel approaches to carry-ons—saddlebags that fit over a briefcase. The handle of the briefcase comes through a slot in the strip connecting the twin saddlebags, so you can unite or separate the two items of luggage very quickly, and when they are together as one unit, they can be carried in one hand. It's a nice idea, but has not proved very popular because the bags tend to slide around on the briefcase and will not contain much before the whole assembly becomes bulky and inconvenient. However, they may work for you on short trips.

The traditional carpet bag, all floppy and voluminous, now comes in a variety of designs and materials. It worked well for Mary Poppins on her frequent flying trips, but she used magic as her carrier and did not have to cope with high overhead luggage bins or cramped under-seat space. Bags like this are difficult to pack and give little protection to their contents because they are so floppy. However, they are flexible and will contain an amazing amount.

The traditional pilot's case, usually in black leather finish, is just right for many travelers, although it takes up a lot of space under the seat, especially in coach. However, if you usually go business or first, or have appropriate physique, you can use a case like this as an extension of the aircraft seat squab during the flight. Position the case upright along the front edge of your seat with your legs over the top. You can get at the contents very easily this way by reaching between your legs into the top-opening pilot's case. A pillow laid on the case makes it more comfortable as an extension of the seat squab to give extra support under your thighs, enabling you to stretch your legs out rather than being forced to bend them sharply at the knee, as is the case if your carry-on bag is farther forward, cluttering up the foot space.

The pilot's case is basically a deep rectangular box that opens at the top, so it is easy to get into during the flight. Files stack vertically and the rigid sides protect the contents, although reducing the flexibility to pack tightly or contain odd-shaped objects. Some models have an expandable outside pocket on one of the long sides, especially practical if it is removable and can be used as a separate document case. A smaller pocket on one of the ends is a boon for holding tickets, wallet, and so on, but it should be deep and have a very secure clasp.

There are also multipurpose one-suiter briefcases, which will take an overnight change of clothes along with the normal business documents and on-the-road accessories.

A word of warning for the style- and status-conscious is that many expensive designer label luggage pieces are victims of the $250-billion-a-year industrial counterfeiting business. If you are offered Gucci, Louis Vuitton, and other famous-name luggage at bargain prices, it's probably a copy without the inherent quality to stand up to the rigors of frequent flying. Some counterfeit luggage looks great at a glance, but the clasps may break, zippers and locks jam, hinges fall apart, and even dyed colors run. On the other hand, some counterfeits are tough and durable, offering better value for money than the originals.

The choice of carry-ons is wide, and the selection has to be an individual one compromising style, cost, and practicality to a particular traveler's needs.

Step 5. Put It on Wheels

Both your checked luggage and your carry-ons should be lifted as little as possible. A fully loaded suitcase can easily weigh 75 pounds. Those of us who make lots of long trips and get expert at packing can make the weight of a single standard-size piece of luggage exceed 100 pounds. Even a small bag can be very tiring and carrying it can cause damage to muscles, ligaments, and joints. It's bad enough having to lift it in and out of cars, taxis, and buses; carrying it even comparatively short distances can add considerably to the physical and mental stress of being on the road.

That is why wheels are such a blessing. If you haven't got your luggage on wheels yet, you don't know what you are missing. I became a wheelie quite early in the technology, when the Nissan Motor Company invited me to visit their factories in Japan and demonstrated their organizational and PR skills well beforehand by sending to my home an ideal set of matching luggage for the trip.

The carry-on bag in simulated leather was perfect for papers, cameras, tape recorder, and other items needed both during the flight and while working in Japan. The suitcase was in tough, molded semirigid plastic and would hold more than enough for three weeks on the road, while being sufficiently tough to withstand many changes of hotels, planes, and other transport. Indeed, it subsequently experienced many mishaps, including falling off a truck in

Australia, and is still strong after more than fifteen years of hectic travel. Still, its main features—novelties then and still not adopted by many travelers—were the pair of high-tech plastic wheels built into the bottom of the suitcase and the flip-out pulling handle on the opposite corner.

It requires very little effort to move that suitcase, even over long distances. I once pulled it fourteen blocks through Washington, D.C., in the middle of the night when I could not find a taxi. The case was so heavily loaded with business papers that without the wheels I would have been immobilized.

Getting luggage with wheels does not automatically bring you all the benefits. For a start, the wheels must be strong, because once you've got them, you'll use them. That means they must be able to support the weight of the fully loaded suitcase without cracking and not wear away quickly, either at the axle or around the rim from abrasion against the different kinds of surface over which they roll. The wheels should be big enough to cope with uneven and cracked surfaces, such as escalators and moving walkways—otherwise they will keep getting stuck—but not so large that they protrude and risk catching in luggage conveyors or being broken off when thrown around baggage handling areas or jammed into airfreight containers.

Those requirements are quite a stiff design and manufacturing challenge, so if shopping for luggage with wheels, it pays to go for quality. Don't hesitate to take prospective purchases for a short test drive round the store, making sure that the bag or suitcase will maneuver easily, that the handle or pull strap extends to a comfortable height for you, and that the quality of materials and construction are up to the job.

Wheels and casters are supposed to be maintenance free, but I lubricate mine sparingly every so often to make them run more easily and eliminate annoying squeaks.

An alternative to having cases and bags with integral wheels is to use a collapsible luggage trolley, now discounted to as little $8. The cheaper ones are of very poor quality, so check the inherent strength of the design and materials as well as features such as the width of the bottom platform and the height of the extended handle. Some platforms are very flimsy and narrow, so they will not take a decent-sized suitcase securely, while others have such short handles that the average person finds them back-breaking to pull along.

In theory we should not have to buy our own wheels or move our baggage around airports because the airport authorities should provide sufficient free luggage carts. In reality the carts never seem to be around when you want them, they are no longer free at many airports, and they have been associated with a new form of airport crime, described in detail elsewhere. So if you want to enjoy the many advantages of getting your baggage on wheels, you must provide them yourself.

Step 6. Label Everything—Inside and Out

Every item of baggage should be labeled with your name, business address, and telephone number at home or business and at your destination. Some women travelers prefer not to reveal either their home telephone number or their addresses, and it is wise for all travelers to use only business addresses on visible external labels for the security reasons mentioned earlier. The address details should be stuck onto the inside of the case and either stuck or tied strongly to the outside, but that's not enough. To minimize the chances of bags being lost or mislaid, monitor every other tag or label attached to them during the trip, as we discussed earlier.

Step 7. Never Lose Sight of Your Bags

Airports in the United States and overseas are plagued with skillful baggage thieves of both sexes and all ages.

You—and your bags—are particularly likely to be targets if you look expensive and tired or preoccupied. It takes but a moment for a thief, or a team working in unison, to distract you and either hide your bags or disappear into the crowd with them, so frequent fliers always keep their baggage fully in view, preferably in touch also, unless handed over into the safekeeping of a uniformed airline or airport official against a valid receipt, or locked away. These precautions are necessary en route to and from the airport as well as when inside the terminal.

On airport buses, which may make several stops at which luggage is loaded or unloaded, I always make a point of sitting by a curbside window so that I can observe the luggage handling and ensure that nobody makes off with my bags, either deliberately or by mistake.

Follow these seven steps, and the stress and hassles associated with traveling with baggage are largely eliminated. The key points are to travel as light and unencumbered as possible, use the check-in facilities, and keep your carry-ons modest to reduce your own travel stress levels and improve air safety for everyone.

Reduce the Stress and Hassles

TAG SERVICES FOR BAGS

One way to avoid advertising your address on your luggage is to use one of the services that provides a central registry of keys and baggage identification tags. Obviously, keys should never contain the owner's address as, even if found and promptly returned, they can be copied very quickly by a thief. Residential addresses displayed on the outside of luggage can alert burglary gangs that your home probably is unoccupied.

Some of these lost-and-found services are very efficient, using computers and functioning internationally; they have toll-free numbers for anyone who finds your bags—or your keys—to call. The service acts as an intermediary, protecting your address but enabling you and your missing bags or keys to be reunited. Sometimes there is a reward as an incentive to the finder.

Typical costs range from $5 to $15 a year, often with an initial additional charge. One such service is the Worldwide Registered Luggage Tag Service at P.O. Box 83914, Los Angeles, CA 90083.

BUY FOR PRACTICAL FEATURES, NOT JUST APPEARANCE

Personal travel luggage is too often bought purely on appearance and not after a detailed evaluation of the many practical tasks it must carry out efficiently while on the road. A classic example of this is that standard item of equipment for Road Warrior, Eagle, Tightrope Walker, and Family Tied—the attache case.

I have been road- and flight-testing attache cases over many years and conclude that some of the best are the least expensive and some of the most costly are so impractical that they rarely get used. For example, to travel internationally with a case made of elephant, crocodile, or other wild animal skin is just asking for trouble these days. Some countries will confiscate at the airport anything made of the skin of an endangered species or made of leather, which may carry infection.

Fine leather attaches may look great in the shop but can be heavy, and they scratch and scuff so easily that they are not practical for rigorous traveling. Rigid attaches in any material may keep papers crisp and uncreased but are very limited in their ability to stretch when you want to accommodate something bulky. I even have one made of antique wood, which looks terrific, but it is too heavy and too prone to scratching to be used on any but very special occasions.

In terms of practicality, an expandable cotton canvas attache can combine remarkable functionality with sufficient good looks to be acceptable in the boardroom. Important exterior features are strong, padded handles and a wide carrying strap that will fit comfortably over the shoulder. The zipper should be strong also, with seams well made so that the attache can expand when—as inevitably happens—the case gets overloaded.

The interior pockets should keep business work tools separated and readily accessible. A key clip on a long strap is a real boon, retaining keys securely while ensuring that they are always readily accessible. An external pocket for ticket, boarding pass, and travel documents keeps these essentials conveniently accessible. External pockets will also keep a personal stereo player, electronic notebook, or small camera within reach. There should be one external pocket big enough to hold a newspaper or paperback book so that it is always easy to get at in the air or on the ground.

A wide top opening is required to enable papers and

TRAVEL WITH A STEAMER

Frequent fliers conscious of the need to look smart in crease-free clothes can take a tip from the rag trade, which has found that steaming clothes to get out the wrinkles is faster and more convenient then conventional ironing.

For around $20 there are lightweight portable travel steamers that do a good job and are faster, easier to use, and lighter than most travel irons. Most are dual voltage, so they can be used in the United States and overseas, where 240 volts is the rule. You fill the unit with water, wait a few minutes until it has heated up and ejects steam from its vents, then pass it over the surface of wrinkled fabrics.

You need no expertise to get good results; simply steam your clothing while it is on a hanger. Pleats and the creases in trouser legs can be restored or made crisper by pinching them together with the fingers and holding them while the steam is directed onto the fold. You can get the form back into shoulder and sleeve areas by stuffing a towel inside the garment to create the desired shape before steaming. Wrinkled neckties come up crisply if you suspend them and pull them into shape while steaming.

These travel steamers are great for sprucing up drapes at home or in the office as well. Instead of having to take down the drapes to iron them, you simply steam them where they hang at the windows. Spies who travel can use them for steaming open envelopes, and there are lots of other legitimate applications in addition to their prime purpose of getting the wrinkles out of clothes while on the road.

Although the manufacturers cannot suggest it, I have heard of travelers putting a few drops of suitable decongestant into the water container, convering their heads with a towel and breathing in the vapors to ease the nasal congestion that often follows a flight. Steaming can be great for rejuvenating travel-stressed skin, opening the pores, and helping the cleansing process. One would need to use an astringent—or cold water—afterwards to close up the pores before exposing them to the dust of the environment. Gentle steaming might be helpful to ease areas of muscle tension or stiffness, but remember that these gadgets are sold only for use with clothes and any other applications are at your own risk and demand that you take care.

so on to be removed or replaced easily, even when sitting cramped in an airline seat. A disadvantage of a flexible attache is that papers tend to get creased if they are not protected in file folders or plastic sleeves. A place for a folding umbrella can be useful, eliminating the need to carry a raincoat in temperate weather.

Enlarged overnighter versions of the flexible attache can hold a change of clothes or a laptop computer or both.

METAL CASES CAN BE LIGHT AND TOUGH

International photographers and television news crews make the toughest demands on luggage. Their bags must withstand the worst that airlines can do to it, yet protect delicate contents from knocks, crushing and climatic ex-

Metal cases can be lighter and far more practical than leather, providing protection for electronic equipment, cameras, and other vulnerable items. (Photo courtesy Zero Halliburton.)

tremes. They rely on rigid cases made of aluminum or an alloy that will resist damage yet is light in weight.

Cameras and sensitive electronic gear such as computers are protected within the cases by high-density polyurethane foam padding. To save space, clothing may be used instead of foam, but it must be packed carefully and really tightly to act as an effective cushion.

This type of metal container is now being styled to look smarter. It comes in a variety of finishes, including the rich silver, gold, graphite, onyx, and Bordeaux colors from Zero Halliburton. Some models have built-in wheels; there is a very useful design in the form of an extra-deep carry-on; one is custom-designed to accommodate a Macintosh computer; and there are matching at-

---

BATTLING THE BAGGAGE PROBLEM

If security considerations do not get in the way, frequent fliers can expect big improvements in easing baggage-related stress problems.

An extremely popular suggestion in the Hyatt travel project research was that hotel and airlines coordinate their services so that baggage is transferred directly from the plane to the hotel. Women voted particularly strongly for such a move as being an important way of improving the quality of business travel.

The viability of the concept of checking-through baggage was demonstrated by Swissair with its service for baggage to be checked through to rail services and on to the station at the passenger's destination. You can check your case in at LAX or JFK and collect it at virtually any railway station in Switzerland.

---

tache cases that will hold and protect a small laptop. Details from Zero Halliburton, 818 897-7777.

Good metal luggage is not cheap. It may cost more than cases or bags made of textiles or glass-reinforced plastic. Indeed, the best metal cases are up in the same price bracket as leather, but far more practical. Cut-price clones being imported from the Far East may well not be worth the cost savings. Compare on quality as well as price, checking in particular for strength, weight, and sturdiness of handles, locks, and hinges.

A golden rule in buying any kind of luggage is to see how well the handle is fastened and if the locks have a

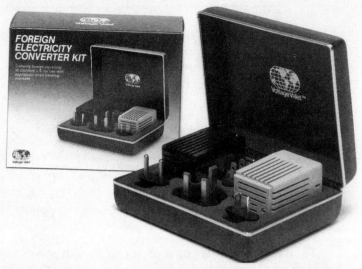

If you don't want to blow your electrical appliances when operating them overseas on different voltages, remember to use the appropriate *type* as well as correct size of converter. The transformer, for traveler's appliances rated up to 50 watts, and the solid state kind, for loads up to 1600 watts, are designed for use with different types of electrical equipment and to cater for variations in load, measured in wattage.

The picture shows a complete traveler's foreign electricity transformer/converter kit with both types of converters, together with the various plugs and adapters required for foreign outlets.

sense of quality and robustness. If a manufacturer skimps in these areas, it is a sign that the hidden aspects of the case or bag may be inferior also.

BE PREPARED FOR VARYING VOLTAGES

Electric voltages and types of plugs vary considerably around the world. It is best to travel prepared with a foreign electricity converter kit. Chose one with automatic overload protection, which will break the circuit in the event of overheating and then reset itself when the overload has been rectified.

There are two main categories of converters for the traveler, and it is a mistake to think that the differences are only in their power rating. There is also a crucial difference in the *type* of electrical power as well as in the quantity of energy required by different kinds of appliances.

The transformer type of travel converter usually is designed to cope with loads of up to 50 watts, while the various solid-state electronic converters for travel purposes range up to 1600 watts. But that is only half the story.

Appliances containing a motor, transformer, or electronic circuitry require a constant "steady state" voltage from a transformer type of converter. Examples are battery chargers, contact lens disinfectors, oral hygiene devices, and tape recorders.

The solid-state converters enable 120-volt appliances to work on 220-volt power supplies by very rapidly making and breaking the current supply, which is practical for such higher-wattage appliances as steamers, irons, curlers, hair dryers, hot plates, and miniature immersion heaters. If in doubt, check with a specialist electrical equipment supplier and read the directions with the converter carefully. Sales clerks in luggage and drug stores where most travel converters are sold are usually not well-informed on these different electrical power needs.

The foreign adapter plug sets sold in travel and electronics stores *do not* convert electricity, but enable the electric plugs standard in one country physically to fit into the variety of electrical sockets found in different parts of the world.

The table on pages 66–7 shows which countries use the 110-volt standard found in the United States and Canada, which use 220 volts, and which have both voltages.

The letter code indicates the types of plugs that fit the sockets in the different countries

Some countries marked with an asterisk still have direct current (DC) in places, usually in very old towns or in

International Electrical Supply Guide

*Country	Voltage	Plug	Country	Voltage	Plug
Afghanistan	220	B	*Germany, Fed. Rep.	110/220	B
Algeria	110/220	A,B,D	Ghana	220	B
Angola	220	B	Gibraltar	220	D
Antigua	110/220	D	*Greece	110/220	B
*Argentina	220	B,D	Greenland	220	B
*Australia	220	C	Guatemala	110/220	A
Austria	220	B	Guinea	220	B
Azores	110/220	B	Guyana	110/220	A,B,D
Bahamas	110/220	A	Haiti	110/220	A
Bahrain	220	B,D	Honduras	110/220	A
Bangladesh	220	B	Hong Kong	220	D
Barbados	110/220	A	Hungary	220	B
Belgium	110/220	B	Iceland	220	B,C
Belize	110/220	A	*India	220	B
Bermuda	110/220	A,D	Indonesia	110/220	B
Bolivia	110/220	A,B	Iraq	220	B,C
Botswana	220	B,D	Ireland	220	B,D
*Brazil	110/220	B	Israel	220	B,C
Bulgaria	110/220	B	Italy	110/220	B
Burma	220	B	Ivory Coast	220	B
Canada	110	A	Jamaica	110/220	A,B,D
Central African Rep.	220	B	Japan	110	A
Chad	220	B	Jerusalem	220	B,C
*Chile	220	B	Jordan	220	B
China, Peo. Rep. of	220	B,C	Kenya	220	B,D
Columbia	110	A	Korea, Rep. of	110	A
Costa Rica	110	A	Kuwait	220	B,D
Cyprus	220	B,D	Laos	110/220	A,B
Czechoslovakia	110/220	B	Lebanon	110/220	B
Denmark	220	B	Liberia	110/220	A
Dominican Rep.	110/220	A	Libya	110/220	B
Ecuador	110/220	A	Luxembourg	110/220	B
Egypt	110/220	B,D	Macao	110/220	B
El Salvador	110	A	*Madeira	220	B
England	220	B,D	Majorca Island	110	B
Ethiopia	110/220	B	Malawi	220	B,D
Fiji	220	C	Malaysia	220	B,D
Finland	220	B	Malta	220	B,D
France	110/220	B	Martinique	110/220	B

Continued

International Electrical Supply Guide (*Cont'd.*)

*Country	Voltage	Plug	Country	Voltage	Plug
Mexico	110	A	So. Africa, Rep. of	220	B,D
Monaco	110/220	B	Spain	110/220	A,B
Morocco	110/220	B	Sudan	220	B
Mozambique	220	B	Swaziland	220	B
Nepal	220	B	*Sweden	110/220	B
Netherlands	110/220	B	Switzerland	110/220	B
Neth. Antilles	110/220	A,B	Syria	110/220	B
New Zealand	220	C	Tahiti	110	A
Nicaragua	110	A	Taiwan	110	A
Niger	220	B	Tanzania	220	B,D
Nigeria	220	B,D	Thailand	220	A
Norway	220	B	Trinidad	110/220	A,B,D
Okinawa	110	A	Tunisia	110/220	B
Oman	220	B,D	Turkey	110/220	B
Pakistan	220	B	Uganda	220	B
Panama	110	A	Upper Volta	220	B
*Paraguay	220	B	Uruguay	220	B,D
Peru	220	A,B	USSR	110/220	A,B
Philippines	110/220	A,B	Venezuela	110	A
Poland	220	B	Viet Nam	110/220	A,B
Portugal	110/220	B	Virgin Is. (American)	110	A
Puerto Rico	110	A	Wales	220	B,D
Romania	110/220	B	Yemen (Aden)	220	A,B
St. Lucia	220	D	Yemen Arab Rep.	220	B
St. Vincent	220	D	Yugoslavia	220	B
Saudi Arabia	110/220	A,B	Zaire	220	B
Scotland	220	B,D	Zambia	220	B,D
Senegal	110	B	Zanzibar	220	B,D
Singapore	110/220	D	Zimbabwe	220	B,D

*Countries using DC in certain areas.
Reproduced by permission of Hybrinetics, Inc., 800 247-6900.

remote areas. Ships and aircraft vary: some have 220 volts, some 110, some both—together with DC supplies for various electrical equipment. Converters will not work with any DC supplies.

In some areas and countries, voltage can vary greatly and is not maintained within the strict tolerances of the developed nations. You may get a 110-volt supply dropping to 90 volts or rising over 140, especially as appliances drawing large loads cut in and out on the same circuit. Such wide fluctuations may damage sensitive equipment. If you are traveling with appliances that are fuse-protected, carry spare fuses of the correct rating and do not be tempted to use silver foil, pins, or any other makeshifts as emergency substitutes for blown fuses.

Before plugging in any appliance, check whether the electric supply is AC or DC and the voltage 110 or 220. Make sure that the converter you are planning to use will cope with the wattage of the appliance. The wattage rating is normally marked on the appliance.

Do not use travel voltage converters for extended periods or with ordinary domestic or business appliances; for example, to run a desktop computer, stereo stystem, power tools, television set, or kitchen blender. These will require a heavier-duty standard transformer. In fact, television sets do not travel well whatever type of converter you use because different parts of the world have radically different methods for transmitting and receiving the broadcast signal. Much of Europe and the rest of the world uses the PAL system, France favors SECAM, while in North America we have NTSC—dubbed by its critics as meaning "Never Twice the Same Color." There is some—but much less—incompatibility between FM radio transmissions in different parts of the world, but this is mainly a problem with receivers with pre-set tuning and for stereo reception. You may not be able to lock in precisely to a station's wavelength, but should still get a signal.

Most countries' electrical supplies alternate at 50 cycles, not the 60 cycles of the United States. This is usually not critical, but it may cause electric motors to operate more slowly, resulting in distortion of tape recordings and disks. When traveling internationally, I run my tape recorders on rechargeable batteries so that the speed of playback and recording is always constant. It makes no difference whether the batteries recharge at 50 or at 60 cycles.

As most portable computers have internal batteries supplying low DC voltages, they come with their own converter/rechargers, and the trend is for these to work on both 110- and 220-volt supplies. The recharger case should be marked accordingly. If you have one marked either for 110 or for 220, check with the supplier about the use of a voltage converter. There should be no problem. Some laptop rechargers sold in the United States are labeled as being suitable only for one voltage but in fact are able to cope with both. However, check first.

DON'T CARRY YOUR VALUABLES AROUND, HANG THEM ON YOUR LEGS OR WAIST

What is the best way to carry money, traveler's checks, passport, driving license, and other essential documents? I have tried all the options and the one that stacks up best in most circumstances is to wrap them round your leg or hang them at your waist.

For years, when going to hazardous places as a foreign correspondent, I preferred a full-size money belt. The first, made of nylon with a metal zipper, was a disaster. It functioned fairly well outside my shirt and under my jacket in cold weather, but that is too visible and too limiting to make the best of a money belt's potentialities. When worn concealed next to my skin, the nylon and metal proved uncomfortable and in hot weather caused perspiration and an uncomfortable allergic reaction.

I replaced it with the most practical of all the full-size money belts, which proved to be one made of thin but strong bleached linen. It has virtually no bulk in itself, so passport, driving license, credit cards, and a few traveler's checks and high-denomination currency notes can be accommodated without adding substantially to my middle-aged spread.

It washes and dries quickly and easily—an essential feature if you wear a money belt frequently next to your skin. There are no metal parts to cause discomfort, as it fastens with a Velcro strip. (An earlier version worked just as well with tape fastenings.)

I have another money belt that is effective but will hold very little. It has proved invaluable in emergencies when I needed fast access to the world's most universally acceptable currencies—British pounds sterling and U.S. dollars. It looks like an ordinary leather dress belt, but a slim zip on the inside gives access to a long thin pocket between the outer and inner surfaces. The pocket can contain a substantial amount of money in the form of high-denomination bills, such as $100 notes, folded singly into tight narrow strips.

This type of money belt, or the larger kind worn underneath clothing, is very secure from pickpockets and will be overlooked by muggers in a high proportion of assault thefts. However, in recent years I have switched to more comfortable and convenient ankle wallets. Again, you can benefit from my early mistakes, because hidden wallets vary considerably in function and efficiency.

Ankle wallets come in various shapes, sizes, and materials. The bulkier, heavier ones—especially those featuring leather or thick synthetic fabrics—should be avoided. One never quite loses the awareness that they are there; some become really uncomfortable after a time. Also intrusive are the elasticized type shaped like the upper part of a sock. They fit very securely, but if too tight will restrict circulation in the leg—which can be a particularly unpleasant effect on long flights.

The ideal leg wallet should fit securely around the lower leg without being restricting or uncomfortable. I have found elasticized Velcro strips the best. While lightweight synthetic washable fabric may be suitable for the outside pocket, the surfaces that come into contact with

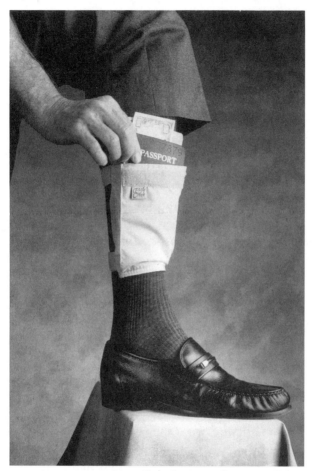

Comfort and security in a leg wallet. This leg wallet meets the prime needs of comfort and security. The parts that come into contact with the skin are faced with a soft cotton fabric backing, which does not get too hot in summer or cold in winter, unlike the tough lightweight nylon of which the wallet itself is made. The lining absorbs perspiration and dries out quickly, while the wallet itself is water-resistant to protect the documents inside. The whole unit can be washed and dried easily in a hotel bathroom.

The fastenings of elasticized Velcro are readily adjustable and will ensure that the wallet remains secure without constricting blood flow in the critical lower leg area.

your skin should be of natural fibers, able to breathe, so that the wallet will feel comfortable even after several hours of walking in hot weather.

If you wear slacks, jeans—any kind of long trousers that are not tight around the lower leg—the ankle wallet is both invisible and inaccessible to pickpockets. Yet the contents can be reached easily at any time by the wearer without the fumbling associated with money belts and body pouches that fit around the neck or under the arm.

You can protect the paper currency, tickets, credit cards, passport, and other small important documents carried in the ankle wallet by placing them in small plastic bags. Better still, for under $2 get a replacement set of stacked windows, the plastic sleeves designed to hold photos and cards in credit card cases and wallets. They will keep credit cards, paper currency, driver's license, stamps, and so on crisp and protected but visible and easy to locate when you need them.

An ankle wallet should accommodate a few keys without becoming heavy and uncomfortable. It is certainly preferable to a conventional wallet or a handbag, both of which can be a nuisance as well as vulnerable to thieves. There aren't many enterprising thieves around who will pick your ankle, although they can easily get into your pockets, even if you are walking quickly along a street.

Attaching anything to yourself is usually better than carrying it, so a fanny pack often figures in my frequent flying packing list. This is the bag or pouch on a belt that is popular among cyclists and hikers. It, or a hunter's or photographer's vest, can contain a surprising amount of the kind of things you need when moving around on foot or public transport, including wallet, a small camera, a microcassette recorder or personal stereo, notebook and pencil, and so on.

An alternative for standard 35mm cameras is to take them out of their usual cases suspended on shoulder straps and put them into the padded accessory cases that fit onto a belt. These cases are available in various sizes and shapes to accommodate different types of cameras and lenses, along with spare film, filters, and a small flash unit.

Putting your camera on your belt is a much more comfortable way of carrying it than slinging it round your neck, and it is at least as readily accessible for use. The belt-mounted case unzips from the top, so you can open it and remove the camera while leaving the case fastened securely to your belt.

If you get one of the larger versions of these belt-mounted camera cases, you may be able to move around comfortably and with both hands free without a fanny pack, money belt, or ankle wallet. I have a belt camera case designed to hold a 35mm camera fitted with a substantial telephoto lens. There is a lot of room left in it when I carry my Pentax with its compact 28mm–35mm zoom—a very versatile lens. In fact, the case will accommodate also my car and hotel room keys, small strobe flash, spare film, small change, passport, traveler's checks and paper currency, miniature FM radio with those tiny phones that fit inside the ear, notebook and pencil, business cards—even a pair of reading glasses or folding binoculars, but not both.

Incidentally, my frequent-flier survival kit includes a pair of drugstore magnifying reading glasses in a flexible case. They cost about $12 a pair, so I don't mind if they get lost or broken. They will slip into my pocket, ankle wallet, belt camera case or in the glove box of the hire car for occasions when I would rather not put my expensive prescription lenses at risk. Also, if the prescription glasses get mislaid or forgotten while on a trip, the drugstore magnifiers are always around for emergency use.

The Ultimate Travel Garment

Neither business suits nor typical leisure clothes are ideal for travel because they do not have enough pockets in the right places to enable you to carry, and have ready access to, the various bits and pieces needed in the airport and on the plane.

The most utilitarian travel garment can be one of the multipocketed vests designed for hunters, fishermen and photographers. Safari jackets also have capacious pockets but are not so easily slipped on and off over other clothing. These vests can be modified for use by travelers, but pick one as a basic that is not padded for outdoor use in cold weather; otherwise it will be too bulky and hot to wear comfortably in the airport or on the plane. The Banana Republic outlets stock a selection at about $85. Good quality hunter's vests can be much cheaper, if less stylish.

Most specialty vests are short on style, but if you put a premium on comfort and convenience, they can be worn during the journey, when appearance is not a critical factor, and then stuffed into an overnight bag before making any business contacts.

Or you can go to the ultimate and either make up a stylish vest to fit your own needs or spend as much as $1700 on a tailor-made Frequent Flier Custom Vest. I am working with California designers to develop this unique travel garment combining frequent flying and fashion styling experience.

The custom vest may be hand cut and sewn of orthopedic leather, or a range of other materials that meet the requirements that enable the vest to be tough and light, resist staining or creasing, and be very comfortable to wear. It can be had in a variety of finishes and colors.

Both inside and external pockets are added according to individual needs. For example, an owner may want to carry both reading spectacles and sunglasses and have a secure inside pocket for money and passport and an external one for an electronic notebook. Some travelers want to carry a personal stereo and a couple of tapes, while others may prefer space for a paperback book. Some will have special medical needs—either readily accessible medication or devices to help breathing.

The Frequent Flier Custom Vest can be worn throughout a journey, as the pockets are positioned not to get in the way of free movement when either walking around or sitting down. They keep objects like keys and wallet away from points where they might press on nerves and cause discomfort.

Get your wallet or billfold out of your back pocket and you will immediately ease a lot of pain on the plane and reduce the risk of loss.

The vest can be fitted with fasteners so that it will fix to the seat in front, with all the pockets within easy reach during a flight. It can be a boon in many situations on the ground also, as a comfortable, practical, and secure way of carrying around all the things you are likely to need when sightseeing or exploring.

Details from me at Studio 250, ICB, Harbor Drive, Sausalito, California 94965.

THE FREQUENT FLIER'S SURVIVAL KIT

Putting together your own on-the-road emergency kit is a worthwhile exercise that need only be done once and will save packing time and offer tangible benefits for years. You may like to consider doubling up on many items and making two kits, one to keep in the car and the other in the suitcase or bag you use most often when flying.

The list that follows is a selection of the most recommended items from travel veterans. Your kit should reflect your own personal needs so that you can produce a really comprehensive, customized on-the-road emergency package.

Although it is not wise to take any kind of medication out of its original packaging, you will not want to carry entire substantial packages, for example of laxatives or aspirin. The need is to have just enough for emergency use, so a few pills or capsules can be taken from their original containers and put into small plastic bags, *which must be individually labeled* with their contents, special warnings, and expiration dates.

I find that the best method is to use small Ziplock self-sealing bags and put everything possible into them. I tackle the labeling by spending a few minutes at the Xerox machine, copying the pack inserts, which give all the details about medication. I copy several inserts at a time onto sheets of letter-size paper, then put the original inserts into the travel pack and the copies into the bulk packaging, which stays at home. Having the original printed inserts with the medication can be a great help at Customs checks when traveling internationally. The inserts give a description of the pills or capsules, which should reassure any Customs officers that you are not carrying illicit drugs.

The creams and some of the medications suggested can be obtained in small sample packs in drug stores—discount drugstores usually have several bins full. These samples make it far easier to put together your kit.

The emergency repair items for clothing—needle, thread, buttons, and so on—can be purchased very cheaply already packaged, or the better hotels give them away to guests.

Checklist for the Frequent Flier's Survival Kit

Written details of your credit cards, driving license, medical insurance, and other important documentation

Copies of prescriptions and details of any special medical problems

Aspirin, codeine, or your other favorite painkiller (which can also double as a cough suppressant and mild sedative)

Throat lozenges

Mild sleeping pills or tranquilizers, or both

Antacid or other preferred digestive aid

Assortment of adhesive bandages

Antiseptic wipes

Antiseptic cream

Hydrocortisone cream for rashes and inflammation

Calamine lotion for insect bites and itchy rashes

Nasal decongestant in squeeze bottle and/or as pills

Eyedrops in squeeze bottle

Mild laxative

Diarrhea preventative and treatment medication

Motion sickness medication

Plastic thermometer (the strip type that goes on your
    forehead is compact, light, and unbreakable)

Sunscreen

Sunglasses

Spare contact lenses or eyeglasses (and prescription)

Antifungal cream or powder

Tweezers

Safety scissors

Sewing kit with safety pins

Ear plugs

Towelette

Spot remover

Shampoo sachet (which can also double for clothes
    washing)

Pair of disposable underpants

A small tablet of soap

Travel pack of feminine hygiene product

Travel pack of paper handkerchiefs

Miniature notepad and pencil or pen, or both

Folding toothbrush and toothpaste

Miniflashlight with long-life leakproof batteries

A $20 bill, two quarters, two dimes and two nickels

A personal check, left blank but endorsed "Not to exceed $100"

Four first-class stamps, two envelopes, two sheets of headed notepaper

Small comb

Shoeshine sachet

Lightweight plastic raincoat or folding umbrella

Small plastic sponge (doubles as clothes brush)

Toothpicks, individually wrapped as supplied in restaurants

It may look like a lot, but all the items on the above list will go into a small bag and will not add significantly to the bulk or weight of your luggage. They will get you through many on-the-road situations. If you only stay in good hotels, you can trim the list down drastically because the hotel should be able to provide you with on-the-spot assistance round the clock—that is one of the reasons for paying premium room rates.

Check through the list with your physician if you have any particular medical needs or problems or allergies.

Pick a quiet time and your neighborhood pharmacist will help you put the medical items together.

If you use anything from the kit, replace it as soon as possible.

CRISIS KIT

The traveler's Crisis Kit from Hartsdale House in Connecticut is typical of the prepackaged selections available for about $2 and up. It contains an assortment of sewing thread together with needle, buttons, safety pins, spot and lint remover, and shoe shiner to deal with clothing problems. The grooming aids include emery board and moist towelette, while for first aid there are aspirin, sterile bandage strips and an antiseptic towelette. A rain bonnet is included as well.

It all fits into a clear plastic wallet no bulkier than a pack of cigarettes. You may want to use a selection such as this as the basis on which to build your own emergency travel kit.

Packing Lists

If you always take the frequent flier's survival kit along with you in its own case, the rest of your packing becomes much faster and easier.

Apart from your business needs, the only other essentials are items of clothing. Here are lists, again a consensus of advice from veteran travelers, of the essentials for trips of up to ten days. They include both formal business wear and leisure clothing, with color matching or coordination to avoid the need to duplicate just for color reasons. For example, as shoes are bulky and heavy, take only shoes that can be worn with any skirt, trousers, or suit.

Each of these wardrobes will go in one carry-on bag if you wear some of the clothes on the flight.

THE TEN-DAY ON-THE-ROAD WARDROBE

Men

One suit

Four shirts

Two neckties

One pair slacks or jeans

Four undershorts

Three undervests

Four pairs socks

One belt (could be reversible)

Two pairs comfortable shoes

One windbreaker

One razor

In cold weather you probably need a topcoat, gloves, and sweater, but just to cope with chilly evenings or the occasional cold snap, wearing two undervests could be sufficient. In hot weather consider adding shorts and swimsuit.

Women

The preferred combination from

One suit

Two blouses

Two dresses or two-piece outfits

One long skirt

One pair slacks or jeans

One sweater or windbreaker

Plus

Two scarves

Four panties

Four pairs pantyhose

Two bras

One belt (could be reversible)

Two pairs comfortable shoes

In cold weather women probably need topcoat and gloves, but layered undervests are compact alternatives for chilly evenings and the occasional cold snap. Women may also wish to add shorts and swimsuit in hot weather.

A significant proportion of both men and women these days sleep naked and so sleepwear is not included in these essential minimum wardrobes. Even in cold weather, most hotel rooms are sufficiently well heated.

However, you may wish to take something along to cope with answering the door to room service, slipping along to the bathroom in inns, guest houses, and private homes where the facilities are not en suite with your bedroom, or to put over a swimsuit on the beach. For both sexes, a smart, loose track suit meets these needs and can be great for leisure activities, exercising, or just lounging around. If it is really cold, you can sleep in a track suit, wear it for flying, use the top as a substitute for a sweater, and many other applications. It is the universal unisex travel garment.

A bathrobe provides a quick coverup in the room, on the beach, or wherever else you need a comfortable slip-on for warmth or concealment. Only the best hotels provide them for guests, and taking one with you adds considerably to baggage bulk. An alternative that will not give much warmth but covers up well is a light travel robe of the kimono style.

If you leave and arrive in cold weather, you will probably be wearing a topcoat, which can double as a robe indoors. If you will only need a topcoat as protection against the risk of rain, a folding plastic coat (listed in the survival kit) is lighter and far more compact. It can be quite warm if you layer additional clothing underneath. Some travelers prefer a folding umbrella for rain protection.

You may notice several omissions from the traveler's packing lists which have been recommended in the past. Well, the times they are a-changing, and our evolving lifestyles and the technological developments aimed at convenience are having a big influence on travel needs. For example, you need fewer clothes overall because the trend is for both men and women to dress more simply in easy-care clothes that can be washed easily and require no pressing.

It is acceptable for men to wear dress shirts that button up and do not require cuff links, which inevitably seem to get lost on a trip. If you rely on cuff links, take two pairs—better, I think, to have shirts that look good without them.

Linen handkerchiefs—lots of them—used to be a requirement. Now I find that both men and women tend to use disposable tissues for all the occasions, except display, on which the linen handkerchief was required. It is a more hygienic practice, for one thing. However, one or two colored handkerchiefs or thin scarves can be valuable fashion accessories to ring the changes.

Customize your packing lists by noting which items you took on previous trips but did not use and those left behind that were needed.

The key to reducing the volume of clothing required for a trip is coordination, making different items work well together in various combinations to cope with practical needs, such as the weather, and from the style point of view also. You do not need to have a large variety of different outfits with you to impress your contacts, just combinations you can put together to be appropriate to the business and leisure situations you can expect to encounter on the trip.

Of course, this is traditionally easier for men than for women. I know a multimillionaire entrepreneur frequent flier who always looks smart and affluent by wearing navy blue blazer, white shirt, and old school tie, gray socks and slacks and black shoes. Anywhere in the world, he can have dinner in smart restaurants, travel, go to the theater, meet his bankers, or attend a football game—all in the same clothes. His packing just requires taking along duplicates of the same basic outfit. He is an object in frequent flying wardrobe discipline whom those of us still striving toward our first million could well emulate.

DON'T FORGET THE STATIONERY

Often forgotten but frequently needed while on the road are your own letterhead, matching envelopes, and stamps. You may not require any of them on two trips, but then on the third time away they could be invaluable—and that is bound to be the time you left your stationery behind.

The trouble with taking such stationery with you is that the paper and envelopes soon get crumpled and the stamps are lost or damaged. So I keep a few sheets of headed paper, some follow-up matching sheets, envelopes with my address printed on them, and a book of stamps of various denominations in a plastic file pocket. In fact, I have three such sets. One stays in the suitcase I use for long trips, including international flights, another in the carry-on garment bag that accompanies me on domestic trips of a few days, and a third in the pocket of the briefcase that I use every day.

The weight of these small mailing sets and the space they take up are insignificant, so it does not matter if they are required only occasionally. The papers stay crisp and uncreased in the file pocket for months.

Animal Frequent Fliers

Living, breathing carry-on baggage is accepted by most airlines—providing it will fit under your seat. In other words, you can take your Yorkie into the cabin, but your Great Dane must be checked.

There are a few frequently flying animals—most of them business travelers—including pedigree breeding and show stock, performers and celebrities such as Spuds McKenzie, and pets of human owners who cannot bear to be separated from them. Queen Elizabeth's corgis are the only four-legged royal frequent fliers, but Elizabeth Taylor's dogs have put in more air miles on commercial flights. One of the most remarkable feats by a four-legged Road Warrior was the 180,000 miles covered by a cat called Felix in the luggage compartment of a Pan Am plane. Felix escaped from his cage and finished up in London before he was discovered and sent back to Los Angeles.

For most of the four thousand or so animals who take to the air every day in the United States, it is a once-in-a-lifetime experience. For some it will prove fatal. Even the worst airlines have not lowered their food and air quality to the point of actually killing off their human passengers, but neglect of animals in the air and at terminals can cause suffering that results in death. However, such instances are comparatively rare and result just as often from ignorance or neglect by the owners of the animals as from faults on the part of the air carrier.

If an airline imposes tough requirements when you want to fly an animal from one place to another, it usually makes sense to comply rather than argue. The airline is responsible for meeting federal, state, and foreign regulations on animals transported and could be found liable if it accepts one in poor health in an improper container or without the required documentation. The precise rules vary from airline to airline—some will not ship animals at all—and on differing routes, so it is important to ascertain the situation at the first opportunity when planning a flight.

Giving advance notice is particularly important if you want to carry a pet on board, as only one animal is allowed in each cabin. The pet must be comfortable in a kennel small enough to go under the seat. This means that the animal must be able to move around and stand up in the kennel and have adequate ventilation. Good pet stores and most of the airlines sell kennels that meet the USDA regulations, and this is a better proposition than trying to make one yourself because the requirements are precise. For example, the kennel must have a ridge around it so that the ventilation air holes do not get blocked if it is stacked up tight against other baggage.

Even if all the advance arrangements are made properly, airline staff can still refuse to accept a pet as carry-on or checked excess baggage or for freight shipment. This may be because the animal appears unhealthy or there is some defect in the container. The labeling on the kennel is particulary important, with the words *LIVE ANIMAL* displayed prominently in letters at least an inch high, arrows showing the up side of the box, clear shipping details with full addresses, and detailed feeding and watering instructions.

Arrive at the airport in good time—at least an hour before domestic flights, more for international trips. The animal should be well exercised beforehand, familiar with its kennel, and not fed for about six hours previously. Do not put anything into the kennel or cage that might injure the animal, for example a leash, which could get tangled around its legs or throat.

Giving any animal a tranquilizer before a flight may be a mixed blessing and should not be done without taking expert advice from a veterinarian. A tranquilizer may have physiological effects on the pet without helping to overcome its fears, and there may be side effects that make it more difficult for the animal to adjust to changes in temperature and pressure during flight. Pekes and other pug-nosed dogs are among animals particularly prone to breathing problems arising from pressure changes and the stress of travel.

Pets checked in as excess baggage must stay in their kennels in a section of the hold on the same plane as the passenger owner, where they should enjoy the same pressure and temperature conditions as in the passenger cabin. If shipped as air cargo, they usually go on a different plane, but still in pressure- and temperature-controlled compartments.

Two animals may be put into the same cage, but they must be compatible and not fight, so this doubling up is usually only practical for young animals. However, the airlines will not usually accept animals under eight weeks of age—one notable exception being the way that animal embryos have been shipped inside adult female rabbits. This is the ultimate cost-effective way to fly cattle, pigs and other livestock around the world. Fertilized eggs are taken from the womb of the expectant mother—perhaps a pedigree Hereford cow in England. They are transferred to the womb of a rabbit and the rabbit flown to, say, an African country in need of new stock lines. At their destination the fertile eggs are transferred to a cow that acts as a surrogate mother. It may be a very ordinary cow but will still give birth to pedigree stock. The saving on air freight costs is enormous!

If shipping animals of any kind internationally, there may be complex health requirements to be met, including quarantine laws that make the whole exercise impractical. Check also for health certification requirements to be met when flying animals between states in the United States, particularly to Hawaii.

The USDA, the Humane Society of the United States, and other animal welfare organizations actually get comparatively few complaints about animals suffering as a result of being flown. When problems do arise, it is rarely in the air but usually on the ground, where the animal may be exposed to extremes of heat or cold or become one of the misplaced baggage statistics and not receive proper care for an extended period.

Travelers' misgivings about loss of control when handing their own destinies over to the airlines can become more intense when they are forced to make similar expressions of trust on behalf of cherished pets. In fact, the risk of anything going wrong is small.

Before You Go

The Frequent Flier's Survival Guide Checklists

BEFORE YOU LEAVE HOME

Domestic Trip

1. Electical appliances unplugged

2. Telephone answering machine switched on

3. Deliveries stopped
   Newspapers
   Milk
   Laundry

4. Bills coming due paid
   Insurances
   Utilities
   Telephone
   Mortgage or rent

5. Arrangements made for pets and houseplants/
   garden/pool

6. Police/security service/neighbors notified

7. Doors and windows secured

8. Car and house keys and itinerary details left with
   neighbor/friend/relatives

9. Baggage packed and checked

10. Medication/toiletries/spectacles and other
    essentials packed

11. Wallet or purse with credit cards (check
    expiration dates)/driving license/checkbook

12. Tickets

13. Business papers and cards

Add for International Trip

14. Passport (with necessary visas; check expiration date)

15. Foreign currency or traveler's checks

16. Health documents (including documentation for prescription drugs)

17. Travel insurance

18. Camera and film

19. Electrical plug and voltage conversion kit

Before You Leave the Office

20. Business papers

21. Agenda

22. Address book

23. Computer and accessories

24. Stationery

25. Business cards

26. Itinerary left with secretary/associates

27. Arrangements made to deal with mail and messages

CREATE YOUR OWN FREQUENT FLIER CHECKLIST

The most effective checklists are those you create yourself from your own experience of your personal needs. The various lists given in this book provide good general guides, but the best list of all will be the one you compile.

Next time you pack for a trip, make two lists of everything you take. Put clothing, medicines, toiletries, and other personal needs on one list, and detail your business travel requirements on the other. When you get back, tick off the things you used and those that were not really necessary. Add anything you did not take but that would have been useful.

After two or three trips, your travel lists will become refined into a much closer match between what you are accustomed to pack and what you need. Make copies of the customized personal list to put inside your suitcase and in your wardrobe or underwear drawer to be readily accessible each time you pack. Keep your business list in your organizer, diary, or a desk drawer at work.

Depending on your travel pattern, you may need modified lists to cover winter and summer, domestic or international, and short or long trips.

Don't Forget the Train

When planning a trip, don't forget the often-overlooked potential of making at least partial use of railways. They can be competitive in real time and cost because they take you from city center to city center.

Trains save the time wasted in getting to and from airports, especially when you have to allow extra time for possible traffic congestion and the additional security checks now becoming commonplace even for domestic flights. Trains in most countries have a remarkable record of leaving—and arriving—on time; new technology makes them faster and more comfortable than the days when they provided the main transportation links between cities; and the locations of the stations offer substantial savings in both time and various travel costs. For example, there are usually good business hotels within easy walk or a short taxi ride of a station, which may make it unnecessary to hire a car.

If your meetings, sales calls or other activities will be predominantly in the city center, you may be able to schedule a very productive working day around the train without needing to check into a hotel at all. Arrive refreshed right in the city center having slept comfortably and breakfasted on the train, leave your baggage at the station while you do business, and perhaps have a social evening or visit the theater before leaving the city again on another sleeper.

That is a routine I have found to work particularly well in Europe, where even short air hops between cities and countries can be subject to long delays, and where less than an hour in the air may involve four or five hours on the ground hanging around the airport and getting to and from it.

It may be easier to work or relax on a train than on a plane, reducing stress and using travel time effectively in a quality way. The baggage restrictions are more flexible, and often Amtrak and overseas rail systems offer incredible bargain packages of reduced fares.

The great thing about trains for the business traveler is that they are so reliable compared with planes. Rarely does bad weather affect their schedules, and trains, unlike planes, are not unduly affected by congestion at peak periods. Next time your flight is locked into a holding pattern or queueing up to take off, think of the trains slipping smoothly in and out of the stations below. If you are on a plane waiting to land, you may still be an hour or more from your city center destination even after the aircraft's wheels have touched the ground. If on the train, you could be in your hotel room within a few minutes.

The big problem with going by train is that the good news is getting around, and overnight accommodation on the most popular services in the United States, Canada, Europe, Africa, and parts of Asia get booked up well in advance. So it is necessary to plan ahead or take a chance on last-minute no-shows.

Amtrak reservations can be made by most travel agents through the same computer systems they use to make airline bookings. However, agents are not so familiar with trains as they are with planes, and you may need to push to get quality information, especially about fare deals. You can cross America by sleeper train for about the same cost as flying first class, and if you get a deal that includes meals or seasonal discounts, it is a financially attractive proposition.

For more information about train travel in the United States, contact Amtrak around the clock on 800 USA-RAIL. Via Rail Canada can be reached from New York,

Rhode Island and Connecticut on 800 361-3677 and from other East Coast locations on 800 561-3949. The number for most of the midwestern, western, and southern United States is 800 665-0200, with the exception of Michigan, Illinois, Indiana, and Ohio, from where you should call 800 387-1144.

Even if Amtrak does not fit into your domestic travel plans, the train can make a lot of sense in territories like Europe and Japan, where distances are shorter and both air and ground traffic congestion generally greater. In Tokyo, for example, the journey to the airport can be so unpredictable that you have to build hours of time into your planning to anticipate delays caused by traffic jams, but the bullet trains are incredibly reliable. Stand by the marker on the platform, and not only will the train arrive at the precise time printed in the schedule, but a door will open immediately opposite you—and close again after you at the precise time scheduled for departure. It's a great way to go!

Travel Planning by Computer

Travel services accessible on electronic bulletin boards by personal computer and modem are becoming more widely available as a tool for business travelers not looked after by in-house or consultant travel specialists. They are one of the most attractive features of Prodigy, the videotext service launched by IBM and Sears. Prodigy is the nearest U.S. equivalent to the remarkable Minitel service in France, which has over four million home and business users. Prodigy is becoming available virtually everywhere in the United States during the early 1990s, and it costs under $10 a month at the time of writing.

Prodigy is linked up with American Airlines' SABRE travel system, enabling you to store information on its database about your personal travel profile, including your credit card number, seat preference, meal requirements, and so on. You can call up from home or office and evaluate available schedules and costs, the type of aircraft and even the track record of particular services in arriving on time. You can make your own reservations on more than three hundred airlines and designate a travel agent to write up the ticket.

Prodigy and other videotext services are evolving rapidly. As personal travel planner facilities have proved among the most popular features, one can expect them to expand steadily and become more sophisticated in the interactive information available on weather, currency rates, and other travel data.

CompuServe, Dow Jones News/Retrieval and Genie are leading databases offering flexible and varied travel services, but the cost of accessing them and the subscriptions are generally higher than for videotext services. CompuServe scores with its hotel and rental car booking services, while the electronic edition of *The Official Airline Guide* on Dow Jones is a superb travel information resource. In effect you become your own travel agent with its comprehensive information on more than 600 airlines and 30,000 hotels and motels around the world. The OAG enables you to compare and investigate the detailed restrictions on discounts, but searching for them can be expensive in time and money when a good travel agent should do much of the work. However, when you are really digging for the cheapest fares and accommodation, it may be worthwhile to do it yourself—and for those controlling corporate travel budgets the computer is a good tool to spot-check on the performance of your agent.

COMPUTER GUIDE FOR FREQUENT FLIERS

An alternative to using a modem and going on-line to a database to do your travel planning is to subscribe to a disk format information resource that is updated regularly.

PC Flight Guide provides independent information on flight options between American cities without any of the bias that can creep into systems owned by airline interests. There are details of 20,000 direct flights and nearly 250,000 connections, hotels, restaurants, parking, aircraft seating charts and other travel topics in the program, all regularly updated with new disks.

Choosing Your Seating and Traveling Companions

Just whom you will sit next to is one of the biggest unknowns in flying and both your seating location and your companions can have a significant influence on the quality of your traveling time. Some elements of this lottery you can influence; others are pure chance. Here is how to improve the odds.

Some women prefer, especially on a long flight, to sit with another woman. Other passengers may not want to be disturbed by infants. You may indicate such choices on booking or when getting your seat allocation at the check-in desk.

Extra legroom is usually to be found in seats by the emergency exits and on some planes in the row immediately in front or behind a bulkhead. However, the seats facing a bulkhead are often used by passengers with infants and may be right up close to the movie screen, so you may not wish to be located there.

Aisle seats give more freedom of movement, but you are likely to be disturbed by other passengers, especially during meals and drinks services. Avoid aisle seats near restrooms and galleys—they can be noisy and you are likely to be disturbed frequently. Choose an aisle seat near one of the main exits if you want to be among the first to leave the plane.

Some planes have single or double rows of seats right at the rear with more legroom and space for baggage than other economy class seating. However, they may be near restrooms or a galley, be noisy, and put you at the end of the queue to get off the plane.

It is generally easier to sleep in a window seat, but they are more difficult to leave, both during the flight when you want to get to the restroom or exercise, and when disembarking. However, you reduce travel stress by relaxing in a window seat and opting out of the scramble to disembark. The time "lost" may well be evened up by delays in the terminal, so that you may get out to your ground transportation just as quickly as those who shoved and pushed.

However, on international trips, especially on jumbos, you can save a lot of time queueing to get through immigration checks if you are among the first passengers off a flight. I have queued for over an hour at Kennedy airport before even getting to the INS desk, and the immigration and health control delays at some overseas terminals are as bad—even worse. However, to be one of the first off the plane demands limited and well-organized carry-on baggage and sitting in an aisle seat near a main exit.

Getting on and off the plane if your seat is some distance from an exit is made far easier and less stressful if your in-flight bag is on wheels with a long strap, so that you can pull it behind you along the narrow aisles. Such a bag also prevents the passengers behind from pushing up against you and, as you can control the distance between yourself and the passenger in front, you feel much less crowded and jostled.

On a lightly booked long flight with plenty of cabin space free, the center block of seats on a wide-bodied plane may be the best choice if you can get a row to yourself and want to stretch out to sleep. Flip up the arm rests soon after takeoff to establish a territorial claim.

Some foreign airlines may put you in a smoking area if all the nonsmoking seats are taken. American airlines are obliged to create nonsmoking areas if passengers insist on their breathing rights. The nonsmoking seats near smoking areas on some planes can subject you to a considerable degree of passive smoking. If this is an important issue for you, establish what the situation will be when getting your seat allocation—it may be too late to change once you are on board a full flight.

If you travel with a cello—or some other fragile, bulky

and precious object—it may be worth booking a separate seat for it. If you have fragile human carry-on baggage, a child under two years of age, you may prefer to book and pay for a seat for it also rather than take advantage of the free concession (or 10 percent of the adult fare on international flights). Airlines do make an effort to arrange empty seats next to passengers with infants—as much in the interests of other passengers as to accommodate the children—but you must tell them in advance.

Indeed, if you have *any* particular seating requirements, make them known well in advance—and book early if you can. Then check again before departure that your requests have been noted.

Children and Traveling

Some children these days are frequent fliers in their own right. Others only travel occasionally, but when they do, the added stress and problems can be a real pain for accompanying adults and for other passengers as well.

Above all, when traveling with children, plan as far ahead as possible and anticipate all the worst-case scenarios that might occur. A fundamental law of travel karma is that most flights alone go reasonably smoothly, but the moment you take a child along the odds are reversed against you.

That advance planning starts with making an early booking. Infants under two years old may travel free as "lap children" on domestic flights and for 10 percent of the adult fare on international trips, but only at the ratio of one per lap. Take two and you will have to pay for one; take only one and it may be worth paying a discounted fare to get it allocated a separate seat.

Indeed, a separate seat can be a worthwhile investment in a young child's safety, because a car safety seat is the best choice for junior's air travel also. It should have a sticker saying that it was manufactured after January 1, 1981, and conforms to federal standards; otherwise it may not be allowed on the plane. Some airlines will let you use an infant safety seat without booking—and paying for—an additional passenger seat if there is space available. Check their different policies, especially as the FAA rules are subject to change also.

An infant restrained in a proper safety seat is far less likely to be injured in an emergency or thrown around in turbulence than is one unrestrained sitting on your lap. But even that is not as bad as strapping a seat belt around both you and the child. In an emergency the weight of the adult being thrown forward against the belt could crush the child.

The fare structure for children is varied and keeps on changing. You should get at least 25 percent off the standard coach fare for a child under eleven who occupies a seat, but there are all kinds of special deals for advance booking and for children traveling with adult passengers.

Children under five years of age are not allowed to travel alone, and those aged five to seven years may go unaccompanied only on direct or nonstop flights. Unaccompanied 8- to 12-year-olds, who are allowed to change flights en route, must be escorted when they make the connection, and that usually incurs a $20 surcharge. Any unaccompanied child should be released from the airline's care on reaching its destination only to someone who has both been designated in advance and can provide proper identification. The airline personnel should follow this rule—but make sure the child knows about it also.

Some airlines are better organized—and motivated—about young passengers than others, so it may pay to shop around on routes where there is a choice. For example, some have special juvenile frequent-flier clubs or children's lounges, which indicate a preparedness to go out of their way in catering for children.

Although it will extend the total traveling time, it is worthwhile to get to the airport well in advance of the mandatory check-in time. That gives a margin in which to try to sort out any advance arrangements that have not been properly followed through or to get the best seat allocation. A crib or bassinet can be booked for infants, but usually only for seats in front of the bulkhead, where the armrests may be fixed. This makes the seating less flexible, which may be a problem, especially if there are other young children along as well.

Traveling children should wear loose, comfortable clothing, layered so that they can add or peel off according to the temperature changes. There should, of course, be spare clothing for accidents. Children are more vulnerable to air sickness than adults, and just the strangeness of the experience may make them throw up. Food and drink are likely to be spilled also by young hands unused to the contortions required to take in sustenance on planes. Disposable diapers, wipes, and sealable plastic bags are essentials for infants, who should also be accompanied by premixed bottles of formula. These can be obtained already made up in disposable bottles, which from the hygiene and convenience viewpoints are not a luxury when traveling, but well worth the extra cost.

Do not rely on the airline to provide anything special for young passengers, either in supplies or services. The flight attendants will heat up a bottle, but they cannot be expected to mix formula or to clean nipples and certainly not to change diapers.

Sucking at a bottle—or a pacifier—will help an infant or toddler cope with the air pressure changes on ascent and descent; older children should be given sweets or chewing gum along with an explanation of why their ears will feel strange.

Special children's meals have to be ordered in advance, but they may not arrive at the most opportune times to coincide with youth's hunger pangs. A plentiful supply of favorite snacks is worth taking, along with favored toys, games, books, and other amusements. Avoid chocolate and other messy, sticky foods that are prone to melting over clothes, seats, and fellow passengers.

The personal stereo and a generous supply of tapes is one of the best forms of entertainment for older children, along with a plentiful supply of favorite reading material. A pair of plastic children's safety scissors takes up no space and can be used for cutting up the pictures in inflight magazines—the best use for many of them! Some airlines also carry crayons, coloring books, packs of cards, and other play items, but they are often not sufficient to occupy a child for long, so you do need to take other toys and games with you.

I read with horror in a family magazine article on traveling with children that it is a good idea to supply them with tape recorders so that they can wander the aisles interviewing passengers and crew. Many adult frequent fliers, even fond parents and grandparents, will find such a prospect appalling and prefer that children on planes stay quietly in their seats, not romping up and down the aisles sticking microphones into other passengers' faces.

One final tip from frequent fliers who are experienced in accompanying children is to have a relative or friend on the ground at each end of the journey. Coping with young children in the airport is bad enough without having to battle with baggage as well, so an extra pair of teenage or adult hands on arrival and departure can prove invaluable.

Take a Tour of Your Ticket

An airline ticket is a valuable legal contract, usually worth its face value in cash. It is also your only record of key data about your trip.

It can be very expensive to lose your ticket. If someone finds it and uses it—even after you have reported the loss—you may get no money back. If you do get a refund, it may take six months, and you may be charged a handling fee as high as $50. Some airlines will not refund cash, only issue a voucher for another trip, which you may not want to take.

Losing your ticket can be as bad as losing cash, so buying it with a credit card is advantageous because you have both consumer credit rights to cancel it and evidence of the purchase. Indeed, if you can produce the credit card slip and identification, you should be able to get a replacement ticket issued without further charge or delay. Policies differ between airlines, so be prepared to argue.

If you have paid cash direct to the airline for the ticket and then lose it, you may find that no record of the transaction is available from the airline's central computer database after twenty-four hours. A cash purchase from a travel agent is easier to substantiate because they usually keep readily accessible records longer.

In any event, you will speed up the replacement or refund process immensely if you can quote the number of the lost ticket—so it pays to note this immediately after the ticket is obtained.

Obviously, the best thing is not to lose the ticket at all, but they are small, flimsy documents, easily misplaced or lifted by pickpockets in busy air terminals. The best compromise between security and convenience for both ticket and boarding pass is in a zipped or Velcro-fastened pocket in your carry-on bag or the clothing you are wearing for a flight or in your leg wallet, money belt, or other safe and accessible document stowage.

A standardized form of air ticket is used by all airlines affiliated with the International Air Transport Association. It is useful for a frequent flier to understand the ticket because it contains a wealth of information about the trip. Passengers who always check that their tickets have been filled in correctly avoid a lot of hassles. Here is a quick tour of your ticket.

Name. Ensure that your names and title—both first and surnames and the Mr. Mrs., Ms., or Dr. have been entered correctly. Tickets may be transferable between flights but not between individuals, so your name on the ticket may well be checked against other identification, particularly your passport on international flights. There have been numerous instances of family members with the same surnames—often the same initials—who got their tickets mixed up, arrived at the check-in independently and had problems being accepted for travel.

Good for passage. This section details points of departure and arrival, with intermediate stops at transfers. Many cities have two or more airports, so the correct airport code should be listed—and followed through with identification on your baggage. Tickets come in carbon sets, and you should be careful to surrender only the appropriate page for the particular leg of the journey. The flight for which any coupon is valid is described within the heavy printed rules.

Fare basis. **Y** denotes economy or coach class, **J** is for business class and **F** for first class.

Baggage allowance. American airlines give their baggage allowances according to the number of items of checked luggage, while internationally there are weight limits. The allowances vary between the different classes;

sometimes the cost of upgrading is attractive if you have excess baggage for your travel class.

Carrier. The code for the airline for which the ticket is issued. Not all tickets are freely interchangeable, even between IATA airlines, if special exclusions are noted.

Flight number. This can be confusing. It is actually the number identifying the route and departure time, not the actual plane you will take, so it is very important to check that the date is correct. On long trips with transfers, the flight numbers will change, and these different numbers should be listed on the relevant sections of the ticket.

Class. This coding may differ from your fare basis. For example, you may pay at the first class rate to fly the Atlantic on Concorde but have an R written here and in the ticket designator box above because Concorde is a single-class plane.

Departure date and time. Check that these tie in with the correct flight number and your schedule. All times are local. Double check the actual *check-in time*, especially overseas, and do not assume it is the customary half-hour for local and one hour for international flights—or that your travel agent knows the latest situation, especially at overseas terminals. These days it is necessary to check in two hours or more before departure at some security-sensitive airports.

Status. It should be marked OK for a confirmed reservation; if left blank or there is any other marking in this box, query your status when you receive the ticket. Check the requirements for reconfirming the reservation before departure or between legs of a trip.

Ticket number. Unique to your ticket. Make a note of it immediately and keep it in a safe place in case the ticket is lost.

Endorsements. Details of routine restrictions such as those applying to APEX fares.

Additional endorsements and restrictions. This box

will contain details of any special conditions applying to this particular ticket for this flight. If the same restrictions do not apply to subsequent legs of the trip or to the return journey, make sure that they have not been duplicated on the pages that follow. Watch out particularly for endorsements giving the airline the right to increase the fare between the issue of the ticket and the actual departure. This may happen if a general fare increase is looming or in countries suffering severe currency inflation.

Fare. This could be important both for your accounting records and if you wish to cash in or change the ticket, especially on an international trip. The box to the right gives the equivalent of the fare if paid for in local currency.

Tax. Airport and other special taxes may apply. Ensure that you know if they have been included or whether you will need to make an additional payment when you check in.

Validity. These dates may be important, especially as there are now such complex restrictions and variations for discounted fares. Normally an IATA ticket remains valid for a year and can be cashed in or renewed within thirty days of expiration. Some airlines are more flexible.

Conjunction tickets. A long or complex trip with more than four stopovers cannot be accommodated within one set of coupons, so additional ones are issued. Reference to them should be made in this section.

Flight coupon number. Coupon number one covers the first leg of the trip, and after you surrender it at check-in, coupon number 2 is revealed for the second leg or return trip. Do not give up the wrong one!

Baggage checked. Details of the weight and number of items checked in will be important if you need to make a claim.

Personal Safety

Traveling Defensively

Don't worry about the things you cannot control, but travel defensively to reduce other risks

Air travel is inherently safe, but there are a number of physical risks to which the frequent flier is exposed. They divide into two broad categories—those you can do something about and those you can't. Understanding and accepting the unavoidable risks does a great deal to reduce travel stress, while defensive tactics do much to protect you against threats you can influence.

The problem is that we worry about both kinds of risk—and the Hyatt Travel Futures Project research indicates that worrying about situations that we cannot control is a major cause of stress and all its unpleasant consequences.

We worry most about aircraft getting so old that they become unsafe, according to a March 1989 poll of adult Americans made for *Time* magazine and Cable News Network. Seventy-two percent thought that aging aircraft were a big problem making it less safe to fly on commercial airplanes. Poor maintenance was close behind with a 70 percent rating; the threat of terrorism ranked third at 60 percent; and the shortage of air traffic controllers scored 58 percent.

An overwhelming 64 percent of those surveyed believed that flying on commercial airplanes had become less safe than five years previously; only 20 percent thought safety had improved; 11 percent considered that there had been no change.

AGING AIRCRAFT

The aging and maintenance of commercial aircraft are related concerns that passengers may think they can do something about because on many flights there is a choice of airlines to use. However, in reality it is almost impossible for passengers—or any "experts" to whom we may turn for help—to make consistent value judgments between the relative theoretical safety of competing fleets.

Deregulation in the United States resulted in an intensely competitive decade. Many carriers failed financially, and most of the survivors were short of cash for replacing aging, tired planes.

In 1989, as a result, the average age of commercial planes flown by the major American carriers was around thirteen years. Several leading fleets use planes averaging over fifteen years. A significant number of the most popular airliners—like the Boeing 727, 737, and 747—are over twenty. We are still remarkably ignorant about the extent to which a properly maintained plane becomes inherently less safe as it ages, especially in the complex deterioration resulting from metal fatigue.

A particular point of concern is that hub-and-spoke flight routing following deregulation has given many of the 3,300 American commercial jets a tough life. They have had to make far more landing and takeoff cycles because of hub-and-spoke and so have been exposed to more stress. So not only has the United States the oldest commercial jet fleet in the Western world, but our planes are also among the most used and abused.

The passenger really concerned about the safety of older aircraft can fly on airlines with the youngest fleet average age, which early in 1989 were Delta, USAir/Piedmont, and American. The oldest averages—all over 15 years—were in the Northwest, TWA, and Eastern fleets. But with so many new planes on order, fleet age averages change all the time.

When traveling internationally, you can reduce the odds of flying on an old plane by picking foreign carriers with particularly young fleets. Singapore Airlines was under five years and Lufthansa under eight years, for example, during 1989. Government subsidies and the high profits possible from regulated fares are among the reasons that some foreign airlines are able to fly a higher proportion of new planes than their American competitors.

But to choose to fly on the basis of the average age of a carrier's fleet is not necessarily to make the safest choice. The American airlines are voluntarily spending $800 million to rejuvenate 1,300 of their older Boeings, and similar action is being taken to give a new lease of life to Lockheed, McDonnell Douglas, and other makes of aircraft.

At the same time, tougher and more effective preventative safety measures, including new ways of monitoring aircraft structures for hidden stress-related problems, are being imposed. An old plane that has been virtually rebuilt—some are actually being reskinned—and subjected to very critical examination may be in better shape than one several years younger that has not been through this process.

The plane on which you actually fly may be a youngster in a predominantly old fleet or a scarred veteran from a fleet that is mainly young. It could be a rebuilt old plane given a new lease of life or a much younger plane badly in need of refurbishing. It may have spent its operating life on long-haul intercontinental trips or on the far more stressful hopping between domestic hubs. Some have made 60,000 hub-and-spoke flights.

So choosing a carrier on the basis of the average age of its aircraft is still very much a lottery.

Air travel buying decisions may also be made on distorted perceptions of which airlines have the younger planes and best maintenance programs. In response to passenger concerns, orders for new aircraft are being publicized intensely, and very clever advertising campaigns have been created to convey deceptive images of reliability and high safety standards. In comparison with the tobacco industry, which can generate strong sales propaganda for a product proven to kill its customers, even an inferior airline's image building is a piece of cake!

Since the issue of the age of aircraft became such a matter of public concern, the airlines have swamped aircraft manufacturers with highly publicized orders that seem to indicate that the graying of the national fleet is a trend rapidly being reversed. Not so; most of those orders will not actually be filled for years, and the expanding airlines have no alternative but to buy venerable aircraft and put them into service. There is such a shortage of jet airliners that few are being scrapped, although there is some consolation in that many of the oldest are being switched from passenger to freight operations. You stand a slightly better chance yourself of going coast-to-coast on reasonably youthful planes than do your air freight packages.

Even if you pick a carrier by an accurate evaluation of the average age of its fleet and actually get to fly on a reasonably new plane, you may be exposed to a theoretically higher risk than necessary because that carrier's maintenance standards are lower than those of a competitor flying the same route with older planes.

To make valid aircraft safety judgments, you must consider the ratio of maintenance staff to planes, allowing for the fact that older planes need more maintenance than younger ones. Then factor in the policies and ethical standards of the airlines, their investment in training and maintenance facilities, whether they pay engineering staff sufficiently well to employ quality people, and whether the morale of those people is high and reflected in the quality of their work.

Companies—or individual travelers—who go to the trouble to make such value judgments still find it very difficult to come to valid conclusions. For example, some leading American airlines spend under $400 in maintenance expenses for every hour that one of their planes is in the air, while others spend almost $700, one even over $800. While the statistics on maintenance expenditures correlate to the average age of a fleet, many discrepancies make this an unreliable standard for evaluating overall maintenance performance.

You can, of course, look at the reports of fines for bad maintenance levied by FAA inspectors, but the inspection system itself has repeatedly been found to be deficient in important respects. The FAA has only about a thousand inspectors to monitor more than four times that number of repair stations in the United States alone. Many U.S. airlines have a significant proportion of their maintenance work done overseas—and there are fewer than twenty FAA inspectors monitoring some two hundred foreign repair stations.

Even if you, your travel agent, consultant, or company travel specialists can make valid suggestions on which airline has the theoretically safest planes, the many human factors involved are far more difficult, if not impossible, to evaluate. Indeed, you are more at risk from deficiences in the aircrew than from mechanical malfunction of the plane. Studies by both the National Transportation Safety Board and Boeing attribute most crashes at least partly to pilot error.

Unpublicized problems may lower the efficiency of a particular airline's flight crews at any given time and so create potentially greater risks for passengers.

A dramatic example of this arose in 1989, during conflict between one leading carrier's union and nonunion pilots. There were suggestions of tampering with pilots' food, discord in cockpits prejudicing the efficient carrying out of preflight safety checks, and a great deal of stress that may erode the aircrew's efficiency in life-threatening emergencies.

"When I go up in an airplane, I want to be in the hands of competent, satisfied employees who are as happy as it is possible to be," Lane Kirkland, president of the AFL-CIO, wrote to the *New York Times* when stressing the importance of airline employee morale. Frequent fliers should agree with that view, but it focuses on only one aspect of safety-related maintenance. Even airlines with high employee morale have cut costs by installing substandard parts or have failed to move as quickly as they should to equip their planes with improved navigational and collision avoidance equipment.

In short, it is well nigh impossible to choose which airlines have the safest aircraft, although growing concerns about aging aircraft, maintenance standards, and aircrew competence will result in "experts" peddling that advice. Their activities will increase frequent fliers' concerns about safety and the consequent unnecessary stress sustained in one of the safest forms of travel ever devised,

GETTING THE TERRORIST THREAT IN PERSPECTIVE

A similar situation exists when travelers try to anticipate and reduce their exposure to their third main concern, terrorism. IBM caused a furor when its travel experts advised the corporation's nearly 400,000 employees not to use American carriers operating out of Europe and the Middle East after the explosion on board Pan American's Flight 103 over Scotland. IBM is not alone; other large corporations routinely advise employees about the perceived security ratings of different airlines. Yet the chances of the business community being able accurately to predict terrorist acts are very small when even government counterterrorist agencies with their vast resources have proved so inadequate at the job.

Your company's security specialists may be getting the best intelligence available from the computer database operated by the Overseas Security Advisory Council of the

---

FEAR IN THE AIR

A survey of Americans who have traveled abroad showed that nearly one in ten have canceled trips because of fear of terrorism.

The study, made by Louis Harris for *Travel & Leisure* magazine in 1989, indicated that the main reason for personal travel is rest, with escape ranked second and adventure third. The top choice for a dream vacation with no limits on the time or money available is Europe for 33 percent, Hawaii for 24 percent, the South Pacific for 16 percent, and the Caribbean for 14 percent of respondents.

State Department. But the quality of that data and how it is interpreted can be very suspect. Indeed, there has been no recorded incident at the time of writing in 1989 of the official U.S. terrorist warning system accurately predicting or preventing any incident involving a civil aircraft.

There will be more disruptions to air travel than terrorists can cause if hysteria builds to the point where, as has been proposed in Congress, the State Department provides travelers with a toll-free line to check out if any threats have been made against the flights they plan to take. That would both increase the already serious problem of hoax threats and make any sensible warning system virtually impossible to operate.

There seems no alternative to delegating the responsibility for making planes as mechanically safe and free from terrorist attack as possible to the airlines, police and other security services, airport authorities and the public agencies which monitor them. It may be frustrating—and they may be found wanting on occasions—but this is all part of the loss of personal control inherent in commercial air travel.

You can phone the State Department's Citizen's Emergency Center at 202 647-5225 or the FAA hot line at 800 255-1111, but you are most unlikely to get specific advice to help make informed decisions about which flights are safe.

FACTS ABOUT ACCIDENTS

About two-thirds of all aircraft accidents occur during descent and landing, about a quarter during takeoff and ascent, and fewer than 10 percent while the aircraft is cruising. So relax during most of the flight knowing that the risks of anything going wrong then are very small.

Even that major worry revealed in the Time/CNN survey—too few air traffic controllers—is largely unjustified. In 1988 there was a marked reduction in errors by air traffic controllers and in the incidence of collisions and near-misses. There is a positive trend for our air traffic control systems to get better at guiding aircraft off and on the ground and at preventing them from running into each other while they are in the air. That mirrors the overall trend toward safer air travel—the 875 people who died in 1988 in accidents involving American commercial air carriers and private planes were the fewest in a decade despite substantial increases in air traffic.

Only one in 257,000 scheduled airline flights that year resulted in an accident, and only one in every 3.6 million flights involved a fatal accident. While these figures relate to accidents only and so exclude the Pan Am terrorist bombing, they demonstrate that the risk to the most frequent flier from geriatric aircraft, poor maintenance, terrorism or a shortage of air traffic controllers is much less than that from other activities we take for granted, such as crossing a busy street and driving a car. Things did get

BEATING THE BIRDS

Ever wondered why the grass at many airports looks far less healthy than fields nearby, or why there is virtually no attempt at landscaping to make them more attractive?

The answer is *birds*. Efficient airports go to a lot of trouble to control insects and small animals—even earthworms—that might encourage birds to collect near runways in the search for food. Various forms of bird scarers, including hawks or falcons, are used to prevent bird strike, when a single bird or a flock collides with a plane.

Bird strike is particularly dangerous during takeoff, when one or a number sucked into the engine can cause loss of power, even damage. Although windshields were vulnerable to bird strike in the earlier days of aviation, modern airliners are fitted with very strong laminated glass that is tested by firing dead chickens at it.

worse in 1989, when there was a series of incidents involving commercial aircraft, but only time will tell if this was just an unfortunate freak situation.

DEFENSIVE FLYING STRATEGIES

If you are concerned about reducing risks even further, use big jets rather than smaller commuter planes, particularly those with fewer than thirty seats that are powered by piston engines and that carry only one pilot. If you do have to use small planes with their worse safety record than that of the big jets, try to avoid bad weather and night flights, when their accident rates are highest. The standards of maintenance, equipment, pilots' skill and other safety-related factors also vary more for commuter airlines than for the bigger carriers.

Dress for Safety

In a crash involving any aircraft, the survival rate of passengers is linked very closely to their ability to get out quickly, before being affected by fire or smoke. Worthwhile precautionary measures for concerned frequent fliers include wearing fire-resistant clothing in which you can move easily. Natural fibers rather than synthetics, and flat, comfortable shoes are desirable. High heels are not the right footwear for air travel; they increase your risk of ankle injury in a variety of situations and are a potential menace to other passengers and to inflatable escape chutes and life rafts.

Select Your Exit

Sit reasonably close to an exit—or at least take careful note where the exits are so that you can find them, even in the dark or if the cabin is filled with smoke and confusion. In an investigation of two hundred survivors of an air crash, 90 percent of them had given advance thought to their escape route in an emergency. Some aviation experts prefer aisle seats near the middle of the aircraft. This gives them a choice of exits if the one nearest gets blocked. Others favor being near the rear, as tail sections tend to remain intact in a crash more than the front and middle areas.

Read the Safety Card

Be familiar with the instructions on the safety card in the seat pocket. If there is time, reread them in an emergency. Postcrash investigations have shown conclusively that you increase your chances of survival substantially if you have read the card and taken a note of the location of the exits. In one study by the National Transportation Safety Board, only 16 percent of passengers who read the card were injured compared with over half who did not.

The Vital Seat Belt

Fasten your seat belt carefully, pulling it as tight as possible low down over your hips and abdomen. If an emergency landing is to be made, pull the belt so tight that it hurts. Put the seat back in the upright position, stow the table, and bend over forward in a fetal attitude with your feet braced against the floor, your head resting on a pillow on your knees, and your arms wrapped around it. If there is room, bend even lower and grasp your ankles.

Some experts advise raising your feet off the floor and bracing them against the seat in front to reduce the risk of injury to your lower legs, but there may not be room for this posture. Even in normal landings, it is sensible to brace your feet slightly forward on the floor and pay particular attention to the tightness and positioning of the seat belt. If it is too high and loose, you can *submarine* in a sudden stop, sliding under the belt and sustaining injury.

As in car accidents, one of the main benefits of a seat belt is not just to reduce injury but to ensure that the passenger remains conscious and so able to evacuate quickly. Unbelted passengers have been knocked unconscious—a few actually killed—when thrown out of their seats when the plane moved violently as a result of turbulence.

Fire and Smoke

The biggest hazards after a crash are smoke, fire, and noxious fumes. You increase your personal risk if you flout the baggage rules—and common sense—and carry on board with you aerosols, butane cartridges, inflammable liquids, and so on.

If the emergency has occurred over water and you put on the life jacket usually found under each seat do *not* inflate it until you get out of the plane. If you inflate the jacket too soon, its extra bulk may prevent you from exiting and impede other passengers also.

Follow the instructions of the flight attendants; don't panic; try to move in an orderly way toward the nearest exit. There may be a lot of competition from other passengers, but the more who get outside the plane, the easier to exit it should become for those remaining.

The Smoke Hood

If smoke or fumes are present in the cabin, get down and crawl along the floor, where the air should be clearer, trying to breathe as little as possible. If you are really well prepared for emergencies, you will carry your own smoke hood until the airlines provide this simple but very effective safety aid. Investigation of a crash and fire of a British Airtours Boeing 737 indicated that forty-five or more lives might have been saved if the passengers had had smoke hoods. Some corporate planes already carry them, but they are optional equipment for scheduled airlines.

Be prepared for obstructions from loose baggage and perhaps from unconscious or injured passengers. Once you are through the exit, the emergency chutes should let you slide smoothly to the ground, but they are flammable, and if there is a fire outside, you must be prepared for a long drop or to use a rope or escape ladder. Once on the ground, move well away to allow other passengers to follow—and to avoid having them collide with you or drop onto you.

Very few emergency evacuations of aircraft occur in water, but if you do finish up in water, inflate the life jacket as shown in the demonstration by the flight attendants and remember that it is designed to keep you afloat on your back with your nose and mouth farthest out of the water. So don't try any fancy swimming. If you have to move through the water to get to the life raft, paddle gently on your back.

Statistics show that many air crashes are survivable and that many more passengers *would* survive accidents if they just paid attention to the preflight safety briefings on how to fasten seat belts properly, use the oxygen masks, put on the life jackets, and find the emergency exits.

TERRORISM AND THIEVES

The terrorist threat to frequent fliers does not justify the concerns expressed by respondents to the Time/CNN survey. Moreover, there are severe limits to what you can do personally to lessen the terrorist threat, apart from cooperating with the security measures being adopted at airports and behaving sensibly during a hijacking or bomb incident.

A basic rule is not to carry any bags or packages for other people—they might contain drugs or bombs—or to allow anyone else access to your own baggage. It makes sense these days, without getting neurotic about it, not to hang around unattended bags or luggage holding areas where bombs might be hidden. Keep away from windows in security-sensitive places—a high proportion of the casualties in bomb explosions is caused by flying or fallen broken glass. Avoid sitting or loitering near waste bins also, as they are a favorite place for concealing delayed-action bombs.

Anyone who travels to hazardous places—and the organizations that employ such travelers—should provide training in antiterrorist and other defensive techniques. Circumstances differ enormously, but here are some basic tactics for a wide range of threatening—or potentially threatening—situations the frequent flier may encounter.

TRAVEL INCENTIVES MAY NOT BE SO ATTRACTIVE NOW

Apprehensions about security in the air and on the ground may prove a big blow to the incentive travel business, which now accounts for a significant proportion of frequent flying.

More than three million Americans a year take trips as rewards for good work performance or as an incentive to do better. The $2.5 billion-a-year business started as stick-and-carrot programs for sales personnel, but in recent years it has extended to virtually all kinds of business activity.

Those who organize competitions know that a travel prize to an exotic destination may generate fewer responses than something of less value but also less threatening in terms of personal challenge or apprehension. Trips to exotic destinations in romantic-sounding foreign countries have become a feature of many incentive travel schemes, but bad publicity about security risks is making them less attractive both to employees and to spouses, who are often invited along.

Bomb Explosions

If there is a bomb explosion, move quickly away from the scene. A second bomb may be planted in case the first does not go off or to target police or military personnel who investigate the first explosion, or both. If an official orders you to stop, do so immediately, assume a non-threatening posture, and keep your hands clearly visible. If shooting breaks out, get down on the floor and cover your head with your hands—both for protection and to make it obvious that you are not concealing a weapon.

Avoid dark and poorly lit areas and places away from the crowd, where you would be more vulnerable to attack. Be particularly careful of public restrooms at night. Be street-smart if you cannot avoid walking in dangerous areas. Pick the busiest, best-lit routes; stay near the curb and away from dark doorways.

If you see any bags or packages unattended in public places, move away from them and alert the nearest security official. Do the same if you see anyone behaving strangely, even if it is something indefinable that arouses your suspicions. That advice applies to fellow passengers on the plane as well as on the ground. If a passenger arouses your suspicion, quietly leave your seat as if to go to the restroom and try to convey your concerns discreetly to a flight attendant. Report any suspect packages or bags you find under seats, in seat pockets, or in the overhead racks. Before leaving a plane at a stopover, saboteurs have planted delayed-action bombs that were missed by cleaners and cabin attendants.

Hijack Attempts

In the event of a hijack attempt, keep calm, do not make any sudden movement, and try to conceal any documents that might make a terrorist more antagonistic toward you. These include military or military style or government or corporate identity cards and passes, sensitive business papers, political and religious literature, and so on.

Literature we consider inoffensive may provoke irrational action by a terrorist or even by a government official in some places. Obviously you would think twice before carrying *The Satanic Verses* on a flight to Beirut, but there could be problem with a copy of *Playboy* in South Africa or the Middle East. It makes sense not to get involved in any kind of discussion with strangers on political, religious, or sexual controversies.

AIRPORT ATTACKED BY CANOE

Mock attacks on airports have been carried out by security forces in a number of countries and have revealed how vulnerable terminals are to terrorists. The most unusual of these security exercises was a raid made by British police in canoes on London's dockland airport. After they landed, the pseudoterrorists easily broke into a locked aircraft and disabled it to prove their point that the airport's security needed to be tightened up.

Do nothing to draw attention to yourself or to cause provocation during a hijack attempt or terrorist incident. Hand over anything they want, including money and valuables. Nothing is more important than your personal safety. Ask permission for anything you need, such as to go to the restroom or take medication, and maintain a subservient, nonchallenging attitude. Follow any instructions from the flight crew immediately, as they may be implementing some tactical procedure to combat the attack. Get down as low as you can and keep still if there is a rescue attempt; then leave the plane immediately when you are told to do so.

Defensive Tactics in Hotels

Special precautions are worth taking in hotels in sensitive places. Do not assume, for example, that there is any confidentiality with the telephone, telex, fax, or message services. Even the room may be bugged if you are a political or industrial espionage target—or visiting a country where the authorities monitor foreigners. Beware of being compromised by trading in personal valuables such as cameras, or in drugs of any kind or by making illicit currency exchanges in countries with strict controls.

Hotel staff may be watching you as accomplices for thieves, kidnappers, your business competitors, or the local police. Be careful what you say directly to them, what they overhear, what they can find out from your papers. Do not hand in your key when you go out, and do leave the radio or television playing. Hang a do not disturb sign on the door when you want to reduce the risk of unauthorized entry to your room.

Taxis and Rental Cars

Taxi drivers may be thieves, kidnappers, informers, or agents of some kind. Reduce the risk by using only licensed cabs and establish routes and fares before beginning a journey. In many places cabs are safer than walking the streets and may be cheaper and preferable to rental cars. Rental cars may be targeted by thieves, and there is the risk of encountering draconian local laws if you are involved in a traffic accident.

State Department Advisories

The State Department provides travel advisories about parts of the world that should be avoided if possible. Don't just miss them out as places to visit, but try to eliminate them as stopovers also. The number to call is 202 647-5225. There are booklets and brochures on security in general and on specific parts of the world obtainable from U.S. Government Printing Office outlets.

Kidnapping

In some places businesspeople and other foreigners are particularly vulnerable to kidnapping. It is a foolish traveler who will not take at least the basic precautions when going there. The threat of kidnapping is not just to the

CEO or other senior management but can extend to junior staff also if it is thought that deep pockets will meet a ransom demand.

The rule in such locations is to keep a low profile and not attract attention to yourself; it's sound advice also if you are on a plane that is hijacked. Nondescript clothing and luggage coupled with discreet behavior reduce your risk of being picked out as a target. It is also good advice for tourists, who too often by flamboyant behavior and dress attract muggers, pickpockets, and other thieves even where the risk of physical attack is not great.

In many countries the traveler should avoid clothing of military style and color, for example khaki safari jackets. Many times having any kind of military association is dangerous.

Do not flash jewelry, wallet, camera, or other valuables; be aware of all the distracting tactics thieves and pickpockets use. In some countries, Italy and Greece for example, children work in gangs and the most innocent-looking one will be used to distract you while your pocket is picked or bag snatched. Bags and cameras on straps should be held close to the body. Do not put them down in public places, such as under your chair in a sidewalk cafe.

The best defensive technique in any kind of threatening situation is to apply common sense and maintain a sense of proportion. Strange places and situations may appear more threatening than they are because of their very strangeness. People living without concern in cities that make the average American apprehensive regard Manhattan and Washington D.C. as two of the most dangerous places on Earth!

TALK FREELY TO TRAVEL MORE SAFELY

An inevitably more familiar aspect of travel in these security-conscious days will be the airport interview. Sometimes frustrating, invariably time-consuming, it is still one of the most cost-effective ways of reducing the risk of sabotage and terrorism in the air.

In some countries, and for some airlines, the preflight screening of passengers has long been a routine. Staff are specially trained to ask questions and watch and listen for responses—in body language as well as spoken replies—from passengers who fit specific profiles that could indicate a threat.

If passengers cooperate, the checks can be made quickly near the boarding gate after passports have been scanned and details compared with intelligence data. If the behavior or attitudes of a passenger, coupled with such factors as his or her nationality and responses to the way the luggage was packed and handled, make the passenger fit a suspect profile, he or she can be taken to one side for more detailed questioning.

This screening—or profiling, as it is sometimes called—is particularly useful to identify passengers whose luggage may have been accessible to a saboteur. Perhaps a suitcase was packed by someone else or the baggage was left unattended so that a bomb could have been placed in it.

Honest answers by honest passengers are easy to handle. The real skill in profiling comes in identifying a passenger who is not telling the truth. So how well profiling will protect us in the air depends very much on the quality of the staff who carry out this key task and how well they are trained. Unfortunately, airlines avoid paying union wages by subcontracting much security to outside firms who may skimp on training and salaries.

In addition to these human checks, dogs are used extensively at major airports in many countries to sniff out explosives as well as drugs. However, dogs have short attention spans, and while they have proved their worth in many bomb-detection tasks, they are not at all effective in monitoring thousands of pieces of luggage for hour after hour because they soon become bored. So the chances are increasing that our luggage will be sniffed by a variety of vapor detection devices that can repeatedly and rapidly analyze the air in and around items of baggage and sound an alarm if explosives are detected.

Our baggage will be exposed to bombardment by the thermal neutron analysis units costing $1 million each. Neutron analysis can detect just traces of explosive chemicals. New and sophisticated x-ray devices give clearer pictures—some in color—and can differentiate more efficiently between harmless objects and those with seemingly innocent silhouettes that are made with the plastic explosives.

Other developments behind the scenes include much greater control over access of airport and airline staff to areas closed to passengers. These include physical checks and electronic gateways to doors leading to such sensitive places as the loading ramps and baggage handling and service areas. It will be a long time before all major airports have tightened up their security in these ways. At Kennedy International Airport in New York, for example, electronic controls will be needed on fifteen hundred doors to sensitive areas.

The vast expense in capital equipment, staff, and operating costs for increased security measures will come largely from airfares. Passengers will pay an additional cost in inevitable delays, most for false alarms. While the most sophisticated of the new devices for identifying explosives are very good at finding bombs, they also raise sufficient false alarms seriously to hinder the efficient handling of baggage and passengers. Even when the rate of false alarms drops substantially—perhaps below 1 percent, much better than most such devices have achieved under test—there will still be several bomb alerts for every jumbo jet, with snap decisions being needed all the time as to which alert requires further investigation.

That is when the passenger profiling near the departure gate will prove especially valuable. The coordinating of the various mechanical security devices with human skills offers our best hope of keeping terrorism out of air traffic.

WHERE IS THE SAFEST PLACE TO SIT?

Ironically, the theoretically safest seats in an aircraft are also the cheapest—right at the back near the tail. That is where the manufacturer installs the flight recorder, usually near the base of the fin well above the heads of the rearmost passengers.

Information about the functioning of the plane's main control systems and conversations in the cockpit, recorded on stainless steel wire, can yield invaluable evidence after a crash in which the rest of the plane may be destroyed. Popularly known as black boxes, they are neither black nor usually boxy, but bright red to make them easier to find and often spherical to withstand the extreme forces likely in a crash.

WINDSHEAR

Windshear, or microburst, has caused a score of commercial airline accidents at a cost of hundreds of lives, but the risk should get less in the near future.

Some airports are particularly vulnerable to windshear, which is a strong downdraft of cold air, usually beneath a thunderstorm or heavy cloud concentration. It can be very dangerous during takeoff and landing, causing a plane to drop sharply and lose air speed. The effect in a bad windshear can be as if the plane has been struck a violent blow.

Unexplained delays in takeoff and landing may occur because the pilot has received a warning of windshear at

> ## KEEP THE RISKS IN PERSPECTIVE
>
> Despite all the alarm about terrorism and the reliability of aging jets, air travel is still one of the least dangerous aspects of contemporary life.
>
> Travel the same route by car, statistics show, and you are as much as seventy times more likely to be killed in an accident than if you catch a scheduled flight.

the airport and is waiting until it passes. However, the radar systems that have been used for many years to give warning of low-level windshear have a reputation among aircrew for a high proportion of false alarms, and their warnings may be ignored if the captain prefers to back his own judgment. Policies on this differ between airlines but are becoming more consistent as the warning systems get more reliable.

A far more accurate Doppler radar system is being installed at U.S. and major airports overseas. It may take several years before all the hundred United States airports that have been using the old low-level windshear alert system get the new Doppler system, but it is being installed first at the busiest ones with the highest incidence of windshear.

Unpredictable turbulence with some similarity to windshear near the ground can occur at altitude in clear air. It can be alarming, shaking the plane without apparent reason and making passengers feel as if they are in a bus with four flat tires bouncing over a rutted road. However, more technologically advanced equipment is making it easier for pilots to anticipate clear-air turbulence and avoid it.

Jet airlines avoid bad weather when they fly at high

altitudes, but the main reason for getting up into the cold air above the lower tropopause is that the engines will perform better. At these high altitudes the pilot also seeks to hitch a ride on a jet stream, whose winds, up to 200 mph, can bring big benefits in shorter flight time and greatly improved fuel consumption.

The Fear Factor

Aviophobia—How to Combat Travel Anxiety

There is nothing unusual about being afraid to fly, even on the big and inherently very safe commercial jets. Research by Boeing and various airlines indicates that about one in every six Americans has apprehensions about flying. These fears range from definite feelings of anxiety right through to a severe phobia. It is an international problem; Britain's Virgin Airways estimates that 20 percent of the population there is worried about flying.

Nor is aviophobia something that afflicts only the novice traveler. Some frequent fliers suddenly fall victim to it in middle or late age. Travel veterans make up a significant proportion of those attending courses to overcome fears; such courses are held in virtually all the developed countries. Typical are the special two-day courses held by Guys Hospital in London. Many of its patients are successful businesspeople who have flown extensively for years, yet suddenly become overanxious about the real and imagined risks involved. These apprehensions have increased all over the world as a result of recent terrorist threats and growing concerns about the age of aircraft and standards of maintenance.

Aviophobia is a considerable problem for the aviation industry, costing the airlines about $2 billion a year in revenues lost from travelers whose fears of flying make them seek alternative ground transport. A Gallup Poll in 1988 indicated that 10 percent of passengers are frightened every time they fly, a further 8 percent most of the time, and a further 26 percent sometimes. In a similar poll in 1983, 67 percent said they were never frightened when they flew, but by 1988 this proportion had dropped to 56 percent. It may well be that the majority of passengers experience fear of flying.

"Millions of Americans have such strong feelings that they won't fly at all; millions more are uncomfortable whenever they do fly," says Fran Grant, cofounder of the nonprofit Fear of Flying Clinic at San Francisco International Airport and a leading consultant on aviophobia. (Grant can be reached at 3802 Kenwood Avenue, San Mateo, CA 94403.)

Sometimes aviophobia is triggered by an event, which may or may not be associated with flying. For example, a traveler may be involved in an emergency landing that triggers an enhanced awareness of personal vulnerability. Perhaps a friend, relative, or business associate is injured or killed, or a crash or hijacking brings subconscious apprehensions about flying to the fore.

It may even be a consequence of many years and hundreds of thousands of miles of uneventful air travel. Travelers may start to believe their luck is due to run out and the next flight could be their last. They mistakenly believe that they have been playing a kind of Russian roulette for just too long and that their numbers are bound to come up soon.

In fact, even a lifetime of frequent flying on scheduled airlines does not expose the traveler to as much physical risk as driving on public roads or to the hazards to health and life present in the environment, or in the foods we eat, the alcohol we drink, or the tobacco we smoke.

Fran Grant stresses that the trigger for an outset of fear of flying frequently has no direct relationship to travel, but could be marital or business problems, fatigue, stress, or other factors.

"It is vital to approach this issue positively, as negative ideas about flying can become embedded and difficult to change," she says. "Fear of flying is generally found in people who are creative, well educated, in charge of others, make decisions for themselves and for others, and are sensitive to their environment.

"When they fly, they have to give up control to professionals whose skills they may not appreciate and who operate in a very different environment. One of the positive, effective ways to overcome such fears is to understand better the personal capabilities of the flying professionals. Visit the cockpit and see the people flying the plane. Talk with them about your concerns and listen carefully to their responses.

"Fear of flying is definitely controllable if you approach it in the correct way and choose to help yourself to overcome it."

Although it has not been accurately quantified, there is no doubt that the extensive publicity given recently to deficiencies in maintenance procedures by some airlines and the risks inherent in the aging commercial airline fleet have increased passengers' anxiety. We are now less likely to trust without question the technology of aviation and the quality of the machines in which we fly and of the human resources that design, maintain, and operate them.

Increasingly we have to adjust mentally to aircraft pushed beyond their anticipated service life, captained by pilots who are tending to get younger and less experienced. Even if you are only slightly nervous when you pass through the plane's door, your apprehensions may be aggravated considerably if the manufacturer's identification plate (located near the entrance at about eye level) shows that the plane was built nearly two decades previously. Then you get a glimpse into the cockpit, and instead of reassuringly experienced gray-haired father figures, you see comparative youngsters. There is such an international shortage of pilots that soon captains in their early thirties may be commonplace. Factors like these aggravate the feeling of loss of control that lies at the root of much fear of flying.

"Being forced into a passive role where they must meekly follow rather than lead, is anathema to the highly motivated, achievement orientated person," commented the Hyatt report. "For most travelers, the only certainty is that something will go wrong."

In the past frequent fliers have usually expected the something wrong to be a delay in the flight, lost luggage, or some other aspect of bad service, not a life-threatening situation. Latterly, however, our awareness of the potential for physical danger has been heightened, and so it is far more likely that something we read, a comment by a fellow traveler, a minor nonroutine event during the journey, even looking out of the cabin window and thinking that the wings are flexing more than usual may act as the catalyst for the onset of aviophobia.

Terrorism directed at air travel—either sabotage of the aircraft or the risk of hijacking—is a particular cause of anxiety for many people. One manifestation is becoming overly apprehensive about fellow travelers and their behavior, which adds a stress factor. This kind of phobic reaction—an irrational fear one cannot readily control—can creep up on you unexpectedly. It happened to me after years of fearless flying, including some hairy experiences as a foreign correspondent traveling around Africa. Sharing it may help readers who have difficulty accepting similar experiences that seem to indicate personal weakness.

I was sitting in a departure lounge one day waiting for a delayed flight when I developed a completely irrational fixation about a fellow passenger and his plastic carrier bag; I suspected him of being a terrorist with a bomb. The feeling passed eventually, but not before I had had some of the classic phobic symptoms, including a racing, erratic heartbeat, sweaty palms, difficulty in breathing, and an overwhelming sense of panic.

There was no justification for these reactions, which I had not experienced to the same degree in far more dangerous situations, including being in a plane hit by lightning, running the gauntlet of antiaircraft fire, getting lost in a single-engine plane short on fuel with a novice pilot, and going into war zones in ancient badly maintained helicopters with reckless mercenary crews playing real-life Rambos. My panic attack was sparked by an innocent fellow passenger with a carrier bag sitting in the security of an airport departure lounge. After that I have treated irrational fears and apprehensions by others far more seriously and sympathetically. They are real and nothing to be ashamed of.

What can you do about them? Is there a cure?

The usual first "treatment" that fliers with anxiety adopt is take some kind of tranquilizing medication or a stiff drink—or both. Neither alcohol nor caffeine is effective, and like drugs, they can develop into dependencies. Far better is to practice relaxation techniques, notably deep breathing, and adopt such travel-smart tactics to reduce stress as arriving at the airport in good time and not being encumbered with lots of hand baggage. Indeed, the most frequent advice I have heard from veteran travelers about reducing stress is to arrive for a flight with time in hand and baggage under control. The most stressful situation, they all say, is to be anxious about being late and coping with excessive, badly organized baggage.

A good book or an entertaining magazine is a distraction from fears. A personal tape player with a recorded book or relaxing music can be even better. There are a number of excellent audiotapes to help you relax, some to the extent of inducing self-hypnosis. The latter are best left until you are inside the plane and seated!

Some passengers with anxiety problems choose seats that make them feel less apprehensive. For example, you may feel more relaxed in an aisle seat, where you will be forced to be in contact with the normal activity going on inside the plane. When sitting by the window, one is inevitably more conscious of the possibly visually traumatic sight of the ground falling farther and farther below and the engines and airframe straining with the stresses of takeoff, or the possibility of crashing as the ground looms closer during landing. However, aviophobia is a very varied and personal thing, and I am one of those who feels less apprehensive sitting by a window and able to see what is going on outside. There is, somehow, a lessening of the disturbing feeling of losing control which the Hyatt research found is such a stress factor for many people.

You get a smoother and quieter ride in most airliners if you sit toward the front, and this helps some apprehensive travelers, although I must admit that I rationalize my preferred seating location on the incontrovertible logic of the statistics that no aircraft has ever reversed into a collision and so feel more secure sitting near the rear! Indeed, on one African airline that should, perhaps, remain nameless as its standards of flight attendant training have since improved, the stewardess announced over the public address before takeoff that there were plenty of spare seats at the rear and passengers might feel safer if they moved back.

On the same flight, the captain jocularly declared: "You may notice that leaving the ground on this flight will take longer than usual. This is because we are overloaded. There is no need for passengers to worry about this as we are doing all the worrying that is necessary up here in the cockpit!" In fairness I should note that there was a civil war raging in the area at the time and if a vote had been taken, both passengers and crew would have preferred to take off overloaded than to remain at the airport.

Most frequent fliers will never face situations that distort the basic truth that flying on scheduled commercial routes is the safest way to get from one place to another. The logic of these statistics is used extensively in most of the available treatments for fear of flying. On some of the tapes, in the books, and at the courses, you are bombarded with such facts as that you are 20,000 times more likely to be murdered than killed in an air crash, or that the chances of a road accident while driving to the airport are far higher than being injured or killed in a plane mishap.

Quality information about the realities of flight can be very reassuring for most people suffering from mild to moderate aviophobia, particularly an understanding of aviation technology—even information about the air through which the plane is flying. Some treatments overcome what many patients find a greatly disconcerting feeling of vulnerability, of being in a void when airborne, by explaining how air has a substance and can support a plane much as a boat floats in water.

Concern about engine failure, which can make some fearful fliers go through agony every time the revolutions change and the engine noise alters, is lessened by explanations of why these variations take place in a normal flight routine and the built-in safety margins that enable planes to land safely even if one or more engines do fail.

Some courses include fear desensitization procedures in which patients are made to go through their worst fears, verbalizing them and discussing them with their group or counselor in an effort to resolve them. There may be visits to airports to see maintenance work in progress, the opportunity to meet and question aircrew, and actual orientation flights.

For example, the various fear of flying programs, which have a good track record going back to 1976 and now operate at more than forty locations worldwide, use volunteer pilots, air traffic controllers, maintenance specialists, and other aviation professionals to give authoritative information to clients. The aim is that passengers' intelligent analysis of the facts about flying will help them to overcome their irrational fears.

The typical programs may feature lectures and discussion sessions at weekly meetings lasting three hours each over an eight-week period. Alternatively, the program can be completed over two full weekends of sessions from nine to five on both Saturday and Sunday. There are weekend workshops in outlying areas, special sessions staged for corporations, and supplementary audiotapes and reading material for self-study. Each group is limited to twenty-five people, and those who wish can graduate with an orientation flight accompanied by their instructors.

A one-day workshop may be sufficient for some fearful fliers and, if taken timeously, prevent more severe aviophobia from developing.

The leading programs typically achieve more than a 90 percent success rate in enabling patients to control their flight phobias, which is impressive considering they must get the more desperate cases. The cost can be about $550—excluding the optional flight. (At the end of this chapter is a list of fear of flying programs in the United States and overseas. The schedule and rates vary from place to place, but most are similar in content and cost.)

Some areas have general phobia centers that offer fear of flying courses or can put you in touch with local facilities. A source of information on all kinds of irrational fears is the Phobia Society of America, P.O. Box 42514, Washington, DC 20015.

If you have a problem over your attitude to flying, or even sense that one is emerging, a logical first step is to talk it over with your doctor or therapist. There may be a link between a fear of flying, especially one that has emerged after extensive trouble-free flying experience, with other emotional, mental, or physical conditions.

Prescription medication such as a beta blocker may help some patients sufficiently for them to cope with travel anxiety, but in most cases, medication—or alcohol—will only mask some symptoms of an irrational fear and not make any contribution to finding a long-term solution. Medication may even reinforce travelers' beliefs that they do not have the ability to control their fears.

One of the most experienced counselors on aviophobia, United Airlines' Captain Tom Bunn, has found after fifteen hundred cases that too much hand-holding can be counterproductive. He prefers helping patients focus on reality and draw on their own resources to overcome their phobias to exposing them to supportive group therapy, physically stroking aircraft on the ground, and getting to know how they are maintained, or similar therapeutic techniques used in some programs.

"One of the most effective methods we have found is to get them to see their problem in the form of a movie—in fact, two movies," Tom explained to me. "The movie they should be focusing on is called *Reality*, and it is what is actually taking place around them as they sit in the plane.

"Think of it frame by frame. There is nothing unusual or frightening taking place in this *Reality* movie, it is all very ordinary. But people who have a fear of flying phobia are playing another movie in their heads. The first few frames are the same in each movie, but in the *Fear* one the imagination runs riot and takes over. In, say, frame three after takeoff in *Reality*, the engine noise dies away and normal activities at the start of a flight are going on in the cabin. In the *Fear* movie the quietness is because the engines have failed and the plane begins to fall. By frame seven or so in *Reality* the flight attendant is leaning over you asking if you want an orange juice. Frame seven in *Fear* may be just before you crash in flames.

"Comparing their fears and the realities of flying in this way works very well for many travelers with aviophobia because they are often highly imaginative, creative people with the natural ability to conjure up strong mental images which they relate to directly and very physically with their own bodies. They are the stars of their own *Fear* movies. It is the loss of control that worries them most—not just of the aircraft going out of control and crashing but of losing control of themselves, perhaps running around the aircraft screaming.

"This fear can happen to frequent fliers who have covered a million miles or more and may be triggered by an incident that has nothing at all to do with flying, perhaps the death of a friend. Often the fear of flying comes as part of a midlife crisis when we come to realize our own vul-

YOUR CREW IS PROFESSIONAL

In a society that tends to measure professional competency in monetary terms, it may help to reassure aviophobics to know that airline pilots can be in similar earnings brackets to the surgeons to whom we also trust our lives.

Airline pilots can earn substantially more than even their executive Road Warrior frequent flier passengers. A twelve-year captain of a Boeing 727 flying the maximum 85 hours in a month can earn $11,964 in basic monthly pay, according to a survey by *The New York Times* in March 1989 drawn from Air Line Pilots Association and individual company data based on labor agreements filed with the federal government.

However, monthly maximum base pay rates vary considerably from airline to airline—to as low as $4735 for a five-year captain flying 83.3 hours per month. Entry-level pay for flight officers in the survey ranged from $1000 to $1800, and for first officers from $2100 to $2288.

nerability. In such cases, the statistics about how safe air travel really is may not help much. It is no good being told that there is only a one-in-a-million chance of you being killed in an air crash if you start off convinced that you are that one!"

Captain Tom Bunn has helped over a thousand fearful fliers at live courses and created audio tapes primarily for those who could not attend the courses. Now he finds the tapes prove just as effective and has put his course material into three audio modules, which cost $95 each.

Some people need only one, others with a more severe problem, two or three. Many people take their favorite tapes along on flights as a sort of parachute. The SOAR course is also available on videocassettes with an audio cassette to take along for on-the-spot reassurance. Tom operates a hot line for aviophobics, 800 332-7359, or you can write to him at P.O. Box 747, Westport, Connecticut 06881.

Another veteran pilot who has pioneered practical ways to help fearful fliers is Captain T. W. Cummings of Florida. He runs seminars and has written *Help for the Fearful Flier* (Simon and Schuster, 1987), also available on audiocassette.

Among other recent books is the one used in the US-Air program, *Fly without Fear*, written by Captain Frank Petee and Carol L. Stauffer and published by Dodd, Mead & Co. Experience gained in the London Guy's Hospital program mentioned earlier features in Dr. Maurice Yaffe's *Taking the Fear out of Flying*, published in the United States by Sterling Publishing Company.

There is a lot of help around. Some approaches to aviophobia are more appropriate to individual needs than others. The universal message is that virtually anyone with a fear of flying can be helped to control it.

Fear of Flying Operations

Alaska
How To Overcome Your Fear
   of Flying
c/o Ronald A. Ohlson, Ph.D.
Wien Air Alaska, Inc.
4100 W. Int'l Airport Road
Anchorage, AK 99502

Arkansas
Dr. Lewis Bracey
1501 N. University, Suite 269
Little Rock, AR 72207

Arizona
John A. Moran, Ph.D.
7530 E. Angus Drive
Scottsdale, AZ 85251
(suburb of Phoenix)
602 947-5739

California
ThAIRapy Flight Relaxation
   Treatment
c/o Glen Arnold, LCSW,
   MFCC

4500 Campus Drive, Suite
628
Newport Beach, CA 92660
714 756-1133

Fear of Flying Clinic, Inc.
A Ninety-Nine Project
1777 Borel Place, #300
San Mateo, CA 94402
415 341-1595

Freedom to Fly
Ronald Doctore, Ph.D.
and Rodney Boone, Ph.D.
941 Westwood Blvd., Suite
207
Los Angeles, CA 90024
213 208-7577

Free to Fly, Inc.
Charles A. Hogan, Ph.D.
659 Third Ave., Suite F
Chula Vista, CA 92010
619 422-8112

Shirley S. Barior, LCSW
Ctr. Anxiety & Stress Treatment
4295 Ibis Street
San Diego, CA 92103
619 543-0510

Colorado
Flight Without Fear
c/o The Ninety-Nines, Inc.,
CO Chapter
14437 West 32d Avenue
Golden, CO 80401
303 795-6564

Craig Angus, Ph.D.
Aspen, CA 81611
303 925-4580

Connecticut
SOAR, Inc.
Seminars on Aeroanxiety Re-
lief
ATTN: Tom Bunn, Pres.
P. O. Box 747
Westport, CT 06881
203 374-4241 *or* 800 332-7359

District of Columbia
See Maryland and Virginia
listings

Florida
Freedom From Fear of Fly-
ing, Inc.
c/o Capt. T. W. Cummings,
Ret.
2021 Country Club Prado
Coral Gables, FL 33134

Georgia
Fear of Flying Seminar
c/o Paulette O'Donnell, Coor-
dinator
Dept. 978—General Office
DELTA AIRLINES
Atlanta Intl. Airport, GA
30320

The Atlanta Phobia Clinic
960 Johnson Ferry Road,
Suite 215
Atlanta, GA 30342

Flight-Fear Orientation Clinic
c/o Ron Jones, Human Fac-
tors Spec.
258 Midvale, N.E.
Atlanta, GA 30342
404 255-9270

Atlanta Phobia & Anxiety
  Clinic
5555 Peachtree Runwood
  Rd., #106
Atlanta, GA 30342

A. Burton Bradley, Ph.D.
1549 Clairmont Road
Decatur, GA 30033
404 982-0327

Illinois
Bert Siegal, Ph.D.
501 W. Odgen Avenue
Hinsdale, IL 60521
312 920-0900

Kansas
W. H. Gunn, Ph.D.
Dept. of Psychiatry
Univ. of Kansas Medical Center
39th Ave. & Rainbow Blvd.
Kansas City, KA

Maryland
Aerodonetic—Become a
  Fearless Flyer
c/o Polly K. Nielsen, Pres.
P. O. Box 8606
Baltimore—Washington Int'l.
  Airport
Baltimore, MD 21240
301 757-5876

Center of Behavioral Medicine
Dr. Robert L. DuPont
6191 Executive Boulevard
Rockville, MD 20852

Phobia Treatment Center of
  Columbia
200 Century Plaza, Suite 311
Columbia, MD 21044

Phobia Treatment Center of
  Chevy Chase
Joseph Mallet, Ph.D.
2 Wisconsin Circle, #700
Chevy Chase, MD 20815

Massachusetts
Fearless Flying
c/o Dr. Albert Forgione
Institute of Psychology of Air
  Travel
25 Huntington Avenue, Suite
  #300
Boston, MA 02116
617 437-1811

The Institute at Newton
Randie Harman Hendrick
30 Lincoln Street
Newton Heights, MA 02161
617 369-5547

Upward Bound Fear of Flying Group
c/o The Fear Clinic
670 Washington St.
Braintree, MA 02184
617 843-7550

New Jersey
Fear of Flying Program
c/o Elaine Spears
Elizabeth General Hospital
925 E. Jersey Street
Elizabeth, NJ 07102

New York
Travel & Fly Without Fear,
    Inc.
c/o Carol & Herb Gross
310 Madison Avenue
New York, NY 10017
212 697-7666 *or* 516 368-4244

Phobia Clinic—Doreen Pow-
    ell
White Plains Hospital Medi-
    cal Center
David Avenue
White Plains, NY 10021
914 949-4500 x2017

Marvin L. Aronson, Ph.D.
120 E. 28th Street
New York, NY 10016
212 532-2135

Phobia Resource Center
c/o Martin Sief & Natalie
    Schor
1430 2nd Avenue
New York, NY 10003
212 288-3400

Dr. Carol Lindeman
New York Psychological Cen-
    ter
245 E. 87th Street
New York, NY 10028
212 860-5560

Dr. Carni Harari
Humanistic Psychological
    Center
473 West End Avenue
New York, NY 10024

North Carolina
Change
c/o Dr. James W. Selby
2915 Providence Road
Charlotte, NC 28211
704 365-0140

Ohio
James Webb, Ph.D.
Wright State University
c/o School of Prof. Psychology
Dayton, OH 45435

Pennsylvania
USAir Fearful Flyers Program
Carol Stauffer, MSW, and
Capt. Frank Petee
Box 100
Glenshaw, PA 15116
412 486-5917

Agrophobia & Anxiety Pro-
    gram
c/o Temple University
112 Bala Avenue
Bala Cynwyd, PA 19004
215 667-6327

Texas
Dr. Bob Ingram
Phobia Center of the South-
    west
12860 Hillcrest, Suite 119
Dallas, TX 75230
214 368-6327

Dr. Habib Nathan
Phobia Center of San Antonio
Oak Hills Medical Center
    #814
San Antonio, TX 98230
512 696-4041

Virginia
Roundhouse Square Psychi-
atric Center
c/o Richard Loebel, Director
1444 Duke Street
Alexandria, VA 22314
and
2771 Hartland Road
Falls Church, VA 22034
703 683-6119

Washington
Fear of Flying Clinic, Inc.
A Ninety-Nine Project
c/o June Blackburn
Seattle Branch
15127 N.D. 24th, Suite 211
Redmond, WA 98052-5530

Australia
Fear of Flying Clinic, Inc.
A Ninety-Nine Project
Sydney Branch
c/o Glenda Philpott
23 Huntingdale Avenue
Miranda N.S.W. 2228 Australia
02-522-8709

Fear of Flying Clinic, Inc.
A Ninety-Nine Project
Melbourne Branch
Steel Creek Road
Yarra Glen, Vic. 3775
03-730-1465

Fear of Flying Clinic, Inc.
A Ninety-Nine Project
Perth Branch
c/o Sylvia Byers
2 Downey Drive

Mosman Park 6012
Western Australia 601
69-384-4836

Fear of Flying Clinic, Inc.
A Ninety-Nine Project
Brisbane Branch
c/o Olga Tarline
11 Fontane Street
Stafford Heights
Queensland 4053
Australia

Canada
Flying Without Fear
(held twice yearly, Apr. &
Nov.)
UBC Center for Continuing
Ed.
5997 Iona Drive
Vancouver, B.C. VyT 2A4
604 222-5237 or 222-5252

Behavior Therapy Institute
Paul Griesbach
62 Charles Street East
Toronto, Ontario
Canada M4Y 1T4
416 928-0858 or 222-5252

England
Air Travel Anxiety Seminar
c/o Dr. Maurice Yaffe
York Clinic, Guy's Hospital
117 Borough High Street
London, England SE1 1NR
01-407-7600 x3428

France
Anne Glanchard Remond,
M.D.

Laboratoire d'Electro-
physiologie
et de Neurophysiologie Ap-
pliquee
Paris, France

Germany
Agentur Silvia Texter
Psychologische Arbeits-Gem-
einschaft
Habsburgerplatz 2
8000 Munich 40, Germany

Ireland
Aer Lingus
Attn: Maeye Byrne, Flight
Service Training

PCB PAI
Dublin, Ireland

Sweden
Captain Bingh Bylander
Varingavagen 3
193000 Sigluna
Sweden

Switzerland
Seminare gegen Glugangst
Dr. med Marc Murwt
Beckenhofstr. 64
CH—Zurich, Switzerland
01 362 73 62

The Health Factor

Health and the Business Traveler

Don't drink the water or breathe the air—they could be hazardous to your health

"I am much pleased that you are going on a very long journey, which may by proper conduct restore your health and prolong your life," Dr. Samuel Johnson wrote to his friend Henry Perkins in 1782. Today's business frequent flier does not regard travel as a health restorative or a life lengthener because it can be a stressful and unhealthful undertaking.

STRESS IS THE MAIN PROBLEM FOR FREQUENT FLIERS

Of all those surveyed in the Hyatt Travel Futures project, 52 percent found overnight business traveling stressful to the point that they lost their effectiveness if they were away for five days or less. Fifty-six percent felt harried or hassled, 47 percent pressured, 29 percent tense and uptight, 20 percent nervous, and 15 percent just generally not in control of the situation. This stress is important economically for the employer in the way it reduces productivity, efficiency and the quality of decision making.

Two-thirds of the business travelers said they could maintain their effectiveness while traveling for only a few days to a week. The most difficult sources of stress for them were being away from their homes and families, the physical stress inherent in travel activities, the lack of control over scheduling, being in an unfamiliar city, and bad service while traveling or in the hotel.

The symptoms of stress manifested in health problems

range widely. Digestive systems can be badly disrupted, resulting in such uncomfortable conditions as nausea, diarrhea or constipation, exacerbation of cardiac trouble, nervous tension, difficulties in breathing, headaches (including migraine attacks) and so on. Such problems rarely become acute but can be very uncomfortable and threatening to the journey's mission.

First Step: Identify the Causes of Stress

The first step in reducing travel-related stress is to identify what causes it. Poor service from airlines topped the list in the survey, with over a third of frequent business travelers finding it very difficult and only 7 percent saying that it was not a problem at all. Hotels that render bad service come next as a stressor, followed by car rental companies. So the planning and selection of travel-related services to reduce the chances of something going wrong are important initial steps toward minimizing at least the stress-related health problems to which the frequent flier is exposed.

The Hyatt Travel Futures project found that the very nature of business travel can cause stress, quite apart from the quality of services encountered on the road.

"The business traveler is under pressure to perform his job in unfamiliar surroundings; his work is dictated by someone else's schedule (the client's or the airline's schedule) rather than his own; he must fill in the time between appointments and meetings, and he must do all this while under the physical stress associated with travel," the report concluded. "A surprising finding was the lack of a significant correlation between travel experience and the traveler's ability to cope with travel-related problems. Neither frequency of travel (i.e., number of trips in the past year) nor the number of years the person has been traveling on business had any correlation with the ability to cope."

Families Influence Stress

Another finding was that stress is influenced by the makeup of the frequent flier's household. Travelers who are singe, divorced, separated, or widowed feel slightly more stress than married travelers unless there are children at home. In that case stress increases for both the traveling parent and the spouse left at home, with the parents of infants and toddlers having the most problems. Also, the children left at home suffer at second-hand, as it were, from the consequences of frequent business travel. Most traveling parents questioned felt their absences stressed their children, most seriously when the children were aged about seven, less when they were toddlers or in their teens.

The majority reported that their traveling puts stress on their spouses, over a quarter of those questioned believing that their spouses suffered a lot of stress, especially if there were children at home. Sexual relationships in particular appear to suffer from frequent flying, and such problems are often attributed to travel-related stress symptoms made manifest in the libidos and emotional states of both spouses.

TRAVELER'S DIARRHEA

In addition to trying to minimize stress, a number of practical actions can make travel more healthful. The number one travel illness still appears to be traveler's diarrhea, sometimes called *turista*, which has been estimated to affect to some degree up to a third of all international travelers. You don't have to eat contaminated food or drink water containing bacteria to get it. Just a change of diet, or minerals present in water to which you are not accustomed, can produce it. Both travelers and medical specialists are somewhat divided on the best techniques to adopt. A mild dose of traveler's tummy may be best left to run its course as a natural reaction to ingested toxins or hostile organisms the body is flushing out. For the same reason some travelers prefer not to use the various prophylactic medications available.

Anyway, most people can avoid traveler's diarrhea by being careful about what they eat and drink. Those more vulnerable—especially on important trips, when one does not want to risk any form of incapacitation—may want to take preventive medication, usually starting on the day before departure and continuing for a couple of days after return. There are several branded products, such as Procter & Gamble's Pepto-Bismol, which can be taken for up to twenty-one days. Some preventives yield unpleasant side effects, such as allergic reactions or increased sensitivity to the sun. Check with your doctor if you have any doubts.

Drinking Water Can Be Dangerous

Even if you predose yourself with antiturista medication, you still need to be careful of what you eat and drink. The main danger stems from contaminated water. Even the drinking water on planes may not be safe. This is a big problem because you should drink as much nonalcoholic liquid as possible in flight to avoid dehydration, and it often is not practical to get the necessary amount in the form of canned or bottled fruit juices and soft drinks from busy or uninterested flight attendants.

Go to the plane's water fountain, and you take a big chance—and the water served to you in your seat by a flight attendant, whether in first class or coach, may well come from the same holding tank. That water, even if you are flying between American or European cities, may have been contaminated by bacteria introduced on another flight to Africa, India, or South America, for example. Say the plane is a Boeing 747 jumbo, with tanks holding two hundred gallons of water for drinking. The plane leaves London with the tanks full of good water, and half of it is consumed on a flight to Greece. The tanks are topped up by suspect water, part of which is consumed on the next leg, and more water—and more bacteria—added at stops in Asia and Africa. By the time the plane gets back to the United States, it may be carrying an international cocktail of water and dangerous bugs.

To prevent passengers from picking up infections, there are various procedures intended to make the water safe, but airlines vary considerably in how conscientiously they follow them, and even the best corporate intentions can be thwarted by slackness by maintenance personnel. The water holding tanks are supposed to be cleaned regularly, but for even the most hygiene-conscious airlines, that is probably not more frequently than once every three months. Even the routine draining of tanks is not practiced very rigorously by most airlines.

In theory, even if the water taken on board or kept in the tanks is hazardous to your health, the risk is controlled by adding chemicals to kill off bacteriological and fungal contaminants and to raise the water to standards of potability stipulated by the World Health Organization. Again, human errors creep into these procedures, and most frequent fliers have encountered water so heavily chlorinated that it tastes awful. If the water does taste all right, it may well be because it has not been treated sufficiently.

The policies adopted by the different airlines on the purity of water on planes vary considerably. Some will not take water on board at all in certain cities and countries; others insist that it be boiled, perhaps under the supervision of their own staff; others take a chance and add varying amounts of chemicals. Air France has had the safest policy. Appropriately for the national carrier of a country that supplies prestige bottled water to the world, Air France has warned passengers not to drink from the holding tanks at all because the only good water comes in bottles.

Some airline crews so distrust their own employers' ability to provide safe water on board that they always carry their own. That is a good tip for health-conscious passengers also.

Ice Cubes May Not Be Safe

The ice cubes served on commercial airlines are usually safe, but where sanitation and general hygiene are suspect, they may not be. It is a myth that freezing or the addition of alcohol will kill the bacteria in contaminated water, although boiling will do so, and coffee and tea should be safe. Even cleaning your teeth in suspect water is risky, as is eating any uncooked vegetables that may have been washed in contaminated water. In many places around the world, salads are hazardous to your health and it is preferable to get fruit and fiber intake from apples, oranges, bananas, and the like, which you can peel.

Boiling the water, or obtaining it in bottles that you can be sure are safer, can present practical problems, so it may pay to take water purification tablets with you. They usually contain iodine or halazone, which kill the bugs but leave a nasty taste. Instant cold tea, concentrated fruit juice, or powdered or crystallized soft drink flavorings make the treated water more palatable. A portable ultraviolet water treatment unit is also available (see Appendix).

Beware of Dairy Products

Other liquids, including dairy products in countries where the milk is not always pasteurized, are suspect too. Many desserts, sauces, and soups use dairy products, so these should be approached with caution in such countries, although usually the international hotels take appropriate precautions to cater for the digestive systems of their overseas clients. You may safely enjoy an ice cream in the Hilton or Sheraton but be dicing with diarrhea if you patronize a food vendor in the street outside.

The basic rules are to eat and drink only what is well cooked and served while still hot or comes in a reputable sealed can or container. Fruit should be limited to what you peel yourself.

Strange foods as well as strange places and climates can set off allergic reactions, which pose a hazard to travelers. If you have allergy problems, consult your doctor before a trip. Indeed, if there are any actual or latent health problems, medical advice before a foreign trip is a worthwhile precaution, also beneficial on journeys within the United States.

Counterfeit Drugs

If you are on a course of medication, take a supply sufficient to last right through your trip, especially if it is overseas. Counterfeit drugs—both generic prescription and proprietary branded products—are a major international problem. Counterfeits range from fake penicillin, a useless chalk solution, to phony eyedrops that can damage healthy eyes, to useless birth control pills.

BASIC TRAVEL MEDICAL KIT

In addition to the antidiarrhea medication, a basic traveler's medical kit should include the following:

> Decongestant or antihistamine
>
> Aspirin or acetaminophen for headaches and other minor pain
>
> Antibiotic ointment for minor wounds
>
> Motion sickness medication if that is a problem

Calamine lotion, sunscreen, and insect repellent if you will be exposed to those hazards at your destination

Throat lozenges

Gentle laxative

Diarrhea medication

First-aid strips

Unbreakable plastic thermometer

If, like me, you have much-filled sensitive teeth with a propensity for crowns dropping off and fillings falling out at the most inconvenient times in the most far-away places, a little bottle of oil of cloves to give relief from toothache is an essential part of your travel medical kit. If going to a high altitude, medication for altitude sickness can prevent considerable discomfort.

Particularly if you have any ongoing medical problems, get your doctor to make out a summarized medical history to take with you—keep it with your passport or credit cards. For travelers with complex health problems, it might be a good idea to get health records microfilmed, so that they can be carried in the wallet or attached to the passport.

If you are crossing time zones, check how you should adjust the dosages of medications you take regularly. "One tablet night and morning" can get really confusing when your body is in Karachi but your internal clock still on Eastern Standard Time. Also make sure that you can check easily on the possible interactions of one drug with another. That means taking them in their original packing, complete with printed instructions—a useful precaution anyway with customs officers particularly sensitive these days about illicit drug smuggling. And of course keep your medicines with you in your carry-on luggage, both for possible need on the journey and to prevent the risk of their being lost or delayed if put into checked bags.

The decongestants are obvious examples of what you may need to keep pain away on the plane.

PRESSURE PROBLEMS

If you suffer from sinus congestion or must fly with a head cold or some other form of respiratory infection, as most of us frequent fliers find unavoidable sometimes, then a decongestant nasal spray, drops, or other form of similar medication is virtually essential. Even when you are fit, flying can be painful because of the changes in atmospheric pressure, and it is as well to be prepared.

Commercial airliners do not maintain cabin pressure at ground level—usually nowhere near it. You may within a few minutes be whisked from sea level to over 30,000 feet real altitude and 6,000 and 8,000 feet of simulated altitude inside the cabin. That plays havoc with the air passages that link your sinuses, ears, nose, and throat. Even if you are perfectly fit, the eustachian tube, a sensitive air valve in your middle ear that equalizes the pressure on each side of the eardrum, cannot adjust readily to this sudden change. If your airways are obstructed by inflammation or mucus, the problem is aggravated. In that case acute pain can come on very quickly, and bleeding and other serious complications may occur.

My first jet flight was on one of the early DeHaviland Comets between London and Nairobi. I left England with a typical mild case of winter snuffles. By the time we were over continental Europe, I was rolling around my seat in agony with excruciating earache. The long flight remains an enduring memory of sustained agony. Commercial airliners do have better cabin pressurization systems these days, but they will always be a long way from perfect because it is not economically feasible to make the fuselage strong enough, or to carry the equipment and burn the fuel necessary, to maintain sea-level pressure inside the cabin at all times. To do so would make the difference between profit and loss, reducing space for passengers by twenty to thirty seats, more on some planes.

Cigarette smoke increases both the work that the plane's ventilation and pressurization systems have to do and the discomfort of passengers throughout the aircraft. It is amazing that smoking is not banned totally on all flights everywhere, as most airlines would prefer because of the economic advantages alone.

Suck, Chew, and Blow

The consequences of pressure changes after takeoff are not usually too bad, and any discomfort should be resolved by swallowing, chewing gum, or sucking on a candy, and gently—repeat, gently—blowing your nose. Coming down, the effect is much more pronounced because the valves and air chambers within your head have become adjusted to high altitude and just cannot respond so rapidly to greater external air pressure as the plane descends toward the ground. Anticipate problems by taking decongestant medication or antihistamines in good time, typically a couple of hours before landing, but check the directions. Sitting upright and using a nasal spray or sniffer will help as well.

Chew and/or swallow vigorously and blow your nose gently, several times if this is what it takes to get the valves adjusting faster. If there is severe discomfort, ask the flight attendants for help. If you anticipate problems, consult them before they get into the prelanding routine. Some airlines provide training in helping passengers adjust to pressure changes, and the attendant may know a new dodge that works for you. Some favor putting cups containing moist hot towels over each ear. The heat and humidity seem to help.

LACK OF HUMIDITY CAUSES PAIN

Humidity—rather, the lack of it—is the cause of much pain on the plane. Passengers suffer because of the sheer economic impracticality of carrying the excess non–revenue generating weight of water that would be required to humidify the air circulated in the cabin. After reading the information a few pages back about the dubious quality of in-flight drinking water, you probably will not wish to drink the glass every hour or so necessary to combat dehydration unless you take it with you in bottles, which is a real drag on any flight and a practical problem on those lasting several hours. Soft drinks or fruit juices will do instead, although too much juice can aggravate travel-related stomach disorders, especially diarrhea, which will make dehydration a much greater problem. Alcohol and coffee also make matters worse because they are diuretics—they increase the rate of urination, further depleting body fluids.

The dry cabin atmosphere hits eyes hard, so a small squeeze bottle of nonprescription eyedrops is an essential item in the frequent flier's survival kit, kept readily accessible in pocket, handbag, or briefcase. Be particularly well prepared if you wear contact lenses—if you do wear contacts, you probably follow that advice already. The first trip that makes your eyes feel as if you have followed Lawrence of Arabia's camel across the Sahara in a sandstorm is a lesson not forgotten.

BEATING BAD BREATH

The dryness, digestive upsets, and battering your throat, mouth, and air passages take during a long flight can also cause halitosis—bad breath. Your spouse or best friend may tell you about the problem after they have got over the initial shock of contact at the arrival gate, but business contacts will be too polite to mention it even if it is souring the deal. There are various proprietary products to suck or chew, and some potent oral sprays provide a quick fix until you can clean your teeth—and brush the fur off your tongue—thoroughly. I have experimented with a tongue scraper, a sort of miniature snowplow common in some cultures for oral hygiene. You don't need water, and you can clean the device by wiping with a tissue, so it is very practical and portable, but no substitute for conventional tooth brushing.

DIGESTIVE UPSETS

Digestive upsets when traveling may cause persistent bad breath and give offense without anyone intimate being around to point out the problem. Combine that situation with eating well-spiced gourmet foods—sauerkraut, certain varieties of European sausages, spirits, and dishes containing garlic are particular villains—and *whew!* It may sound a small and not particularly significant point to make in a book on the practicalities of frequent business travel, but you ignore it at your peril. I once moved some lucrative printing business away from one company because my staff and I really could not take any longer poring over page proofs with a representative who suffered badly from halitosis. Incidentally, offensive body odor can be a reason for being bumped from a flight. USAir recently disembarked a husband and wife from a flight out of Seattle because the flight attendant considered their personal hygiene below acceptable standards.

AIR QUALITY CONSIDERATIONS

As we become more conscious of the dangers of passive smoking, airlines may be forced to compete more effectively in offering better air to breathe. (The first definitive study of cabin conditions during flight and their effect on health was being performed by the U.S. Department of Transportation in 1989–1990.)

Significant fuel economies can be achieved by recirculating half the air in the passenger compartment rather than fully air conditioning the plane and recirculating all the air. Such cost cutting is bad news for passengers trying to reduce travel stress and resenting the sore throats and eye irritation that can come from exposure to other people's cigarette smoke.

Even sitting in a nonsmoking section can still expose you to the unpleasant effects of passive smoking. *The Journal of the American Medical Association* reported research showing that the type of aircraft ventilation is more significant than where you sit in reducing exposure to tobacco smoke. Fresh air circulation significantly reduces the nicotine content of cabin air compared to the cost-saving practice of mixing fresh air with recirculated air to reduce the energy consumed by the plane's air conditioning system.

Tests on passengers and crew on four commercial flights by Boeing 767s—two with fresh air and two with half recirculated air—showed elevated levels of a nicotine metabolite in urine of passengers exposed to recirculated air for up to three days after the journey. The researchers also produced evidence of annoyance—and consequent indications of stress—rising quickly after passengers were exposed to nicotine-laden cabin air. The best air is usually found near the front of the plane. If air quality is really poor—complain. The pilot—who gets the freshest air—can usually do something to improve things.

BEWARE OF ALTITUDE SICKNESS

Symptoms similar to those of influenza and jet lag, including headaches, disturbed sleep, nausea, and feeling tired, may be due to altitude sickness. Some people experience discomfort at altitudes as low as seven thousand feet. The cabin pressure in your plane may be the equivalent of a higher altitude than that. Usually it is somewhere between five thousand and eight thousand feet, but the factors responsible for altitude sickness—notably lower oxygen and higher ozone levels in the air—may be accentuated by the inferior environmental quality controls encountered on many flights.

Many people are vulnerable to altitude sickness. The *Journal of American Medicine* reported on a study of doctors attending medical meetings at Rocky Mountain resorts; the research indicated that about one in four suffered from it.

Like jet lag, altitude sickness can affect any traveler of any age. It is a natural consequence of the rapid change in environment resulting from jet travel. Altitude sickness occurs as the body adjusts to a lower oxygen content in the air, which may take several days. Rest, eating light meals, and drinking plenty of fluids (not alcohol) should help. Carbonated drinks and fatty or other foods difficult to digest may make things worse. If you feel bloated and uncomfortable during a flight, it usually is not a direct reflection on the airline's food but the fact that the lower cabin pressure is causing gases in your intestines and other parts of your body to expand.

Temporary relief may be obtained by using the same quick fix that works so well for hyperventilation—breathing in and out of a paper bag to increase the amount of carbon dioxide inhaled and so boost blood flow to the brain.

EXCESS OZONE

Ozone levels are greater at higher altitudes. There is conflicting evidence about the dangers of ozone to both air passengers and crew. Levels vary enormously between types of plane and the air filtration systems they use and indeed between one flight and another on the same plane. Wind and air currents cause unpredictable concentrations of ozone at the altitudes that commercial jets fly, and the weather, the time of the year, and the geographic location cause fluctuations.

The main result of excessive ozone appears to be only temporary discomfort—symptoms such as dry sore throat and itchy eyes also arise from dehydration. However, when you add the ozone to the other environmental stresses of frequent flying, there is the possibility of a cumulative long-term effect on frequent fliers. There is a woeful lack of evidence about this—and very little you can do about it. However, you need not make the quality of the air you take in worse by sitting in the smoking section; you should avoid flying if you have pulmonary problems; and you can get outside and exercise, or indulge in deep breathing, as soon as possible after your arrival. Such exercise is one of the best ways of overcoming the lethargic feelings that often follow a flight—whether those are symptoms of jet lag, dehydration, excessive ozone, or other in-flight air hazards.

ION BALANCE

An even grayer area of knowledge about the dangers in the air that frequent fliers breathe is the question of ions. The study of ions, still not very far advanced, remains highly controversial. We know that the balance of electric charges in the air molecules inside an aircraft can be affected by the many electromagnetic changes that take place within the plane, by the movement of air within the cabin, by the friction between the plane's external skin and the outside air, by smoking, even by the action of passengers walking on the carpets, wriggling in their seats, and just breathing.

A buildup of positive or negative ions in the cabin air can have a whole range of effects on the bodily functions of the passengers and crew. An imbalance may contribute to the symptoms of jet leg, cause headaches, affect the ability to metabolize essential elements such as potassium and calcium, alter blood chemistry, and cause depression or irrational behavior. The list of potential consequences of an imbalance in the ratio of positive to negative ions in an aircraft cabin is very long. Some people are especially sensitive to ions and react particularly strongly on the ground or in the air to the imbalances caused by smoking or air conditioning.

Military aerospace research into ionization—much of it still classified—indicates that it should be subjected to serious investigation as a possible hazard in commercial air travel. It is certainly a stressor that may play a significant role in many problems, from aggravating cardiovascular disorders among Road Warriors to creating fluctuations in the menstrual cycle of Tightrope Walkers.

Some studies have linked ion sensitivity to reactions in the body's immune system, with indications that infections are more likely to spread when excess positive ions are present. That is why some hospitals have used negative ion generators in their burn units. Experiments with rats and mice indicate that physiological reactions to excessive ion imbalances can be fatal and may increase susceptibility to infectious diseases.

Some airline personnel claim to have benefited from using portable ion generators, particularly to help them sleep after a long flight across several time zones. If you travel frequently and think your sensitivity to ions is causing you problems, it may be worth experimenting with a generator, although there is a dearth of scientific evidence as to whether they really do much good. As with virtually every other frequent flying tip—if it works for you, go for it!

As the immune system is believed to be sensitive to

ion imbalances, frequent fliers may find themselves con-
tracting far more virus infections—colds and influenza,
gastric and pulmonary disorders, for example—than colleagues who do not travel. They may not be able to blame
their problems, at this stage of scientific knowledge, on
ion imbalances or ozone or other specific adverse aspects
of the air quality on board. Cosmic radiation, for example,
may be twice as great at cruising altitude as at sea level.
We know very little about these potential dangers. Still,
what seems irrefutable is that frequent fliers are being
subjected to a large number of known stressors, which can
have a cumulative effect both singly and in combination
over an extended period.

SYMPTOMS OF DEHYDRATION

The physical stressor that is most readily apparent to us
when we fly—dehydration—is the easiest to combat. The
dry throat, nose, mouth, lips, and skin are tangible symptoms of how the typical humidity levels between 5 percent and 20 percent in an aircraft cabin deplete body
fluids. Humidity of 25 percent to 45 percent is considered
the most desirable range for human beings, but is rarely
achieved on commercial aircraft. Significantly below that
the body loses excessive amounts of fluid in perspiration
and respiration.

Visits to the restroom become less frequent—have
you noticed how much more widely spaced is your need
to urinate when on a long flight, and how much more
deeply colored and concentrated your urine may appear?
These are visible symptoms of dehydration and are caused
by low humidity in the cabin.

Blood volume decreases also, with consequent problems arising from lower oxygen and blood sugar levels.
This contributes to jet lag, tiredness, depression, and so
on. So drink plenty of the right kind of nonalcoholic

fluids—several pints on the longest flights. Alcohol and coffee, being diuretics, increase urine production and aggravate dehydration. Every cup of coffee can stimulate by diuretic action the loss of a cup and a half of body fluid.

The dryness of the cabin air can bother wearers of contact lenses. This effect is heightened by air pressure changes. Some frequent fliers take out their contact lenses before a flight and use conventional spectacles while they are airborne.

Anyone can suffer from dry, sore eyes, which may be eased temporarily by rapid blinking. Take eyedrops on board with you and use them frequently. Also, if reading for long periods, make a point of breaking every so often and letting your eyes focus as far way as possible, either out of the window or as far as you can see down the cabin. This exercises the eye muscles and reduces eyestrain. That's why computer users are being advised now to position their monitors so that they can take periodic breaks from gazing at the screen and focus on infinity by looking out of the window, for example.

BLOOD SUGAR LEVELS

Dehydration in combination with the other stress factors associated with flying—especially for fearful passengers— can cause temporary hypoglycemia, or abnormally low blood sugar. Some research indicates that the incidence of diabetes may be higher among flight crews and cabin attendants than in the general population. However, not enough research has been conducted to draw firm conclusions. It is not known whether frequent flying can result in long-term, possibly permanent damage to the body's ability to metabolize carbohydrates efficiently and manufacture insulin to maintain normal blood sugar levels.

The symptoms of low blood sugar are easily confused with other consequences of the cabin environment, such as general fatigue, irritability, cold feet and hands, irregular heartbeat, feelings of nausea, and so on. More distinctive is the craving for something sweet, which depleted blood sugar can prompt after several hours in the air. The solution is not to pour extra packets of white sugar into your tea or coffee. A quick hit of refined sugar can aggravate the extreme swings in blood sugar levels set up when travel stress is causing excessive hormonal activity, particularly of adrenaline, and the pancreas is getting various conflicting messages about the insulin production required to balance blood sugar levels.

It is far better to try to get the swings smoothed out by snacking frequently on high-protein and natural carbohydrate foods such as fruit and fruit juices and nuts.

Nicotine really plays havoc with blood sugar levels, even on the ground. Although smokers may not think so, they would benefit along with everybody else from a complete ban on smoking on aircraft.

NOISE STRESS

While we can do much to tackle the problems of dehydration and unbalanced blood sugar levels, there is not a lot of control we can exert on noise in aircraft, which even on modern jets can make a significant contribution to travel stress.

The cabin of a commercial airliner may seem remarkably quiet because the noise settles into a reasonably constant pattern once the cruising level has been reached. In fact, the ambient noise is higher than it seems. If this were not so, you would be far more conscious of the inevitable babble of voices in the conversations between several hundred people confined within such a small space.

It is well established that noise is a stress factor, its potency varying by type and frequency as well as by volume or intensity. At times during a flight you will hear

noise levels similar in intensity to those in a busy street or
on a factory floor. Even if not loud enough to cause permanent damage to hearing, the sustained noise during
flight may be a significant cause of stress in some travelers, especially the millions of us who suffer from tinnitus, the most usual symptom of which is ringing in the
ears.

I am a tinnitus sufferer, and my condition gets far
worse when I am tired or under stress, so I cannot blame
the discomfort from ringing in my ears during flights directly on the noise levels in the cabin. My discomfort may
be a direct consequence of the combination of other frequent flying stress factors that together make me fatigued
and stressed out.

However, I know I am particularly sensitive to noise
when flying, so I avoid sitting near a galley or toilet or
close to the engines, as these are the noisiest seats. Other
frequent fliers tell me that they find particular types of
music, especially with a heavy beat or strong bass, dis-
comforting—and so, presumably, stressful—during a
flight.

Earplugs may help, or suitable music at a comfortable
volume from a personal tape player or the aircraft's earphones. I find that earplugs accentuate tinnitus, while soft
music masks the internal ringing and hisses. Tinnitus is
such a personal thing, with so much variation in symptoms, that it is best for the individual traveler to experiment. If you have a particular problem with noise on aircraft, you might even try getting a tape of the white noise
that is so effective at masking sounds in office buildings
and playing it in your personal stereo.

VIBRATION STRESS

Integral with the noise levels on aircraft are vibrations and
very-low-frequency sound waves, which can bother some

passengers. They are set up by movement, flexing, and resonance in the structure of the plane and in its many components. Vibration has been linked to both sea- and airsickness in some susceptible travelers. While in the Royal Navy, I always felt nauseous in the areas of the destroyer on which I served that picked up the worst vibrations from the engines and propeller shafts.

If you think vibration is aggravating your frequent flying stress, it could be worth experimenting with several different seating positions on the type of aircraft you use regularly until you find the best. The vibrations set up in galley equipment are another reason I keep away from the galley areas, in addition to the general noisiness of food preparation, cleaning up, and chattering flight attendants.

CLAUSTROPHOBIA

Not to be overlooked is the extreme stress some people experience in confined environments. Claustrophobia is a very complex and highly variable condition in which mental distress and various physical symptoms can combine into acute stress reactions. Laboratory rats kept in confined, crowded conditions become highly stressed and aggressive, and they reveal excessive hormone activity. It is not surprising that we experience similar physiological reactions when crammed into a small space in a metal tube that is projected rapidly through the air, accompanied by loud noises and violent movement. These factors combine with the sense of loss of control, which is such a stress factor in business travel, and many other physiological changes. So someone who ordinarily does not feel claustrophobic may experience acute distress on an aircraft, particularly a crowded one. These symptoms of claustrophobia may develop into, or mistakenly be interpreted as, an acquired fear of flying.

The tips in the section on aviophobia may suggest ways to tackle specific stress problems associated with claustrophobia. Various forms of meditation seem to work well for many frequent fliers; others swear by detective stories or other light reading in which they can become immersed, as a distraction from the disturbing closeness and feeling of confinement within an aircraft. The bigger jets seem to cause less discomfort, having a spaciousness that the older, smaller ones lack.

An interesting phenomenon revealed during the research for this book is that, for some travelers, listening to a personal stereo or wearing the plane's earphones can acutally increase claustrophobia in certain circumstances.

There are no pat, easy, and universal answers to all the environmental and other causes of stress when flying because reactions to this alien environment vary so considerably between individuals. However, the pointers I have given to the main stressors encountered during frequent flying can be evaluated for their effect on you, and there are ways to minimize the consequences of those to which you are most susceptible. It's well worth the effort in the returns in enhanced quality of your traveling time.

SWOLLEN ANKLES

The one place on a plane where there is too much liquid after a few hours in the air is in your feet and ankles. The effect of fluid build-up in the extremities is caused by a combination of the lower air pressure in the cabin and immobility. Blood collects in the lower limbs and may clot more readily. As a result, feet swell, and the relief obtained by slipping off your shoes may not be sufficient compensation for the embarrassment and inconvenience after landing when you cannot get them back on again. Experienced frequent fliers often wear or carry light, soft, and flexible shoes to enable them to cope with this problem. Fabric slip-ons may feature as giveaways in premium-priced sections of the cabin, but I have found they tend to be too flexible to contain the swelling of feet during a long flight, and you may still not be able to get your shoes back on again when coming in to land.

Elastic bandages or support-type hose may provide enough pressure to contain swelling, but be careful not to have them too tight, or blood circulation will be affected and then your pain on the plane will be aggravated by cramps or pins and needles. Cramp can be a particular problem for some people during flights, so remember to move your feet around at frequent intervals and walk up and down the aisle if this is practical. I usually get hit by an agonizing bunching up of muscles in my calves, for which the only quick fix is to grab hold of my big toe and bend it up as far as it will go. When this becomes necessary, especially in the restricted seating space of coach class, the contortions required for a six-foot-four man weighing 240 pounds to reach and manipulate his toes give a whole new dimension to in-flight entertainment.

If you have varicose veins or have suffered from phlebitis, it is particularly important to exercise during a flight. Simple stretching and flexing isometric exercises can make all the difference, especially if there is a footrest or suitably located mounting for the seat in front against which you can brace your feet.

BATTLING WITH BACKACHE

Backache sufferers have such a wide range of conditions that there is no simple cure-all technique to reduce their pain on the plane. The ergonomical design of aircraft seats has improved a lot in recent years, and you can increase the chances of getting comfortable by identifying seat locations that give you the room to twist or stretch in the way that helps you most. If your backache is serious, the premium price for the more spacious and comfortable seating in business and first class becomes much more worthwhile. If you can afford only coach and have particular discomfort during a trip, ask for an upgrade on the next flight. The check-in clerk or flight attendant may be sympathetic if the booking situation permits.

Even an uncomfortable seat that is stressing your back can be improved by the judicious use of pillows, for example by sitting upright and putting them in the small of your back. Short people may get relief by resting their feet on a bag on the floor. Tall people in aircraft find space for long legs and big feet in an aisle seat or by moving from an assigned seat in a congested row to one where it may be possible to get two empty seats together.

One pain on the plane problem very easily resolved is something in your pocket pressing on a nerve. A bunch of keys or a wallet can send pain signals up into the back or down the legs.

Backache sufferers also have problems with the different types of mattresses encountered on the road. It is not only Crocodile Dundee who has found it more comfortable to sleep on the floor of a hotel bedroom! Good hotels are geared to cope with such guest idiosyncrasies and may be able to provide a bed with an orthopedic mattress or a bed board.

Much back trouble when traveling stems from the wrong shoes and luggage. Take only comfortable shoes with you, even if that means compromising on appearance. The effect of elegant feet will be ruined if your face is screwed up in pain. Luggage was covered fully earlier, but the main health-related points worth repeating are to keep luggage down to a minimum, pack in lightweight bags that you can lift easily, and put everything possible on wheels. A heavy garment bag—or any other very heavy carry-on—can soon cause discomfort in your arms and shoulders, with consequent back pain later.

HEADACHES CAUSED BY ANGER

Headaches are another common in-flight ailment. The director of a California headache clinic told me that most pain in the head is a direct consequence of muscle and blood vessel contraction and expansion resulting from suppressed anger. As the Hyatt Travel Futures project found so much cause for anger in business travel, the link is obvious, and prevention is better than any available cure. Avoid stress; try not to get too angry at bad service or delays; and relax as much as possible. The experts in chronic head pain condemn frequent dosing with aspirin or any other painkillers, which tend to be less effective the more you use them.

The best quick fix I have found for a headache while traveling is to apply pressure by squeezing on the nerves and muscle in the fleshy junction between forefinger and thumb on the other hand. Press hard—the more it hurts, the more good it seems to do. Treat each hand in turn and maintain the pressure for two or three minutes.

Don't ask me why it works. Western medical science is still baffled by the effects of the manipulation of acupuncture pressure points, although they are believed to be endorphin reactions in the body's system for feeling pain and pleasure. Anyway, squeezing this point on your hand is the cheapest, safest, cleanest, most convenient way of dealing with headaches on the road that I have ever come across.

HEART AND LUNG PROBLEMS

Travelers with heart and lung disease problems are particularly affected by the lower oxygen pressure on flights and should always have medical advice before traveling. If extra oxygen will be needed during the journey, don't expect to be able to get a quick whiff from the emergency equipment over your seat. That's an automatic system, and although every commercial aircraft is equipped with oxygen, it is not readily available to passengers except in dire emergencies. If your doctor advises supplemental oxygen, make arrangements with the airline at least forty-eight hours before the flight. Their policies vary, but most prefer to supply the necessary equipment themselves for security reasons and because their cabin staff will be familiar with it. Others will let you take your own equipment on board, although the recent tightening up of security is making this less likely. In either case, you need a letter from your doctor which should spell out clearly the need for supplementary oxygen without overstating your medical problem to the extent that the airline might think you unfit to fly at all!

That's an interesting point. In theory, American airlines are not legally within their rights to deny travel to anyone with a disability, but there may be practical issues involved in individual cases, and the law varies from country to country. The Eastern Paralyzed Veterans Association has put together a useful guide particularly appropriate to wheelchair users. It is available from them at 7520 Astoria Boulevard, Jackson Heights, NY 11370. The telephone number is 718 803-3782.

WHEELCHAIRS AND SPECIAL DIETS

Of course, wheelchair users should make their particular needs known well in advance when booking flights. Travel agents and airline staff can identify the seats of easiest access for disabled passengers.

The airlines require advance notice also if you need a special diet, and they are generally quite good at coping with such common requirements as meals for diabetics or passengers needing to restrict their cholesterol, salt, and fat intakes. Diabetics should keep their insulin in their carry-on luggage, as temperatures in the baggage hold may drop to freezing point or below. Special care should be taken to monitor blood sugar levels when crossing time zones, because the normal insulin dose routine and body chemistry will probably be disrupted.

Cardiac patients with pacemakers often worry too

much about the risks of these devices being affected by magnetic or ultrasonic radiations associated with traveling. The fields you will encounter in airports and on board planes should not cause any problems, and you need to follow only normal precautions. Do get the pacemaker—including the batteries—checked before a long trip and make sure details of it are included on the medical data list described earlier.

MOTION SICKNESS COMES FROM CONFLICT

Motion sickness should not be much of a physical problem any more for anyone flying in a big commercial jet, although the psychosomatic symptoms can be real for travel sickness sufferers whatever their mode of transport. Research by the British Royal Navy found that 30 percent of seasickness cases were psychological in origin, although the subjects threw up just as vigorously as victims who had physiological reactions to travel motion in the body's sensory systems.

The cause of most motion sickness is a discrepancy between what the eye sees and what the body feels. Your ears, which react so much to changes in air pressure, are also very sensitive to motion. The tubes containing liquid in the inner ear interact with sensory signals of motion and enable the body to maintain its balance. This mechanism gets confused when the eyes receive motion signals that differ from those fed in by the other senses, most commonly demonstrated by people who can travel by car with no problems unless they try to read. Then the eyes pick up an image of a motionless page, while the rest of the body is sending signals of movement to the brain.

So one of the worst things you can do if a bumpy flight is making you feel nauseous is to try to hold a book still and carry on reading. Conversely, I found when bouncing around in a Royal Navy destroyer during a mid-Atlantic gale that looking at the horizon, the only thing around that didn't move, was a great help for seasickness. It might also help some fliers during rough weather to focus on the horizon through the plane window. In cars, buses, and trains, however, motion sickness is aggravated by looking through side windows as blurred scenery flashes past. The general rule is to look at distant rather than near objects, or to close your eyes.

Ships move in six different directions. The vertical heaving is more likely to make you feel ill than the seesaw pitching movement, the rolling, yawing from side to side, the fore-and-aft surging or the side-to-side swaying. Small planes mimic these motions, but big ones spend most of their time high enough to miss most of the weather and air turbulence.

THE PLACE FOR A SMOOTH RIDE

If you are subject to motion sickness, you will get a smoother ride seated over the wing, where the plane's movements are felt least. A drink or two may both relax you and have some as yet not fully researched beneficial effect on the body chemistry of travel sickness. University of Southampton researchers in England who studied 20,000 passengers on the rough seas around Britain found a much lower incidence of sea sickness among those who had taken alcohol. However, there has been ample previous evidence that overindulgence aggravates motion sickness, and there is absolutely nothing worse than being travel sick during a hangover or when overindulging.

SYMPTOMS OF SICKNESS

The first symptoms which should prompt a quick reassuring check that the sickness bag is in the seat pocket in

180 Savvy Business Flying

front of you are tiredness and sweating, particularly cold sweating. You will go pale, feel disoriented and restless, probably tired and maybe salivating more than normal despite the dryness of the cabin air. React fast if you notice these symptoms in children, who are particularly vulnerable to motion sickness and who can progress from the first signs of discomfort to actually throwing up very quickly. People in late middle and old age are much less likely to get travel sick; no one knows quite why, but it's great for the cruise business. Indeed, teenagers and older people who take motion sickness prophylactics as a routine precaution because of previous past bad experiences might try stopping them to see if they have outgrown the problem.

If you are ill with motion sickness, the prognosis is excellent. When the motion stops, so does the malady and the relief is usually so great that there is a psychological high. A headache may linger for a while, and if there has been considerable vomiting, the body may be dehydrated, but generally recovery is very quick and complete.

SIDE EFFECTS OF MEDICATION

Medication, both to prevent and to treat motion sickness, is quite effective, but take it with caution because of the risk of side effects and some risk of addiction if used to excess or for a sustained period. Various forms of hyoscine hydrobromide, which helped the Allies to win the Second World War by alleviating seasickness during the D-Day landings in Europe, can stave off the nausea if taken a couple of hours before the journey. Like the antihistamine prophylactics, however, they also produce drowsiness, which may be beneficial if you are a passenger who wants to doze but is dangerous if you are driving a car, skippering a boat, or piloting a plane.

There are various products for easing sickness after it has started; those containing phenergan are among the most effective—and fast-acting if injected or taken as a suppository. The preventive medications are available now as slow-release patches. You put one containing hyoscine hydrobromide behind your ear, where the drug is slowly but effectively released through the skin into the bloodstream to reach the sensitive balance mechanism of the inner ear.

HOMEOPATHIC TRAVEL AIDS

There are also homeopathic travel sickness products and devices that work on acupuncture principles and that you wear around your wrists. Called Sea-Bands, they have been found to help combat nausea in cancer patients undergoing chemotherapy, and many travelers swear by them, especially as, unlike the conventional drugs, they have no undesirable side effects.

A recent unfortunate trend, which might cause problems at Customs if you are carrying an unusually large quantity of some kinds of travel sickness pills containing cyclizines, is that they are being abused by drug addicts to enhance the effects of heroin.

EMERGENCY ACTION FOR TEETH PROBLEMS

One of the few physical health hazards that could cause pain on the plane and is not covered so far stems from all the in-flight eating we do. If you crack a tooth or dislodge a filling or crown, covering what's left with chewing gum can make it more comfortable until you get to a dentist. I have heard of candle wax being used as well, but candles are not easy to find on airliners—unless you are sitting next to an Eskimo with a packed lunch! Avoid hot and cold liquids, spicy foods, and sweet things if you have a mishap with your teeth, as these can all set off a pain cycle. A small piece of cotton wool moistened with oil of cloves and held to the affected area can deaden tooth pain remarkably effectively, but using aspirin in this way as a local anesthetic can lead to soreness as a result of the chemical reaction with skin tissue.

If a crown comes off, don't be tempted to stick it back on with superglue! Wrap it carefully in a tissue and keep it safe until you can get to a dentist. You might try putting some Vaseline in the crown and pushing it back on if it is a really tight fit and you place a lot of importance on your smile, for example if you are on your way to a television appearance, photo session, or important presentation. However, it is tempting fate—it may drop off again and you may swallow or lose it. Superglue is also not the answer if there is an accident with dentures, which require special adhesives and which may be damaged by the solvents in ordinary glues. Just collect all the bits and keep them safely until you can get the denture repaired professionally.

Try not to fly at all for two or three days after any serious dental work until your mouth has settled down again. Otherwise the changes in cabin air pressure can set off bleeding or painful reactions. If a partially healed recent tooth extraction starts bleeding, a moist tea bag over the socket could ease it. Preferably use chamomile tea bags, which are great traveler's aids—you can use them to make a cheering cuppa and then put the bags over your eyes to refresh them. Slices of cucumber are also great for tired eyes.

IS IT REALLY INFLUENZA?

One of the trickiest preflight health-related situations is if you are feeling a bit off-color but uncertain whether your condition will get worse and so you should not travel, or it is safe to press ahead with your plans in the expectation of getting better. Those are particularly difficult shots to call when trying to distinguish between a common cold and influenza. If the symptoms are severe, come on suddenly, and include fever, severe headache, and other pain, accompanied by tiredness and a very weak feeling, then the odds favor flu, and you should definitely stay at home.

HELP OVER THE TELEPHONE

While it is impossible to anticipate every health problem that may arise while on the road, you are never far from expert help in the United States because of the proliferation of telephone advisory services. These vary from place to place, and not all are available around the clock, but there is bound to be someone to turn to for advice. The central point to get a lead on the service that can help you best is the National Health Information Center in Washington, D.C., 800 336-4797. A growing number of areas have sponsored Ask-A-Nurse services, where you dial and speak to a qualified nurse who is able to answer a variety of medical problems. Hotel porters and the Traveler's Aid points at airports will usually be able to steer you to whatever is available locally.

RENT-A-NURSE

If it is necessary to travel when seriously ill, handicapped, or infirm, then renting a nurse to go on the trip as well can be a cost-effective solution.

For example, the best way to cope with a valued employee taken ill on the other side of the country—or the world—may be to rent a nurse to bring the patient back to family and medical care rather than to fly out relatives or colleagues and cope with the additional problems of organizing medical care from a distance.

No one who is sick or incapacitated should fly at all without a physician's express approval—in writing—or permission to board may be denied. Advance notice of any special facilities required should be given as far ahead as possible.

Nurses can be rented by the hour, day, week, or longer through a number of agencies, a few of which specifically offer medical escort services. At the time of writing, in 1989, the Langlois Medical Escort Service in North Carolina was charging $295 a day plus expenses with reductions possible for longer periods. Some medical insurance and other traveler's policies will cover escort and other expenses incurred in flying a sick person back to the point of departure, but there are lots of restrictions.

Lynn L. Langlois, executive director of the Langlois Medical Escort Service, spends 50 percent of her working life as a frequent flier. She says her experience accompanying passengers shows that their greatest fear is how they would cope if anything happened to the aircraft— another reflection of the sense of loss of control that emerged in the Hyatt Travel Futures survey as a significant stress factor for even fit and unhandicapped business travelers. A qualified nurse gives a greater sense of security than relatives, friends, or flight attendants may be able to supply, says Ms. Langlois. It has been her experience that the cabin staff do not have the time—or often the inclination—to cope with the special needs of sick or infirm passengers, such as accompanying them to the restroom.

She finds that no one particular aspect of flying causes the greatest problem for ill passengers; rather they appear to respond in different ways to the combination of stress factors involved. The various stressors detailed earlier give pointers to the kinds of difficulties that should be anticipated if anyone is forced to fly with health problems.

For example, the varying pressure and quality of the air have greater effect on passengers with pulmonary problems.

Lynn Langlois and her medical escort service can be contacted at PO Box 51418, Durham, N.C. 27717, 800 628-2828, x 392.

VIRUSES ARE FREQUENT FLIERS ALSO

If you suffer a health problem after a visit overseas—or after being in contact with someone recently overseas—make sure that your physician is informed about your possible exposure to alien viruses.

Intercontinental jet travel is responsible for the rapid spread of many types of virus, and a frequent flier may pick up a bug somewhere and return home unaware that he or she is infected and can be spreading that infection before any symptoms become obvious.

Medical knowledge of viruses is still limited, and the typical family physician cannot be expected to keep abreast of developments in the thousands of strains active in remote places now just a few flying hours away. For example, dengue and other infections are spread by mosquitoes in parts of South and Central America, Mexico, and the Caribbean, and the Delta virus found in Europe can easily get to the United States and cause obscure symptoms only a specialist might be able to assess accurately.

A particular problem in developing countries is the spread of new infections by large-scale migrations from rural to urban areas. Your new, modern, clean Western-style hotel in a city center may be only a short distance away from unsanitary squatter communities; it may even draw its staff from among former rural dwellers who have migrated—along with their health problems—to the big cities in search of work.

Consequently, the foreign traveler is exposed to unknown and new virus strains from even the most remote areas well away from his or her itinerary. This situation underlines the need for greater attention to health matters while traveling and for investigating possible links with overseas infections if sickness occurs after a trip. In the old days of slow travel by surface transport, most infections hit their victims during the journey. Now the ability to travel rapidly over vast distances means that the traveler can be back at home or in the office from the other side of the world with memories of the trip fading before the disease has finished incubating and produced symptoms.

BEWARE SHELLFISH

Delicious as they may be, shellfish are a frequent cause of food poisoning, and it makes a lot of sense to pass them by when traveling. Some airlines even prohibit their pilots from eating shellfish before or during flights and take further precautions against the risk of food poisoning by having the captain and the copilot eat different meals. So if the captain staggers past you clutching his stomach and heading for the restroom as fast as he can go, there should be no need to panic because the odds are good that there is still a pilot left up front who is fit and well!

BEATING HEARTBURN

Nearly 30 million Americans suffer from heartburn at any given time—and many of them will be flying when they experience this uncomfortable burning sensation in the chest.

The gastric reflux that causes heartburn can be aggravated by the positions we have to adopt in a plane. Acid is produced in the stomach, then causes problems when it flows up into the tube connecting the stomach with the throat. Overeating—particularly of fatty foods—smoking, heavy drinking, and bending over are among the many factors that can increase the production of stomach acid and the chances of its getting into the esophagus and causing heartburn.

Moderating food, alcohol, and smoking; exercising; and cutting back on coffee are among the preventive measures that travelers can take. If heartburn when trying to get to sleep is a problem, try elevating your head well above your feet with extra pillows, and do not eat just before you go to bed.

WARNING—YOU MAY NOT HAVE SUITABLE MEDICAL INSURANCE

Do not assume that you have sufficient health insurance when traveling just because you are well covered when at home. Lots of employee medical schemes are hedged around with restrictions to keep down premiums and may be invalid or not readily acceptable away from base, especially in another state or country. Schemes and policies vary in the coverage they give against sickness and accidents overseas. Don't rely on "free" socialized medicine in other countries, which may not be able to offer the kind of medical care you feel you need and usually is not free for foreigners.

Frequent business travelers should have clear instructions from their employers on procedures for getting treatment while away. If the employer's standard policy does not offer sufficient coverage while on the road, it should be extended at the employer's expense. Good employers also provide—

or pay for—any additional accident and baggage insurance needed to assemble a comprehensive travel insurance package for the frequent flier. Often the best and most economical coverage can be obtained by extending existing homeowner and other policies rather than by taking out specific short-term travel insurance.

Even if Medicare or your normal medical insurance will cover you overseas, you may have to pay the cost of treatment immediately or provide convincing evidence that the bills will be paid.

WARNING FOR CONTACT LENS WEARERS

Dehydration, changes of climate, and other particular problems arise for the frequent flier who wears contact lenses. Maintaining hygiene standards becomes even more important when on the road despite the practical difficulties.

The Food and Drug Administration has issued a Safety Alert about the importance of hygiene standards for saline solutions, particularly those made by dissolving salt tablets or capsules in distilled water. Such homemade solutions are not sterile, may contain infections that can cause blindness, and should never by used as eyedrops or to wet lenses.

The FDA recommends that homemade saline solutions be used only before or during heat disinfection of the lenses, never afterwards or in conjunction with the chemical disinfection adopted by many contact lens wearers while on the road. The risk of eye infection is ever-present when traveling and can be reduced by not swimming or using a hot tub while wearing contact lenses. Always wash your hands before handling your lenses and disinfect soft lenses every time they are removed.

TALK TO YOUR COMPUTER TO IDENTIFY TRAVEL STRESS

Companies that take seriously the true cost of business travel, particularly the impact on the health and efficiency of their people, can help to overcome the critical lack of authoritative data by conducting their own research—and establishing treatment procedures.

Interactive computerized employee assistance programs can be adapted to this role. Such software enables employees to detail personal problems and helps to identify the causes. The stress of frequent travel is often overlooked. It is not unduly difficult to create or modify existing software for use by the frequent fliers in an organization, helping the company to collect useful data and assisting the travelers to identify the possible travel-related causes of illness, stress, and other personal problems.

TIPS ON SUNSCREEN

Traveling to very sunny places, especially those by the water, which have high-intensity reflected light, or at high altitudes, where ultraviolet light is stronger, can pose problems. Skin not accustomed to regular sunshine can be very sensitive, and heightened public awareness of skin cancer makes us all more cautious.

Standard advice from skin care authorities is to use generous applications of proprietary sunscreen products with a sun protective factor (SPF) of fifteen or more. The SPF rates the degree of protection from ultraviolet B rays, which cause most burning and danger of skin cancer. The

A rays, which are of longer frequency, can also do damage. The broad-spectrum sunscreens claim to offer a wide range of protection but vary in their effectiveness against the A rays.

Consult your doctor or dermatologist if you have a particularly sensitive skin or your journey is likely to expose you to large amounts of sunshine. Try switching brands if you prove allergic to one sunscreen, as they can vary a lot in their content.

In an emergency, zinc oxide ointment is helpful but messy, while lip balm can moisturize and offer some protection for your nose and ears as well as your lips.

Sometimes the intensity of the sun in a window seat on the plane can be troublesome, although it is unlikely to burn. Sunglasses in your carry-on baggage can make looking out of the window more comfortable.

RISKS OF INFECTION

One particularly sensitive issue seems to bother many travelers, especially those for whom being on the road is not a frequent experience. The use of public lavatories, extensive casual contacts with strangers in confined places, eating out, and other similar "strange" experiences can cause apprehension about being exposed to infectious diseases.

I once had a colleague who never traveled without his own sleeping bag made from a bedsheet. He had heard that some hotels do not always change the sheets between guests but turn them over if they appear clean. Being apprehensive about coming into contact with sheets another human body might have touched the night before, he always played safe by putting his bag between himself and the possibly offensive linen!

TAKE NEEDLES WITH YOU
TO BE EXTRA SAFE

Now that AIDS, hepatitis, and certain other diseases that can be transmitted through contaminated hypodermic needles have become such an international concern, some frequent fliers are following the example set by staff of the United Nations agencies who have to visit developing countries.

In some places disposable syringes are not readily available and the sterilization of reusable needles is suspect. So consider taking sealed packets of sterile hypodermic syringes and needles for use in an emergency. The disposable kind are not bulky or heavy, but you should always have with them an impressive document from a doctor or clinic giving justification for your possession of what customs officials may suspect is illicit drug-taking paraphernalia.

Little can be done to anticipate the risk of being exposed to infected blood if an emergency requires transfusions. However, special solutions called blood expanders can provide temporary help in maintaining the necessary volume of blood in the body.

AIDS and Other Infections

AIDS has become such a serious issue that attention is focused on the whole issue of exposure to infectious diseases while traveling, especially as the publicity about the initial spread of AIDS in North America by a gay flight attendant has generated many myths. In fact, the risk of catching any contagious disease through the exposure to infection in normal business travel in the United States, Canada, most of Europe, Japan, Australia, New Zealand, and other developed countries is not exceptional if you take the same precautions as in your own home town. Some Third World and Eastern bloc countries present very little extra risk, but others with low standards can expose you to far higher possibilities of infection.

Flight attendants in particular have become very hygiene-conscious, and their risk of exposure to bugs from passengers is far greater than your risk of catching anything from them.

Of course, you may get head lice or fleas from hotel bedding, but they are more likely to come home from school with one of your children. You may pick up athlete's foot from a bathmat while attending a sales convention a thousand miles from home, but the risk is just as great every time you shower at the neighborhood racquet club. There may be worms in the raw fish in San Francisco's Japantown, but look first for the caterpillar in your mother-in-law's salad! In other words, while familiar things and environments are reassuring, those strange and distant can seem irrationally threatening. As one veteran traveler commented: "Get paranoic about all the possible health risks when traveling and you take all the fun out of it—it's digging a grave in your field of happiness."

We started this section with Dr. Johnson, so let's permit him the last word on healthful travel in his farewell message to his friend Henry Perkins. This is Samuel Johnson's six-point plan for healthful travel, almost as practical today as it was in 1782, although you have to substitute "plane" for "chaise."

DR. JOHNSON'S SIX-POINT PLAN

"1. Turn all care out of your head as soon as you mount the chaise.

"2. Do not think about frugality; your health is worth more than it can cost.

"3. Do not continue any day's journey to fatigue.

"4. Take now and then a day's rest.

"5. Get a smart sea-sickness [remedy], if you can.

"6. Cast away all anxiety, and keep your mind easy."

The One-Minute Travel Stress Audit

The single most effective action you can take to reduce travel-induced stress and so improve the quality of your life on the road is to give yourself a periodic *Travel Stress Audit*. It is easy and free, takes only a few seconds—and works!

Using this technique will reduce or eliminate pain on the plane from abused muscles and joints, help you to relax and enjoy business travel more and enable you to function with greater efficiency to the benefit of your company and your career.

It is a technique particularly effective against *Traveler's Elbow, Frequent Flier's Back, Road Warrior's Neck* and *Tightrope Walker's Tension*—all business travel–related health problems that affect millions of frequent fliers but are largely preventable.

The *Travel Stress Audit* simply involves pausing regularly during a journey to review your mental and physical state. If this self-appraisal indicates stress building up, you can act in good time to ease it and prevent more serious problems from arising. The technique has been refined from the Work Stress Inventory developed by Dr. Roy Forest of Mill Valley, California, a specialist in disabling and painful conditions arising from work and travel. His patients include both professional airline crews and frequent business fliers.

Dr. Forest takes pain on the plane very seriously. "You can injure yourself and suffer persistent, chronic pain just carrying your bag to the departure gate or falling asleep in your seat," he says.

The chances of doing so are reduced dramatically if you follow these simple tips.

The Hyatt Travel Futures project found that poor service from airlines is the most difficult stress factor for frequent business travelers. We get tensed up and put abnormal strain on muscles and joints just in *anticipation* of hassles on a trip, so we start to suffer travel-related stress before we even leave for the airport. Then we compound the condition with the physical stress associated with the journey itself. A majority of frequent travelers surveyed found it difficult to cope with physical stress, and they could clearly differentiate the causes and symptoms of mental stressors from those of physical ones.

The more stress reactions build up in the body, the more acute become the symptoms and the more difficult it is to get rid of them. Stress is an important factor in the two areas of the human body most afflicted by neuromuscular and musculoskeletal pain—in the lower back and in the neck and shoulders. Both are major problem areas for frequent fliers. Regular *Travel Stress Audits* can be the best preventive medicine.

THE ONE-MINUTE TRAVEL STRESS AUDIT

The neck, shoulder, arm, and back pains resulting from travel are similar to and often more acute than those incurred in the workplace. For example, anyone who works for long periods at a computer, probably concentrating hard and under pressure to solve a problem or finish a task, will soon start to display characteristic symptoms of stress-related discomfort and pain. Bad posture and keeping one unnatural position will make neck and shoulder muscles tighten up, even go into spasm. Particularly vulnerable are middle-aged and older people who can suffer degeneration of the disks between the seven vertebrae in the cervical spine of the neck, coupled with loss of flexibility in fibrous tissue between and around disks.

Similar problems show up in the lower back. While

orthopedically designed chairs and the correct ergonomic placement of the keyboard and screen can help, the only really effective preventive measure for these neck and back problems is periodically to stop what you are doing and consciously carry out a stress inventory.

Delay Is Dangerous

"Regularly take a momentary break to review what inputs you are giving your body, the effects they are having, and the actions needed to put things right," says Dr. Forest. "It takes only a few seconds to pause, realize that your position is becoming fixed and uncomfortable and that you need to shrug your shoulders or move around to break the pattern and get relief. If you fail to carry out regular stress inventories, the tension and consequent muscle and joint stresses get steadily worse and more difficult to remedy.

"I have had computer operators requiring weeks of traction and difficult treatment before their necks and shoulders could be relaxed sufficiently for chiropractic manipulation. They could avoid all those problems if after, say, every screenful of work completed, they would pause for a brief stress inventory.

"The *Travel Stress Audit* works the same way. To reduce stress and muscle and joint pain, stop regularly during every trip to carry out a stress audit, find out what inputs are creating problems, and put them right."

Start before Your Flight

The technique begins as you prepare for the journey to the airport. Remember, anticipation is beginning to set up stress and tension. You need a regular cue to prompt you to undertake a stress audit, and that is automatically provided during the preflight period. Monitoring the behavior of colleagues and associates I have accompanied on business trips, or at least taken to the airport and seen off, reveals that typical travelers look at their watches at least five times in the two hours before departure. Some do so far more frequently.

If you carry out a quick stress audit every time you look at your watch, you can identify the sources of tension and deal with them far more easily than if you allow them to produce actual physical symptoms. You may, for example, begin to develop underlying apprehensions about timing—a clear warning to leave a comfortable margin for the journey to the airport in case there are traffic jams, which can cause major stress if your timing is allowed to become too tight.

Traveler's Elbow

You may be hurrying along the corridor toward the departure gate, glance at your watch, be prompted to carry out a stress audit, and realize that there is a pain in the elbow of the arm carrying your briefcase.

"*Traveler's Elbow* is a common affliction among my frequent-flier patients, and rarely do they even guess the cause of this pain, which can travel from the elbow right up into the shoulder and neck, even causing headaches," says Dr. Forest. "Once you do a travel audit and observe your fellow travelers' habits more closely, you realize how often and unconsciously we carry a briefcase, bag, or suitcase with our arms slightly bent. That puts a lot of strain on the elbow joint, especially if the traveler is stressed already and has tensed muscles.

"Far better to carry any case with the arm extended and straight, so that the main strain is on the much stronger shoulder muscles, not the vulnerable elbow. Carry out a regular *Travel Stress Audit*, and you will be reminded to carry your bags properly."

Road Warrior's Neck

Similarly, a quick stress audit as you settle into your seat on the plane will remind you to reduce the stress on your neck and lower back from the design deficiencies of the seat, which become more apparent as the journey progresses. Action at this point will dramatically reduce stress later on, helping to minimize such complaints as **Road Warrior's Neck**, a stiff and painful condition that restricts movement in and around the cervical column. It stems from tension and/or sleeping during a flight with the neck in an awkward and stressed position. Older people, with their less flexible fibrous tissue and degenerating disks, are particularly vulnerable.

Many such problems are caused by aircraft seats, the world's great seating compromise because they have to meet such conflicting requirements. They must be as light in weight and small as possible, because every pound and inch costs money for the airline in reduced payload and increased fuel consumption. Yet a seat may have to accommodate a petite ninety-five-pound senior citizen, next a three-hundred-pound truck driver, then a tall slim model replaced on the following flight by a short dumpy waitress. The same seat must be strong and firm enough for a truck driver with his beer belly, yet have sufficient resilience to give a cushioned ride for the diminutive elderly lady; provide enough room for the model's long legs, yet allow the short waitress's feet to rest comfortably on the floor.

It must incorporate a reclining mechanism yet leave enough space underneath for carry-on bags and the feet of the passenger behind. It has to pass elaborate crash and fire-resistance tests but not be excessively expensive or adversely affect load factors that eat into the airline's often slender profit margins. It must be easily taken in and out and moved, as the internal configuration of commercial planes can change frequently. The list of often conflicting requirements goes on and on. It is not surprising that so many of us find airline seats costing thousands of dollars still miserably uncomfortable, and we have to customize them as much as possible to our individual body shapes and requirements.

Additional Pillows

That is why the canny frequent fliers, memory jogged by their stress audits, make sure they bring additional cushions with them or get at least two of those that the airline provides.

"Never—ever—sit for any length of time in an aircraft seat without extra support for your lower back," advises Dr. Forest. "The better auto seats have lumbar adjustment, but until this becomes available on aircraft, the least you should do is put a pillow as support between the curve in your lower back and the seat."

Dr. Forest regularly gets patients who have actually injured their necks by falling asleep during a flight, so to avoid neck pain that may persist long after the flight is over, he recommends at least one pillow to help support your neck and head.

"You sit in an awkward position on a plane, and just dozing off can result in your head flopping heavily to one side, putting considerable strain on your neck and shoulders. If possible, get a window seat if you intend to sleep and take a special neck pillow with you or get extra pillows, perhaps blankets as well, to provide support for your head."

Find Your Cues

If you forget to take these precautions around takeoff time, you should be prompted to do so when you take subsequent *Travel Stress Audits* during the flight—although by then you may have dozed off and already be suffering neck problems. Travelers look at their watches far less frequently during a flight than before it, so until it becomes a habit, you may need to create special cue reminders to take periodic audits while in the air. Depending on the flight, these could be such regular occurrences as when an attendant comes to one of the seats in your vicinity, every time there is an announcement over the public address system, every five pages in your book, or when the tape in your cassette player needs changing.

Every audit will make you stop and think about inputs that are likely to cause discomfort or stress. You should, for example, get an early warning about the consequences of crossing your legs, which in the confined space of an aircraft can restrict blood circulation in your lower body and twist your pelvis. Staying in that position for any length of time will progressively aggravate the situation.

If watching the movie, you will be reminded by your audits not to adopt an incorrect position for your head and neck, which you may need to do to get the best view and then hold unconsciously for a long period while you concentrate on the film. Sitting for prolonged periods with your chin thrust up and forward and your head leaning back, a common position to get the best view of the screen over the seats in front, causes tension and pain. Far less stressful is to keep your chin tucked in and your neck drawn back.

Exercise Every Hour or Two

Travel Stress Audits also compensate for the longer intervals between the visits to the restroom that result from dehydration. We may not actually *need* to leave our seats for several hours, but Dr. Forest recommends still getting up every one to two hours to stretch and exercise—preferably using the occasion to collect a fruit juice or drink of water.

Usually you can find a place to do basic stretching exercises without disturbing other passengers. These are similar to the limbering up and cooling off exercises for jogging, tennis, and other sports.

To do *The Leg Stretch* stand up, put your hands at shoulder level against a wall or door, and lean on them while stretching one leg out behind you and bringing the heel down to the floor. Lean into the wall and hold that position for thirty seconds, stretching the muscles right up the back of your extended leg. Repeat with the other leg and with your head alternately up and down.

If the plane is too busy or there is not enough space, try **The Flamingo Position**, standing on one leg and pulling the other tightly up against your chest. The **In-flight Squat** takes up little space and is not likely to disturb other passengers. To do this, squat down, put your hands over your knees and push your lower back upright, flattening the curve that it has probably got into from slouching in your seat.

Exercises in Your Seat
Many **Travel Stress Audit** exercises can be performed without leaving your seat or while standing in a queue for the restroom or to get a drink. **Neck** and **Shoulder Rolls** are great for relieving stress and tension. Let your head flop loosely and roll it and your neck clockwise for a few seconds, then repeat counterclockwise.

The **Head Tilt** is another mild but effective in-flight exercise. Relax your arms and shoulders and tilt your head sideways in each direction, getting your ear as close to the point of the shoulder as possible without straining.

The **Shoulder Shrug** may hardly look like an exercise at all, but it works well. Simply relax your upper body and keep shrugging your shoulders, first forward, then back.

Various isometric exercises, when performed regularly for a few seconds during **Travel Stress Audits**, will help to prevent muscle tension or to ease it if it does occur.

The **Forehead Push** involves leaning back, placing the palm of your hand on your forehead and pushing foward with your head and back with your hand at the same time. Nothing much moves, but your muscles work and the blood courses more freely through them.

Alternate the Forehead Push with a few seconds of **Sideways Head Pushing**, pressing your right and left hands alternatively against the sides of your head—not your chin—and pushing your head toward your shoulder. Maintain the pressure for a few seconds, then relax for a moment before letting your head move freely down toward your shoulder as far as it will go comfortably. Repeat in the other direction. This is a great way of easing neck and shoulder tension, and you will find it can give much greater mobility to your neck and head.

The *Seat Lift* involves dropping your arms to your side and getting a grip underneath the seat squab. Gently pull up as if you are trying to lift the seat with yourself in it.

The *Thigh Squeeze* will exercise other muscles in arms, legs, and particularly the chest, which stiffen up after a long period sitting in a confined space. Put your hands flat on your thighs, lock your elbows, and try to lift your knees.

The *Knee Butterfly* also involves stimulating exercise without actual movement. Slightly spread your legs, put your hands on the insides of your knees, and try to close your legs as a butterfly's wings go together when it is resting. Repeat in the other direction—legs together, trying to open like wings against the pressure of the hands on the outside of the knees.

You need only a minute of these exercises every hour or two to reduce muscular and joint pain on the plane— and ease both the physical and the mental stresses of flying.

Tightrope Walker's Tension

Dr. Forest says that some women travelers have distinctive physical reactions to the stresses of flying at certain points in their menstrual cycle, especially when their ligament structure becomes more lax around the time of menstruation. They may even become more susceptible to joint injuries, such as from the abnormal strain caused by lifting heavy bags, and may benefit by particularly careful stress audits at those times.

Tightrope Walker's Tension can be a problem for this category of business traveler, identified in the Hyatt Travel Futures Project research as young women under thirty-five years of age without much experience of frequent business travel who feel especially powerful when on the road but are harried and tense. That tension and stress during a trip often lead to prolonged pain and discomfort, necessitating treatment from specialists like Dr. Forest.

Many painful complications of flying—for Eagles, Family Tieds, Tightrope Walkers and Road Warriors alike—can be prevented by the simple technique of regular *Travel Stress Audits*, which soon become second nature. Just as it is good business practice to audit your financial records periodically, so it pays during travel to run an audit of your physical and mental balances and take timely action to prevent them from slipping into the red.

Intellectual Overdosing

In one strange form of travel-related stress, the culture and other emotional and intellectual aspects of a strange environment cause extreme reactions in susceptible people.

This condition has been observed for many years in Florence, where it is known as the Stendhal syndrome after the French writer, who experienced irregular heartbeats and disorientation during a visit to the Italian city. Other symptoms include stomach pains, excessive perspiration, hallucinations, and depression, elation, and other emotional extremes.

Medical opinion differs on the causes of this mysterious traveler's condition, but the consensus seems to be that the unreality and emotional impact of an exotic place on impressionable people, when compounded with all the other stressors associated with travel, have this extreme effect.

Most of us who travel on either business or leisure have either felt something similar ourselves or know of such symptoms arising in other travelers who have not been exposed to the unusually rich diet of art that Florence offers. Obviously, other intellectual and emotional stimuli may have the same effect. Some professional conferences, for example, can be intellectually very intensive and stimulating, giving the effect of a high, which when coupled with travel stress, can backfire into conditions similar to the Stendhal syndrome.

This whole subject is one of the great unknowns of travel-related stress, but there are reassurances. At least as far as the experience with over a hundred cases of Stendhal Syndrome in Florence is concerned, sufferers tend to be novice travelers, not Eagle or Road Warrior types. Most victims seem to be traveling alone, not in groups, of U.S. or north European origin, and to be particularly sensitive to cultural influences.

The prognosis is for complete recovery from a cultural overdose after a few days of rest. This indicates that an intellectually demanding business trip is best timed so that it ends with a weekend of relaxation and does not dump the traveler straight back into an intensive work routine.

There's a Masseur in Every Hotel Bathroom

Warmth and a gentle massage are excellent treatments for the cervical strain and neck discomfort that so often follow a flight. Both are readily available in every hotel bathroom—just switch on the shower.

An increasing number of hotels are fitting the special shower heads that produce variable pulsating jets to give a massaging effect, but an ordinary shower can bring a great deal of relief very quickly.

Turn up the temperature of the water as hot as you can comfortably bear it and let it play on your neck and shoulders for at least five minutes. Try to relax, letting your shoulders slump and rolling your head and stretching your neck gently, as in the in-flight cervical stress reduction exercises described in detail on pp. 201–202. In particular, turn your head slowly as far it will go comfortably to the right and left, then rock it gently from side to side, trying to get each ear touching its adjoining shoulder.

Relax between each movement and let the hot water wash over and gently aid the massaging effect of the muscle movements taking place during these exercises. Finish by getting the rest of your body toned up with a final round of stretching exercises that involve the legs as well

Hook your thumbs together behind your back and pull back and down while trying to make your shoulder blades meet as your back is braced and you take a deep breath. Raise up onto your tiptoes and bend your back gently until you can look at the point on the ceiling immediately above you. Hold this position for a slow count of five, then relax, exhaling as you do so. Repeat the exercise five to ten times.

These special in-shower exercises can work wonders after a tiring, stressful journey. The combination of the heat from the shower water and the muscle movements simulates many of the benefits of a professional massage. Within fifteen minutes, from undressing through to dressing again, you can get toned up for your first business meeting.

The shower exercises are also great as a relaxant before going to bed and will help to combat some of the symptoms of jet lag. Demonstrate to yourself that they work by comparing the amount of comfortable neck movement you have before getting into the shower and afterwards. In some people with moderate to severe cervical strain, the improvement is dramatic.

Jet Lag

*Take it seriously—the consequences are
usually unpleasant and expensive; they
may even be fatal.*

Jet lag is the most serious common health problem facing
travelers who cross time zones—and it costs their employers dearly. Ignore jet lag at your peril. It is a major
stress factor in international and transcontinental business
travel, and can even have fatal consequences. But it is a
largely avoidable charge on the business community, representing many millions of dollars wasted annually in lost
productivity and reduced work performance.

Research by the Upjohn Company found that 90 percent of those suffering from jet lag were tired and sleepy
during the day, and almost as many could not sleep at
night. Sixty-nine percent had difficulty concentrating; the
reflexes were slowed in 66 percent; about half were irrita-
ble and had upset digestive systems; almost a third suffered from depression.

Eagles, Road Warriors, and other frequent fliers who
may be tempted to dismiss jet lag as a symptom of weakness in coping with travel miss the whole point of this
phenomenon. There is nothing macho in claiming that jet
lag does not affect you. It cannot be overcome by tough-
ness and determination, as you can jog an extra mile or
play another set at tennis by calling on physical and psychological reserves. Nor can you take a pill and press on
bravely. Flying across time zones creates tangible physiological disturbances that adversely affect the functioning
of the human brain and body. These symptoms are as real
and as much outside your control as the consequences of
being infected by an influenza virus or suffering from seasickness.

When I served in the Navy in my teens, the old dogs would make fun of all us young sailors if we were ill during rough weather. Seasickness was equated with lack of experience and self-discipline. Some frequent fliers have a tendency to look on jet lag in the same way. True, familiarity with the conditions that bring on motion sickness does enhance many people's resistance to the problem, but for a surprising number of experienced sailors, it is something that just does not go away. That great nautical hero Admiral Horatio Nelson suffered seasickness throughout his eventful career, just as the most hardened Road Warrior or the most self-confident young Eagle will feel the symptoms of jet lag, however many frequent flier bonuses they collect.

CUMULATIVE EFFECT

All managers, particularly human resource specialists, need to be conscious of the potentially serious and cumulative effects that jet lag can have on frequently flying personnel because their efficiency, productivity, motivation, and relationships can all be adversely affected.

Crossing time zones, coupled with the environmental and other stresses inherent in flying, affects your body and mind in many well-defined ways, whether you are old or young, male or female, hero or coward. Your heart rate, the pressure and clotting characteristics of your blood, your mental processes, your bowel movements, your hormone levels, the rate at which your hair grows, even your body temperature change as a result of the disruption in normal human cycles. Women on a business trip who break a nail more easily than usual or who find their hair suddenly becomes difficult to groom may have symptoms of jet lag that are tangible and easy to identify. Just as real but more subjective are the feelings of depression, the irritability, forgetfulness, and other emotional and psychological symptoms that afflict all ages and both sexes of long-distance travelers.

MAKE ALLOWANCES

As a result, flying from Los Angeles to New York or London to San Francisco, or other long flights across time zones is hazardous to your health and the quality of performance of any task you undertake after your arrival. Frequent fliers—and the employers or clients for whom they are making business trips—must take these facts seriously and make appropriate allowances. Some companies forbid staff to undertake negotiations or engage in critical work for one, two, or more days after significant time zone changes. Others do not consider jet lag important, but expect their people to get on with the job quickly. The latter is a short-sighted policy because the enormous expense associated with long-distance business travel can be justified only in terms of investment in the quality of expertise and thinking that the employee will bring to the assignment. If effectiveness is reduced by a third or more by jet lag, then the exercise can become a very poor investment.

TAKE PRECAUTIONS

Medical knowledge about jet lag is still comparatively restricted, and the extent of the problem has never been comprehensively quantified, but ignorance of the details does not alter the basic realities. Fortunately, there is much good news about jet lag. Its effects can be reduced dramatically by taking precautions before the flight, modifying your activities during the journey, and by taking simple actions after your arrival.

First, let's dispel some popular myths about jet lag. One is that it does not seriously affect younger, healthy people and that women are less susceptible than men. Everyone is vulnerable. However, older travelers as a rule do seem to suffer jet lag symptoms more severely than younger people. A study by one of the European airlines indicated that young members of flight crews cope with jet lag better than those in middle age. It seems that the aging process naturally makes the synchronization of our internal clocks less efficient, so some people find they get jet lag more easily and its consequences last longer as they get older. A complication for women is that anything that disrupts the circadian rhythms can also affect the menstrual cycle, a problem for both female shift workers in factories and flight attendants.

While jet lag can be particularly unpleasant for some older people and for some women, the effects on the young and healthy of both sexes can be significant. In a military experiment, a group of eighty-one healthy American soldiers aged between eighteen and thirty-four were meticulously monitored on how they reacted to an eastward journey across six time zones. Most of them suffered fatigue, irritability, sleepiness, headaches, and other symptoms that significantly reduced their strength and performance for up to five days.

EXTREME DEPRESSION

Suicides in apparently normal men, both young and old, have been linked to the extreme depression that can be an important symptom of jet lag. In other investigations, both men and women subjected to emotional stress tests after crossing time zones have shown such extreme reactions as breaking into tears and displaying excessive anger, which demonstrate why personality conflicts and poor decision making so often occur among jet-lagged business travelers.

Another myth is that alcohol relaxes your body and

helps to mask the symptoms of jet lag. In fact, drinking, either as a prophylactic or cure for jet lag, invariably makes things worse. There is considerable evidence that compulsory abstention from alcohol before and during a flight is a major factor in enabling aircrew to cope better with jet lag than their passengers who drink liberally, despite the extra stress that aircrew experience during the journey.

EAST AND WEST

Some people believe that you get jet lag only when flying eastward, when you lose time, rather than westward, when the days and nights are extended. The westward journey may cross as many time zones, but the changes are partially canceled out by the actual time spent traveling. On an eastbound flight, the transit time and the zone changes combine to create greater disruption of circadian rhythms. A major international study of fatigue in airline flight crews showed that they slept better immediately after westbound flights than eastbound ones but that the differences tend to start to even out, as the quality of sleep often declines on the second night after a westbound flight.

The main practical advantage of a westbound flight is that it is usually easier to stay up late on your first day at the destination and then go to sleep when all the locals do. Trying to get into the rhythm of a new eastward zone, when time has been lost, is inherently more difficult. The body and mind have to adjust to a difference of three hours when crossing the United States west to east, at least six hours when crossing the Atlantic toward Europe, and by as much as twelve hours from the United States or Canada to parts of Asia and the Orient.

Many people suffer severe jet lag after trips in either direction, and we all have our circadian rhythms upset to a significant degree when crossing more than one or two time zones.

NOT PSYCHOSOMATIC

Another fallacy is the view many Road Warriors have expressed to me. They believe that "if you don't think about jet lag, it will not bother you—only those who worry about it, experience it." The assumption is that it is a psychosomatic complaint. However, both children and animals, who have no knowledge or understanding of jet lag, still suffer badly from the same symptoms as do informed adult humans, so there is no way they could generate the physical symptoms by their psychic or emotional processes.

TRAVELER'S AMNESIA

Yet another of the many myths is that taking sleeping pills to help you get to sleep during the flight or to help you acclimatize to the sleep patterns of the new time zone after arrival will combat other symptoms of jet lag in addition to insomnia. In fact, sleeping pills and alcohol may seriously aggravate jet lag symptoms. Neither promotes quality sleep, and both have aftereffects that can make mental and physical symptoms of jet lag worse and extend by a day or more the time taken for the body to adjust to a new time zone.

It became quite trendy for a time among frequent fliers to take a short-acting sedative called triazolam, which did not appear to have significant aftereffects, as a way of combating jet lag on eastbound flights. Then the *Journal* of the *American Medical Association* reported three cases of physicians who suffered ***Traveler's Amnesia*** as a result of this practice. They checked through immigration, collected their baggage, changed money, caught cabs, had meals, and even attended meetings and apparently behaved normally after their arrival. Subsequently, however, they could remember nothing of these activities, in one case for eleven hours after taking the sleeping pill. The three neuroscientists also took alcohol, which aggravated the consequences. This kind of anterograde amnesia has occurred with other sleeping pills taken by travelers.

By all means take drugs to help you sleep, either on the plane or after your arrival, but only if actual sleeping time is vital to your peace of mind. Your body needs quality more than duration in sleep, especially to reduce the consequences of jet lag. We tend to worry too much about missed sleep, whether traveling or not, and those who complain of insomnia usually subconsciously exaggerate the number of hours of sleep they miss. But it still makes sound business sense to allow for sleep disruption after long east-west trips.

DIVERGENT AND CONVERGENT THINKING

Even one night's loss of sleep can have a big difference on the divergent thinking processes, although convergent thinking may still be comparatively unaffected even after two sleepless nights. The ability to perform well in divergent thinking is very important to many business travelers because this is the more creative type of mental process, involving being flexible and coming up with fresh solutions to unusual problems.

Convergent thinking, in contrast, relates more to manual or routine tasks. An experienced accountant can draw up a simple balance sheet, and an artist can produce a routine representational drawing, using mainly convergent thinking processes. If the accountant needs to do some creative reallocation of resources to minimize tax liabilities or the artist produce imaginative visualizations, then the divergent thinking processes come into play.

Loss of sleep—as little as one disturbed night—and other symptoms of jet lag seem to have far more impact on divergent than convergent mental processes. So if your business trip crosses time zones and you are required to do creative, spontaneous, or original thinking when you reach your destination, take the jet lag threat very seriously. You could be as much as two-thirds less competent at crucial tasks if you rush into business situations soon after your arrival.

PHYSICAL AND MENTAL CHANGES

It is difficult to measure the quality of thinking, but evidence that jet lag causes real changes in physical and mental processes can be seen in other reactions. For example, in two dramatic cases reported by the Eastern Virginia Medical Authority, a thirty-year-old man and a thirty-year-old woman both experienced isolated sleep paralysis after a transcontinental flight. They suddenly could not perform simple voluntary movements at the point of either going to sleep or waking up. Both the man and woman had auditory and visual hallucinations and suffered from extreme anxiety.

Investigators believed that these symptoms stemmed from the altered rapid eye movements—REMs—that characterize a certain type of sleep. The rapid change of time zones caused by the transatlantic flight so altered the sleep behavior of these two passengers that they were literally paralyzed and suffered disturbing hallucinations. Fortunately, they recovered quickly, but the cases show that there is a lot more behind the often unusual behavior of travelers after long flights than simply tiredness or an upset stomach.

Having emphasized the importance of jet lag, let us

look at the main reasons for it and the best ways to minimize the consequences.

INTERNAL CLOCKS

The body's activities are governed not by one but by many internal clocks, or cycles. Some are rapid, such as the rhythm of your heartbeat and eye blinks, others more leisurely, like those that trigger hunger at mealtimes, drowsiness when it is time to sleep, and the almost reflexive desires to move the bowels or urinate at regular intervals.

Still longer cycles regulate such body functions as menstruation and hormone levels. All these internal timekeepers are affected when we cross several time zones. In effect, our main clock in the brain and the many other keepers of time and rhythm directing biochemical processes throughout the body become temporarily unregulated, breaking into a discord of unsynchronized rhythms when they receive confusing, unfamiliar signals. The effects can be likened to the discord produced by members of an orchestra all playing the same melody but to a different beat. The conductor, the central internal clock, wavers between the rhythm of the strings and the beat of the percussion section.

CUES SET THE RHYTHMS

The body's various timekeepers take several days to adjust to a new set of cues, and the systems they control are seriously out of balance until the new synchronized rhythms are firmly up and running. The rhythms are established both by environmental influences and by our own patterns of behavior. Light cues are particularly influential—medical science is just starting to realize how important. We are all vulnerable to some degree to SAD—seasonal affective disorder—a specific type of depression brought on by lower levels and intensity of light during bad weather or winter. In the same way, we are affected by rapid variations in the cycles of light during travel or shift work.

Many travelers have experienced a dramatic demonstration of this after a long flight during which the main time routines of home have been maintained. If it was a night flight, you may have slept well; if a daytime one, you pushed ahead with the paperwork you brought with you. You may feel great until you step out of the plane and get a light cue—perhaps blazing sunshine to indicate day or darkness for night—that conflicts with what your body is expecting. Then the body and mind react quickly with symptoms of jet lag. These get worse during conflicts between what you would be doing according to your internal body clocks and what you are expected to do according to the time on your wristwatch. The watch, being just a machine, has adjusted immediately when set to local time, and unlike our far more complicated body clocks, has no built-in memory of its previous setting to confuse it.

The sun shines at your destination, sending a message to get on with the day, while your body tells you it is still dark at home and time for bed. The visual, audible, and other environmental cues are linked with many social behavioral signals. You have an engagement for lunch and a meeting, but your body and mind resist participating in these normal activities because for them it is the middle of the night and they should be in bed resting.

Changes in temperatures may be an important influence also. Some research indicates that you are biologically predisposed to sleep at certain times that are closely related to body temperature variations. The international research on flight crews showed that many slept only for a short period after an eastbound journey because their body clocks controlling temperature were still on home time, and their body temperatures began to rise as a preliminary to waking up as if they were still at home.

LONG-TERM EFFECT

Other research suggests that jet lag, or even any major change of time zones that does not occur so rapidly, can have very long-term, not just transitory effects. Some people with body clocks particularly resistant to change have problems with changes in latitude also. Patients with depression have been deprived of sleep in an attempt to reset their circadian rhythms after they changed countries of residence and experienced significant differences in latitude. The theory is that the changes in temperature and light have put their circadian rhythms permanently out of synchronization with their new environment and the society in which they have to function. Their internal clocks make them biologically programmed to be sleeping when those around them are busily interacting. The results of such research are still not conclusive.

There is conflicting scientific evidence whether some symptoms of jet lag, such as sleep disorders and depression, can be permanent. However, there is no dispute that we are not designed as a species to change our cycles or rhythms rapidly, nor have we evolved the capacity to do so. Consequently, our physical and mental processes malfunction until the well-established rhythms have adjusted to the cues and cycles of the new time zone. This process can take several days in normal, healthy people.

THE JET LAG PILL

It may take a week for the production of melatonin in the brain to become adjusted. It is called the nightime hormone because the brain releases melatonin into the body during sleep in one of many biochemical reactions governed by our internal timekeepers. Scientists have found that the judicious taking of melatonin capsules during long flights across time zones helps to reduce some of the symptoms of jet lag by speeding up the rate at which our internal clocks adjust. Naturally, pharmaceutical companies are keenly interested in this potential for a jet lag pill, and one based on melatonin may become available in the future.

Australian and European scientists expect to have a melatonin medication on the international market early in the 1990s. Take a couple of pills at night after a long flight across time zones, and they compensate for the pineal gland still being on home time and not producing enough melatonin at the new bedtime to stimulate natural sleep. Initial trials have shown a dramatic decrease in jet lag symptoms and few side effects.

Another possibility is that very low doses of nitrous oxide or oxygen or both may prove very effective. Hospital staff, aircrew, and divers all know how oxygen can help settle body systems disrupted by a hangover, a condition of dysfunction that shares many physiological symptoms with jet lag. A decade of research into the action of nitrous oxide on the internal opioid system—the endogenous opiates—by the South African Brain Research Institute has pointed to the dentist's laughing gas as a possible quick fix for jet lag. Already it has yielded spectacular results in treating seven thousand cases of withdrawal from alcohol addiction. It is still a dream that we will be able to pop a pill or take a sniff of a gas to get instant relief for jet lag, but in the meantime there are other ways of helping our internal clocks to adjust.

EXERCISE AND LIGHT HELP

The most practical treatment for jet lag so far is also very healthful. Hamsters in a trial at the University of Toronto adapted far more quickly to changes in light and dark if they were encouraged to exercise. The hamsters who were left alone to idle in their cages took more than eleven days to adapt to what was effectively a different time zone in which night arrived eight hours earlier. Those put into exercise wheels spun their circadian rhythms back into synch very quickly so that their sleep-wake cycles were in tune with their new environment after only a day and a half.

This experiment demonstrated in the laboratory what many frequent fliers who exercise regularly know works well in practice also. Even a modest exercise routine can work wonders, either to boost the psyche and the body to cope with a busy day or as a prelude to a restful night's sleep in an alien time zone. According to Dr. Mark Gillman, Director of the South African Brain Research Institute (SABRI), exercise has many effects on the endorphins and on brain and central nervous system functions. It directly stimulates the release of opiate substances created within the body; your body makes druglike substances much more specifically tailored to its particular needs at any given time than anything you can swallow or inject. If you are an inveterate pill-popper, try to substitute a brisk run round the block for the latest highly publicized wonder drug and let your body generate the high itself.

Exercising in bright daylight is particularly beneficial because the light gives strong visual cues to help reset your body clocks and lift depression. The renowned Max Planck Institute for Psychiatry in West Germany and other European researchers have obtained some very promising results using light to treat jet lag. The general conclusion from the international research into the effects of light on human and animal behavior indicates that normal artificial illumination is not sufficiently bright to influence human circadian systems. You really need to get out into the sunshine to absorb enough light to ease jet lag quickly; sitting in an artificially illuminated room, especially the low light typical in hotels, just will not do it.

Because so many guests leave the lights burning when
not in their rooms, some hotels have a policy of using low-
wattage globes. Those dimmer room lights may save a hotel chain a lot of money over a year, but guests may suffer
eyestrain because the light intensity in parts of the room
is insufficient.

Some veteran travelers carry high-wattage globes with
them; others complain and get brighter lights installed;
most do not notice. If you carry a globe as a temporary
replacement for the low-wattage one supplied by a mi-
serly hotel, it is best packed with padding in a plastic box.
Failing that, wrap it in socks and tuck it into a shoe for
protection.

DIET IS IMPORTANT

There is substantial scientific evidence about the effect of
diet on jet lag, and some frequent fliers who use dietary
techniques swear by them. Overeating—particularly a
craving for carbohydrates—is a common problem among
shift workers, who disrupt their circadian rhythms in the
same way that frequent fliers do. So a common symptom
of jet lag is a strong desire for fatty, unhealthful foods,
which can aggravate various problems associated with
traveler's tummy. As blood sugar levels seem to be closely
linked to circadian rhythms—and are certainly related to
the physical consequences of travel—diet undoubtedly
should play an important role in smart frequent fliers'
strategy.

Dietary techniques to combat jet lag have been refined most extensively by research at the Argonne National Laboratory in Illinois. This has resulted in a three-
phase program widely adopted by much-traveled executives of *Fortune* 500 companies, as well as by the U.S.
Army Rapid Deployment Forces and leading politicians.
It is not always practical for even the most privileged to
adopt President Johnson's autocratic practice of keeping to

home time and forcing everyone else on foreign trips to fit in with his unchanged internal body clock.

You can find out about the diet by sending a stamped self-addressed envelope to the Anti-Jet-Lag-Diet at Argonne National Labortory, 9700 South Cass Avenue, Argonne, Illinois 60439, or get a comprehensive description of it in *Overcoming Jet Lag*, by Dr. Charles F. Ehret and Lynne Waller Scanlon, published by Berkeley Books at $5.95. This details the dietary techniques required to trick your body clock to adjust rapidly by changing your food intake, starting three days before takeoff, running right through your period in the different time zone, and continuing after your return home. The program can get quite complicated, but the basic message is that high-protein breakfasts and lunches give an energy boost that is useful during the day, while carbohydrates are downers, good for dinner to help you sleep.

The diet uses feasting and fasting techniques and the methylated xanathines in many soft drinks, tea, and coffee to advance or retard internal body clocks. Although rather complex and requiring discipline, the regimen makes sense and has too many loyal adherents not to be taken seriously. (There are more details on pages 226–227).

OTHER TECHNIQUES

A popular anti–jet lag technique used by many business frequent fliers is to set their watches to the destination time zone as soon as they board the plane and then try to establish the routine most appropriate to it. Some international airlines help to achieve this, but the activities of other passengers, the timing of meals and movie screenings, whether the main cabin lighting is on or off or window screens drawn, all create complications. In particular, an extra meal when traveling westward can make adjusting to the new time zone far more difficult for some people. It is best to get into the eating pattern of the destination time zone as soon as possible and to avoid overeating.

Flights that leave very early or very late also tend to aggravate the disruption of sleep patterns. Business fliers who economize on red-eye specials may lose out on the lowered quality of their performance when they arrive and have serious work to do. Arrival times are very important, as reaching your destination when it is difficult to adjust quickly to the local timescale can aggravate jet lag. Once an important business trip from Europe to New York brought me into John F. Kennedy about two in the morning, when most of even the Big Apple is asleep. In theory, traveling westward should not have been too much of a problem, but by the time I had battled through immigration and customs, transferred to Manhattan and got into my hotel room—a bustle of activity in complete contrast to the environmental messages I was receiving from the dark, sleeping city—I was physically exhausted, mentally hyped up, and suffered severe jet lag for several days.

Indeed, for over a week, my sleep patterns were still disrupted by daytime drowsiness and nightime insomnia. In contrast, an eastward flight into London had far less effect because I arrived as the late-morning commuters were going to work and was able to carry through with those around me the normal daytime activities in daylight. It was a long and exhausting day, but my circadian rhythms adjusted to local time far more quickly.

DON'T WORRY

Sleep disruption is the most common complaint about the symptoms of jet lag, and is aggravated by unnecessary worry about losing sleep during or immediately after a long flight. Transient or short-term insomnia is a natural symptom of jet lag and should go away leaving no long-term adverse consequences, but worrying about the possibility of its developing into persistent and chronic insomnia can become a self-fulfilling prophecy.

If you cannot sleep, don't fret about it; instead try various relaxation techniques. The most difficult aspect of sleeping on a plane for most people is getting the head positioned comfortably. That is usually easiest in a window seat, where the side of the plane provides some support, and more difficult in a center or aisle seat, where those silly little pillows won't stay in place. Taking a special neck pillow with you can bring major benefits. An eye mask and earplugs also help to insulate you from the environment. I use a mask with built-in earphones, which I plug into a tape player with a relaxation program cassette, and it proves a very effective sleep-promoting combination.

There are more practical tips on sleeping on planes under Travel Stress and Pain on the Plane.

NAPS CAN BE GOOD—AND BAD

Getting to sleep in the hotel is easier because there is a conventional bed on which you can lie down. The majority opinion, from both research and practical experience by frequent long-distance fliers, is that if you arrive during the day, you should try to stay awake until a normal early bedtime at your destination. Your internal body clock may interpret a daytime nap after your arrival as a confirmation of its own memory programming and decide that whatever the sun is saying, it is actually night and you should be asleep. The nap can turn into a long, deep sleep from which you awake firmly out of synchronization with your new time zone.

If you arrive near local bedtime but your internal clock is still set on waking hours, try to get some sleep. At least go to bed and watch television or read, which may well send you to sleep anyway. If you wake exceptionally early, say at four in the morning, it just doesn't matter because you are a long way on the road to adjusting to new sleep patterns and the worst is that you face a somewhat longer waking day than usual. Indeed, millions of people routinely start their day well before dawn and have no problem with it.

DISRUPTED SLEEP PATTERNS

Your sleeping pattern may remain disrupted for several days, but staying in bed trying to sleep for the seven or eight hours you think are normal in the hope of getting in the appropriate quota of sleeping time can be counterproductive. It usually results in spasmodic shallow sleeping with regular waking up. This sleeping pattern can become a habit, and a characteristic of this type of insomnia is that one usually remembers only the times awake. This can easily produce a fixation that virtually the whole night was spent without sleep, causing worry and that self-perpetuating prophecy typical of insomnia. It makes sense to go to bed and get up at normal times, but relax and accept the fact that your body may not easily adapt to a new rhythm and that you will not sleep as long as normal.

Some commercial aircrew swear by the practice of going straight to the hotel and going to sleep, whatever time the flight arrives. It may work for them, but their whole life-style is different from that of the passenger. Aircrew have to work during the flight, and so they arrive physically and emotionally far more tired than the passengers. Also, they are probably on a routine that gives them exceptionally frequent time zone changes, so that their circadian rhythms are all over the place and it is difficult for them to adjust to a new pattern before it has to be changed again.

For passengers and crew alike, the worst remedy is

alcohol or sleeping pills to induce sleep. Both can make matters worse with a whole variety of side effects, not least the reduction in effect from frequent use with the attendant risk of addiction. Neither alcohol nor sleeping pills produce quality sleep. Even after being unconscious for several hours of artificially induced sleep, you can still wake up tired with the additional problem of a hangover, which just complicates the other physiological problems of jet lag.

Diet and sleep quality are closely linked. Heavy meals, unusual spicy or rich foods and other changes in diet can worsen both nightime insomnia and daytime drowsiness as well as the digestive disorders that are a frequent consequence of jet lag.

DRINK A LOT OF WATER AND JUICE

Drinking plenty of water or fruit juice both helps to combat dehydration during the flight and seems to ease the general malaise of jet lag symptoms. A pint of liquid every three hours is the often recommended minimum consumption to combat dehydration in the air, but excessive quantities of juice and fizzy carbonated drinks may aggravate digestive upsets. Fatty and fried foods—indeed, anything that poses a challenge to your digestive system—are best avoided.

Avoid compounding jet lag symptoms by additional avoidable stress factors. That practice should start before you ever get to the airport by having a good sleep on the night before departure, eliminating last-minute panics, and planning a flight schedule that will make the trip as smooth as possible by avoiding unnecessary, frustrating changes. Careful routing and selection of airlines may make a complex international flight quicker and easier than taking the first schedule offered by your travel agent. Or you can look for ways to ease the time zone transitions by allowing inexpensive stopovers. For example, I always try to get a Hong Kong break on trips from Europe or Africa to Australia and the Far East.

AVOID THE SMOKE

Even when I was stupid enough to be a heavy smoker, I usually flew in the nonsmoking section on long trips because I found that the carbon monoxide poisoning, blood sugar fluctuations, and other consequences of my own and fellow passengers' smoke aggravate jet lag symptoms seriously. Ironically, however, some research has indicated that small doses of nicotine and other substances contained in tobacco smoke may help a nonsmoker's circadian rhythms to adjust by stimulating the same cell receptors that respond to light. It is a long way from being proven, and anyway, smokers cannot expect to benefit because their systems have probably developed a tolerance for any constituents of tobacco smoke that may have this beneficial effect.

LEAVE TIME TO ADJUST

Plan your business schedule to give you time to adjust to the new time zone, preferably with at least one free or routine day in which you do not have to meet difficult mental challenges. Allow for the fact that your mental processes and other skills may be seriously below par for several days if there has been a marked time shift. Include in that schedule ample opportunity for relaxation and exercise during daylight. You get all kinds of cues from being active in the new environment that help your various internal clocks to reset their rhythms.

Proper planning can be a critical element in minimizing the consequences of jet lag. The other defensive tech-

FEAST AND FAST TO COUNTER JET LAG

Alternate feasting and fasting, and protein foods to stimulate activity and carbohydrates to encourage sleep, are the key elements of the Argonne National Laboratory's anti–jet lag diet.

The theory, which many frequent fliers swear works very effectively, is that the fast days reduce the amount of carbohydrates stored in the liver and make the body's internal clocks adjust more readily to a new zone. High-protein breakfasts and lunches get the body up and active, while taking foods high in carbohydrates later in the day stimulates sleep. Begin juggling these factors in a well-researched diet regimen starting three days before departure so that by the normal time for breakfast *at your destination* on the fourth day, your body clocks adjust comparatively easily.

Three days before departure—feast. Eat a high-protein breakfast and lunch and a high-carbohydrate dinner.

Two days before departure—fast. Eat sparingly of only light foods, especially salads and fruit.

The day before departure—feast. Eat a high-protein breakfast and lunch and a high-carbohydrate dinner.

Departure day—fast. Eat sparingly. Drink coffee and caffeinated beverages before noon when traveling west, in the evening when traveling east. The fast can be cut to half a day when going westward.

Arrival day—break fast. The key moment is the normal time for breakfast at your destination, even if you are still on the plane. Sleep until that time if you can and if the flight is sufficiently long. Then wake up and try to stay active, eating a high-protein breakfast as soon as possible, then get into the mealtime routine at your destination.

NOTES: Caffeinated beverages, such as coffee, tea, and colas, are allowed only in the afternoons between three and five on the first three days. Do not drink alcohol on the plane.

High-protein foods include eggs, red meats, high-protein cereals, fish, most nuts, cheeses, soya beans, and green beans.

High-carbohydrate foods are starches and sugars, including potatoes and other starchy vegetables, pastas and spaghetti, bread and sweet desserts.

Fasting foods include toast without butter, salads without dressing, fruit, and light broths.

(Source: Argonne National Laboratory, 9700 South Cass Avenue, Argonne, IL 60439. U.S. Government Printing Office, 1984-754-904)

niques are mainly applied common sense about sleeping, eating, and drinking. However, one needs to be conscious also of the important psychological consequences of jet lag, which are not fully understood yet. Depression is one that can creep up unexpectedly, especially when alone at night and unable to sleep because your body clock is set to be awake back home. That is when a telephone call home can achieve a much-needed mood change and should be as justifiable a business expense as entertaining clients.

THE FIRST AIRLINE ANTI–JET
LAG SERVICE

The first airline to make a really determined effort
to help passengers combat jet lag was Continental,
which in 1989 introduced a version of the Argonne
National Laboratory's program on its flights from
the United States to Tokyo.

Dr. Charles Ehret helped Continental develop
menus and a cabin schedule of meals, rest periods,
movie screenings, exercises, management of the
light levels, and other activities to help first and
business class passengers adjust their body clocks to
Tokyo time after leaving American territory. If you
traveled coach, you had to do it yourself by
studying Dr. Ehret's book.

The most surprising feature of the service is that
it took so long for an airline to introduce it. This
notable first by Continental is bound to find more
imitators.

STRANGE CHEST PAINS

To end this section on a serious note, be particularly careful if the symptoms of jet lag are accompanied by chest
pains, which you may be tempted to dismiss as being indigestion, muscle pain after sleeping for many hours
cramped into an aircraft seat, or a chest infection from the
rotten air on many planes.

While the symptoms of jet lag have frequently been
wrongly diagnosed as heart attacks, there appear to be
links between a particular form of thrombosis and long-

distance flying that is potentially fatal and may not be treated properly if confused with jet lag. When you sit with your legs cramped for hour after hour, breathing air deficient in oxygen, suffering from dehydration and probably drinking alcohol, everything is conspiring to increase the clotting of blood in your legs. These clots may travel to the lungs and cause a pulmonary embolism after you have left the plane.

Pulmonary embolism was found to be the cause of eleven of the sixty-one sudden deaths over a three-year period among passengers arriving at London's Heathrow Airport after long flights. When three physicians reported in the leading British medical journal *The Lancet* that they had suffered mild thrombosis attacks after long flights, many other similar cases came to light, some having been wrongly diagnosed as muscle pain or infection. We still have very limited knowledge of the causes and consequences of jet lag.

Sitting Comfortably and Safely

TAKE A TOUR AROUND YOUR SEAT

Excruciatingly uncomfortable as it may seem after a long, crowded flight, your seat on a modern airliner cost a lot of money and reflects thousands of hours of research and development to find acceptable compromises between safety, lightness of weight, compact dimensions, ergonomic attributes, and other requirements.

However, most still lack the variable lumbar support and other adjustments now commonplace in auto seating, so to customize the shape to your particular needs requires judicious use of pillows, blankets—even baggage. Some tips on getting comfortable are contained in the health section on pp. 152–234.

Annoying as it may be, the request from the flight attendants to put your seat in the upright position for take-off and landing is a vital safety precaution. When upright, the back locks into place sufficiently strongly to give you some protection from impact from the passenger or luggage behind you in the event of an emergency sudden stop. If the sudden deceleration is particularly severe and the passenger behind is thrown forward with sufficient force, the back of your seat will break forward in a predictable way and help to protect both of you.

Although your seat and those next to it are designed to be removed quickly and easily if the interior configuration of the aircraft needs to be changed, they should still remain anchored to the floor in quite severe crashes. In the United States and a number of other countries, a seat containing a passenger will not break away from its floor mounting until a forward force of at least nine times that of gravity has been exerted, and there are stringent requirements for resisting sideways and rearward pressures.

The seat is your first and very effective line of defense in an emergency—but only if you stay in it by fastening your seat belt securely. Even many frequent fliers have not learned to fasten their belts in the best way to protect themselves. The belt should be around your hips and below your stomach, across the point at which your body will pivot if you are thrown forward. Fastening the belt across your stomach can cause unnecessary injury in the event of rapid deceleration, and although probably not serious in the long term, could incapacitate enough to hinder or delay your escape from the plane. However, even a badly positioned belt that is fastened is infinitely better than one left dangling down by the side of your seat. The latter will do nothing to prevent you from becoming a missile in an emergency deceleration, risking killing yourself and any other passengers with whom you collide.

Every so often, the suggestion for rearward-facing airliner seats is revived in the cause of greater safety. Although it is commonplace for military aircraft, and some private and corporate planes, to have the seats facing backward, the safety benefits are questionable. The exposure to injury—particularly to the neck and spine—could be worse when facing to the rear, as your upper body would be whipped forward and back in severe deceleration. The seat back would need to be much stronger—and consequently heavier—to withstand this load, and it could not break away as effectively as one facing forward. Also, few accidents in either autos or planes involve straight, direct forces. Almost invariably there are sideways movements as well, and studies have shown that on balance, your body may be better able to cope with being thrown sideways if you are leaning forward in the direction of travel than if you are pushed backward and sideways at the same time.

Rearward seating can also be uncomfortable in a modern plane, which climbs to operating altitude quickly after takeoff, often as a legal requirement to reduce its noise footprint on residential areas below. Being pressed back into the seat as the plane accelerates and climbs is far less uncomfortable than when the seats face to the rear and the forces tend to drag you out of it so that you partly hang by the seat belt. It is also more pleasant to look out of the window and see where you are going instead of where you have been.

Another factor is the way that cabin baggage is thrown violently around if a plane comes to a sudden stop, breaking out from the overhead racks and other storage areas. The backs of forward-facing seats offer some protection, especially if passengers adopt the correct emergency position. If you were facing to the rear, these missiles would be coming straight toward you and could do more damage.

The arguments will continue to rage, especially when there has been a crash in which the seating has been an important factor in the passenger survival rate. There are lots of pros and cons, but the reality is that forward-facing seats are likely to be a permanent feature of commercial air travel, and they do not make the risk of injury or death in the rare event of a crash any greater, if at all.

There are strict regulations about the flame-resistant qualities of seat upholstery materials, although still plenty of room for improvement in their overall performance if they do burn, particularly in generating noxious fumes. The seat upholstery fabrics now in use also represent substantial technical advances in their resistance to soiling and staining.

The drop-down or folding tables vary widely, as does the layout of the controls on each seat. Controls for the reading light, attendant call, and audio system may be more easily reached when set into the seat's armrest than into the overhead rack above, but in any case you have to

take what you can get once you are on board. However, if
the seat next to you is not occupied, you may be able to
ease one frequent cause of annoyance—the headset
socket. Particularly in small economy class seats, the
socket may be difficult to reach. Often, with the type that
transmits the sound to the ears along a flexible hollow
tube, the sound becomes distorted or cut off altogether as
the tube is pinched or is partially dislodged from its socket
as you move around in the seat. You may overcome these
hassles by plugging the headset into the control panel on
the adjoining seat if it is not occupied and the tubing or
cord will reach.

Another boon of having the adjoining seat free is that
you can use its table for drinks and snacks, giving you
more space and freedom of movement. It is becoming increasingly common for the center seat in a row of three to
have a back that will flip forward and form a table. On a
flight with unoccupied seats, you can create space to
stretch out by folding the back of the seat in front of you
forward and putting your legs and feet on top of it. However, that could be offensive if any of the other nearby
seats in the row in front are occupied. Moving the back of
an unoccupied seat in front of you may also substantially
improve your view of the movie.

If only neighboring passengers could cooperate in
using empty seats more effectively, we would sleep more
comfortably and enhance our enjoyment of in-flight
movies. A particular cause of annoyance is the passenger,
especially one who is tall, whose head bobs around to obscure the view of the screen for the passenger behind,
who in turn has to keep moving to follow the action and so
causes problems for the next passenger, and so on. There
is no easy solution, although a polite request will often
bring an improvement, especially if the owner of the offending head was not aware of the problems arising behind.

Your seat usually provides storage for a life jacket, and

the cushion may be designed to float as well. The design of aircraft life jackets has improved a great deal in recent years, and they are easier and more logical to put on than they used to be, even if you did not pay attention to preflight demonstration by the cabin staff. The instructions not to inflate the life jacket while still in the aircraft must be taken seriously or your ability to move quickly toward the exits could be severely impeded. If several passengers blow up their jackets too soon, the whole evacuation process can be jeopardized.

In the pocket of the seat in front will be a selection of literature, including a card showing the layout of the aircraft, evacuation drill, and location of the emergency exits. The details are worth memorizing. Research into air crashes repeatedly shows that survivors read the card and so acquired information that helped to save their lives. Unfortunately, one of the cheapest and most effective emergency aids will not be in the seat pocket for a long time to come. It is the smoke hood, which I first encountered in a Tokyo hotel many years ago.

The Efficiency Factor

The Savvy Business Traveler in the Electronic Age
Keeping in touch and working on the move

In the pretransistor age, neckties and handkerchiefs predominated among the unwanted gifts that businesspeople stashed away at the back of drawers. Now, because business and travel are so closely linked in the minds of our friends and relatives, we get bombarded with electronic, folding, or inflatable gadgets that loved ones less experienced with frequent flying think will help to ease our travel.

There are a number of basic truths about travel gadgets, the most important being that 95 percent of them are both overpriced and useless. Another is that, unless the traveler chooses the gadget personally after long deliberation, it won't get used. Also, unless you are really locked into yuppie status symbolism, anything bought primarily to sharpen your image, lacking tangible practical value, will soon get left at home.

Those rules eliminate from serious consideration pocket microchip devices that give you the time in two dozen different zones or produce liquid crystal displays of useful phrases for taxi drivers in foreign countries, together with tooled leather wallets with compartments for passports, credit cards, and maps; watches and pocket computers that store telephone numbers and birthdays; fancy miniaturized manicure and sewing sets; slim, elegant briefcases that will hold only a few sheets of paper and a pencil; and such exotica as a portable environmental sound machine to produce rain, surf, and waterfall noises to help you get to sleep in strange beds.

However, without the expensive gimmicky junk, there

is room in your luggage for some really useful high- and low-tech aids to business travel efficiency. Here is a list of the best:

LAPTOP COMPUTERS

Hailed as the ultimate electronic business travel aid, the laptop computer delivers on its promises only to a minority of business travelers, but for them it is invaluable. Before making the plunge, ruthlessly assess your computing travel needs. If you do a lot of complicated data processing in faraway places, must have ready access to large quantities of information, and generally are dependent on computing power, then you need a very different type of portable computer than does someone like me, a writer, who needs simply to work with words.

Every laptop now on the market or in development is a compromise between weight, size, processing power, features, and the ability to function under adverse conditions. Despite all the advertising, you rarely see anyone actually working on a laptop on a plane or in an airport terminal. This is not because portable computers are not being sold in large numbers, but because most people buy the wrong one for their particular needs and so leave it at home.

The biggest mistake, particularly if the company is footing the bill, is to go too far up market, buying a Maserati for perceived power and image when you really need a Ford for practical transportation. A sophisticated laptop with hard disk and all the bells and whistles can be too large and too heavy and can consume too much battery power to be convenient and practical for most business travel applications. If it is the latest, most sophisticated design, it may be too expensive to be really cost-efficient.

It does not matter how clever the machine is if you have urgent work to do and it won't fit on the drop-down

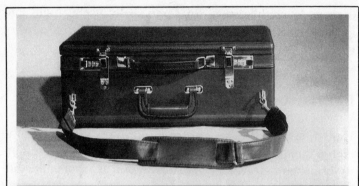

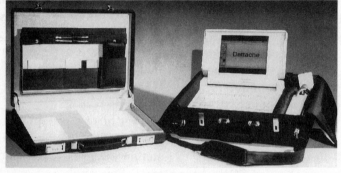

ELEGANT PROTECTION

Research has shown that business travelers can become very emotionally attached to the things that we take with us on the road. The distress when an airline loses bags is often out of all proportion to the value of the contents. Having the portable equipment to which we "bond" most readily, our laptop computers, damaged can be very upsetting also, as well as very inconvenient if data on the hard disk is lost, as can happen as a result of just a knock while in transit.

The soft cases normally supplied to carry portable computer gear have practical benefits, but they offer minimum physical protection and usually not much elegance if they have to double up as attaches. Lance Miller, a Californian frequent flier, knew there had to be a better way and came up with this neat two-in-one idea. It looks like a large conventional carry-on case, until you find that the top section removes completely and functions as a briefcase when you are able to leave the bulkier, heavier bottom half containing the computer and accessories behind.

The frame of light wood with shock dampening foam lining gives a lot more protection to the computer than a soft fabric case. The two-in-one concept means that you can carry a briefcase, a computer in its own case, and a garment bag into the cabin and still be within the two bag limit.

Details from Lance Miller, Technological Evolution Corporation, 603 Begonia, Corona del Mar, CA 92625.

table in the plane, or the hard disk consumes so much power running your sophisticated software that the batteries go flat between New York and Chicago. The ten to fifteen pounds your wonder machine weighs may have seemed of little consequence in the store, but it becomes a real drag when it has been lugged in and out of taxis all day and pulled your arm almost out of its socket getting to gate 56 on the far side of the terminal.

For a fraction of the price, your traveling computing needs may be better met by a small, less expensive machine, providing you can live with the compromise in legibility of the screen, size of the keyboard, and limited memory and data processing ability. Other points to be considered include your real need to work in places where there is no ready electric power—in airport terminals and on planes, for example—or whether most of your computing when traveling will be done in offices, hotel rooms, and other places where you can plug in easily.

Do you need to print out information? In that case you may have to plan to take a portable printer with you, which adds weight, bulk, and other problems. Do you need to communicate with head office or remote databases? If so, you will need a modem. Will you have to transfer files to desktop machines? That gets you into a whole maze of decision making about disk size, compatibility, serial or parallel ports and their cables, and so on.

Draw up a checklist to assess which of the main features available on portable computers are most appropriate for your particular needs. If you go through it carefully, you will build a specification that should enable you to make the right choice—and probably save both a great deal of money and numerous hassles on the road.

The bag in which you carry a laptop is crucial. Airlines are getting really tough about carry-on baggage, especially the two-item rule, so adding a computer to your business traveling kit needs careful planning.

If you usually carry a garment bag onto the plane with you, then you may have to accommodate the computer in the compact second piece of luggage with reading and toilet items, paperwork, and other paraphernalia that normally go into a briefcase or shoulder bag. Most rigid briefcases do not have enough space or flexibility, and the expensive custom cases for portables stocked by computer outlets are usually too limiting also. So get the biggest legal soft-sided carry-on bag that will comfortably—and protectively—contain the computer and its accessories, together with all your carry-on gear. Its pockets and compartments should enable you to separate different items for ease of access. If you need to turn up for meetings with a smart case for your paperwork, get a good-quality slim leather document case that will go inside either of your carry-on items. I always keep mine in the garment bag, where it and the papers it contain stay flat and take up very little room.

Careful selection of software for your laptop can save you considerable weight and hassle. Above all, avoid taking the bulky manuals with you, so get easy-to-use software with good help screens. If you need to carry out several different computing tasks while traveling, consider some of the very competent and easy-to-use integrated programs that combine word processing, spreadsheet, database, and communication applications on one or two diskettes. Pick one that exchanges data readily with your desktop system, does not take up too much memory, and that you know already or that has adequate screen help so that you do not need the manual.

You can modify a sophisticated program, one that you use on a desktop machine with a hard disk, so that it will run on the more limited power of a basic portable. Then you can stick with the program that is familiar to you and easily transfer the data you have processed on the road to your main system. For example, I use the very powerful latest version of Microsoft Word on my desktop machine with its hard disk, but I need very few of its more sophisticated features when working away from the office. So I have loaded onto one diskette just the Word features I will need on a journey together with the DOS operating system. Pop it in, switch on, and my laptop boots up and puts me into Word quickly and easily. If I am going to need other functions in addition to word processing, I take along the PFS:First Choice program diskette with its built-in word processor, spreadsheet, database, and communications software. It doesn't take up much memory, and it functions fine on a basic laptop. My documents can be stored in ASCII code and loaded straight into the desktop computer for more powerful formatting and other publishing procedures when I get back to base.

If you do need to travel with software that requires special routines you cannot remember, or your portable does not have the capacity to hold the help screens, or there is other computing information you may need while traveling, it pays to summarize it on paper and slip it in with the computer or to carry it in the form of a saved document file you can call up at will for quick reference.

In theory, with a laptop, modem, and telephone, you are in instant touch with the world—including your office and any database services that you use. In practice, even the most expensive hotels may make life difficult for the computerized business traveler. However, for a few dollars you can put together a communications survival kit that will cope with almost any situation.

Here is the shopping list, which any good electronics store or Radio Shack outlet can fill from stock:

Modular line cord, the familiar standard hookup cord between a telephone receiver and the wall outlet, with a modular RJ-11 plug at each end. I prefer one that is coiled like a spring so it doesn't get tangled up.

Modular in-line coupler, which is a connector with two RJ-11 sockets. It takes up virtually no space and can be very useful in enabling you to extend the cord to the hotel telephone by connecting it to your own modular line cord, or for turning a male coupler into a female socket.

Modular duplex jack, which has one male RJ-11 connection and two female. This enables you to plug your computer and the telephone in to the same outlet at the same time.

Most hotels these days have modular sockets, so you can plug in your duplex jack and your computer with no problem. Some of the leading, larger, newer—and more expensive!—hotels have special data transfer jacks. Otherwise, explore two immediate first routes to hook up your portable computer. If the telephone itself has modular connections, detach the cable at the phone end and use your in-line coupler and duplex jack to make the male to female plug conversion and hookups for the phone and computer. Alternatively, and preferable if the wall socket is located conveniently, plug your duplex jack directly in to this socket and then run the phone and computer from it. Often the hotel telephone cord disappears through a cover plate into the wall, and you may have to remove the plate to get at the modular jack behind it. So carry a small screwdriver, the double-ended kind that copes with both conventional slotted and cross-cut screws.

If the hotel room does not have any modular jacks that you can access, check the telephone in the bathroom. Often a phone was installed in the bathroom of an older hotel as part of an upgrading and so is more likely to be modular than the one in the room.

If all else fails, you can still hook up if you have come prepared with a special cable that is quite easy to assemble yourself. Buy a phone cord with a modular plug at one end and the wires exposed at the other or cut up a conventional modular line cord. The exposed red and green wires are fastened to miniature alligator clips, small versions of the spring clamps with teethed jaws used to jumpstart the car or charge the battery. The black and yellow leads in the phone cable are not needed. Trim them and tape them over, making sure that they do not have exposed ends that could cause a short.

To hook up the computer, unscrew the telephone mouthpiece and fasten the alligator clips to the wires inside, red to red and green to green. Or clip directly onto the terminals of the wall socket wiring block. This direct hookup may require moving a bed or table and getting down on hands and knees, but it often eliminates interference and other transmission problems that may arise when connecting to the telephone instrument. If you have some electrical knowledge, you can try to minimize interference by fastening the alligator clips to alternative connections within the telephone that bypass the transformer.

This small, cheap connector kit should enable you to hook up the modem in most situations and is more convenient than carrying around an acoustic coupler, which has rubber cups to go over the telephone handset and makes the communications link acoustically instead of electrically. A few hotel and office telephone systems will not accept a direct connection with your computer modem, and you may be forced to use an acoustic coupler in such circumstances. They are also useful for making connections to pay phones. But in this day and age, certainly in the United States, the connector kit should be sufficient for most travelers.

One tip often forgotten is that hotels usually require you to key in a number—8 or 9—to get an outside line. Get the outside line manually before using your modem, or program in a couple of seconds of delay after the 8 or 9 digit if the modem is doing all the dialing.

The most convenient modem is one that is built into your laptop. Most of the newer models of portable computers either come with a modem as standard or are ready to accept one as an accessory. However, special internal modems tend to be expensive. Separate ones are cheaper and take up very little space—they need not be much bigger than a pack of cigarettes. If you travel overseas, get one that will work to both the U.S. and international telephone standards.

Get a modem that is Hayes-compatible and that has the most appropriate baud rate for your needs. The baud rate, e.g., 1200 or 2400, is the speed with which the modem sends and receives data. It's worth watching out for special deals in which a modem is part of a package price with software or as an incentive to subscribe to one of the on-line services.

Most travelers use the communications ability of their laptops to send and receive data from their base office, for an electronic mail service, or to tap into one of the commercial database systems. There is also software that allows a traveler to operate the home or office PC by using a laptop and modem—truly remote computing. It has also become possible to make a computer emulate a fax or a

How to take a complete library on the road. Frequent fliers who need to take a great deal of computer software or reference material with them on the road have a new option in the CD-ROM technology. There is a new generation of portable computer systems with a significant difference—built-in CD-ROM drives.

Just one CD disk can contain a whole reference library of material for such specialist occupations as the law, engineering, or medicine. William Liu, President of California's C.D. Technology, Inc., says that this kind of package is the ultimate in complete office portability for the business traveler. When he pioneered the concept in 1989 he proved his point by putting 1,200 of the most popular public domain software onto one CD disk.

So with just one portable computer and a few CDs you can carry onto the plane the equivalent of a very comprehensive office reference library, filing system and powerful desktop computer complete with an enormous selection of software. Add a pair of portable speakers and it becomes a high fidelity sound system also!

The computer—including the 1,200 software programs—costs under $5,000 from CD Technology, 780 Montague Expressway, Suite 407, San Jose CA 95131. (408-432-8698). Other manufacturers are introducing similar equipment.

telex machine if the information is already processed by the computer, so that you can send messages and other data direct from the laptop in your hotel room to anyone in the world who has a fax or telex number. It can cost less than $50 to turn either your traveling laptop or your office PC into a fax substitute with software that enables it to transmit and receive files ranging from conventional business correspondence to charts and graphics. Useful contacts for more information are MCI Mail at 800 444-6245, or Xpedite Systems, Inc., who produce software, at 800 227-9379.

A neat portable PC fax from Quadram Corporation will transmit documents straight from your word processing program to anyone anywhere who has a fax receiver. If full fax facilities are vital to you when on the road and you need to transmit or receive documents or visuals not available in computerized bits and bytes, investigate the increasingly compact and sophisticated portable fax machines.

If you use hotel telephone facilities extensively—and an on-line computer communications exercise can take much longer than one anticipates—then your final bill may be greatly inflated. Many hotels have a policy of inflating the cost of telephone calls and turning them into a lucrative profit center instead of one of the essential services supplied to clients. This is as deplorable as the way car rental companies make hidden profits from insurance waivers and gas. A number of hotels, including some of the leading chains, have now seen the light and no longer mark up telephone charges exorbitantly. Others are receptive to some hard bargaining from regular customers who are heavy telephone users. It pays to shop around, especially if you have to make a number of international or long-distance calls. At hotels overseas, the higher cost of telephone calls plus the hotel's mark-up can quickly generate phone bills in the hundreds of dollars.

Controlling the cost of telephone calls from hotel rooms begins with establishing the hotel's policy on surcharging. For example, find out if it belongs to a scheme like AT&T's Teleplan, which limits surcharges. Use telephone credit cards or reverse the charges where such tactics will reduce costs, especially from overseas. Establish contact, then hang up so your home or office can call you back—or prearrange times at which they will call you.

The traveling executive with a computer who needs to produce good-quality hard copy documentation has a very limited choice of portable printers. Some printers are small and light enough to carry around, but their output often is not the letter quality we have come to expect for business documents. There are so many PCs around now in homes and offices that it may be convenient to get someone to do your printouts for you when traveling rather than carry a printer with you. You are seldom refused. However, it's a good idea to carry your own printer cable—the flat ribbon type is lighter and takes up less space—so that you can make a fast hookup to a borrowed printer without having to fumble around disconnecting the cable from the back of a desktop machine. Easier still, of course, is to get someone to run your disk on the house system if it is compatible, although in these days of computer viruses, that may be as welcome a request as seeking to share a toothbrush with a stranger!

Another alternative is to go to one of the many desktop publishing and business service boutiques with computers and printers you can hire by the hour. They can be a big boon and enable you to do advanced work while traveling. You could, for example, customize or modify software for preparing sophisticated quotations or presentations on your laptop and then take it to one of these desktop publishing service centers to produce immaculate documentation, overhead transparencies, presentation charts, and so on.

A tip worth remembering is that your laptop PC will probably be able to drive a Macintosh ImageWriter printer if that is all that is available to you. Unless you have a great deal of trouble and expertise, expect to get only the basic ASCII character set, as there will be compatibility problems with formatting, boldface, underlining, and so forth.

Some travelers will need to take software and cables that allow information to be transferred between the laptop and a PC, although more desktop machines now have the three-and-a-half-inch disk drives that are the norm on portables, and so it should only be a question of swapping disks, with no need for a direct machine-to-machine connection. Another practical alternative when exchanging information between machines is to hook them up by modem and telephone line, even if they are standing side by side. It may be the easiest way to enable them to talk to each other.

Often a laptop could be used if only it were possible to work comfortably with it on your lap. For many machines the name laptop is a misnomer because they are too big, too heavy, or too awkward. Being forced to balance a laptop on your lap is a pain. One frequent flier, Jack Weaver, president of Input Systems, invented a telescoping monopod that takes much of the weight and helps to stabilize the machine between your knees. He sells it for $24.95 and can be reached at 305 252-1550. Alternatively, if you travel with much photographic gear, you could modify a photographic tripod or monopod to do the same job.

Beware of Computer Viruses While on the Road

The frequent flier who uses a computer while on the road is now at considerable risk of picking up a computer virus. At the least this could destroy or alter data of work in progress. It can result in a business catastrophe by introducing infection that spreads right through an organization's system, destroying information necessary to render invoices, pursue research and development projects, make sales, and carry out other vital functions.

"Be very, very careful about using strange systems or exposing your own laptop and your diskettes to infection while on the road," warns Computer Virus Industry Association chairman John McAfee. "Some small companies have already been brought to their knees by these dangerous programs, which contain self-replicating code enabling them to reproduce very rapidly and destroy or damage computerized data."

The potential for picking up a virus while traveling is demonstrated by one of the worst cases on record, when a consultant went to a conference in Canada and was given what he thought was a harmless diskette containing a computer game. He took it home to the United States, tried out the game on his Mac, and then got on with a consultancy project for Aldus, a major manufacturer of branded software.

The virus, the notorious Peace strain, was hidden on the diskette he brought from Canada, and it got into his home system when he loaded the game. It multiplied among his Mac files without giving any indication that it was there and infected the demonstration program on which he was working for the Aldus company.

He sent that project off to Aldus, and when it got there, the virus infection spread into commercial packages of the Aldus Freehand program. Soon many thousands of Macs throughout the United States and many foreign countries were hit by a chain of infection that led directly back to a diskette picked up innocently by a traveler visiting Canada.

"Computer viruses are an international problem, with some of the most virulent and damaging strains coming from Europe," warns John McAfee. "But the business traveler could also pick up an infection to his system on just a short domestic trip when he is given a diskette, uses his own diskette on a strange system, or hooks into a network via a modem from his hotel room. Infection is being spread also through the establishments providing desktop publishing or computer hire services, which can be so useful to the traveler but now also pose potential dangers."

The best way of keeping on top of the constantly developing virus epidemic is through the International Computer Virus Institute (ICVI). Membership details and more information on this important issue are available from The Computer Virus Industry Association, 4423 Cheeney Street, Santa Clara, CA 95054, 408 988-3832.

John McAfee, the leading authority on the virus epidemic, and the ICVI have developed specially for *Savvy Business Flying* the following guidelines to *Safe Computing on the Road*. Follow their advice and minimize the risk that you—and your organization—will join the statistics of the hundreds of thousands of virus victims.

In the interests of spreading the message about safe computing, the guidelines may be copied or reproduced, providing the acknowledgment to the ICVI and *Savvy Business Travel* is included. You may, for example, wish to distribute copies to colleagues who use laptops on business trips and who, if they do not practice these safe computing principles, could easily bring back an infection that spreads to your system.

Safe Computing on the Road

Practice safe computing and reduce the risk of bringing home a virus infection.

The Ten Golden Rules for Safe Computing

1. Do not load unknown diskettes into your system while on the road.

2. Do not use your diskettes in an unknown system unless the write protect tab is set.

3. Do not accept gifts, loans, or samples of programming unless you can be absolutely certain that they are virus-free.

4. Be very careful if renting a computer, or using business or desktop publishing centers that do not have stringent antiviral precautions in force.

5. If it is essential to exchange diskettes, or run your programs or data on strange systems, adopt an effective isolation procedure. For example, do not run possibly infected diskettes on your main system, especially if it has a hard disk. Check them out first on a nonessential isolated system, for example a stand-alone desktop or laptop without a hard disk and without a diskette in the second drive. Be warned that even this procedure is not completely safe. If running your own programs or data on strange systems, transfer them first to backup disks and destroy these when the task is completed. Do not bring them away with you and run the risk of their being inadvertently loaded into your home or office system. Diskettes are cheap—data is not!

6. Do not download programs from bulletin boards or strange networks.

7. Do not let other people use your computer unsupervised, especially if there is the possibility that they may load their own diskettes into it. Remember—infection can easily be spread by the friendliest of hands!

8. Watch for unexplained changes in the way your system functions, for example disk drives running for no good reason or loads or saving taking longer than usual.

9. Use write protect tabs extensively and create volume labels that record the size of your programs. Check the volumes regularly whenever you run the programs for unexplained increases that could indicate virus replication activity.

10. To protect against physical loss or damage as well as a precaution if a virus infection occurs, do not

take any diskette on the road without first
creating a backup to leave behind in a safe place.

How to Minimize the Loss and Aid Recovery if a Virus Attack Occurs

1. Don't panic. A careful, methodical approach can minimize the consequences of most virus attacks.

2. Switch off the computer. A virus infection or damage to data may occur in microseconds, but it cannot get any worse while the system is powered down.

3. Do not execute any program from a disk that might be infected.

4. Seek expert help (or if you think you have adequate computing skills, follow steps five through eight).

5. Reboot your system from an original system diskette.

6. Back up all the nonexecutable files.

7. Perform a low-level format of the disk.

8. Replace both the system and the executable programs.

9. Restore your data.

10. Contact and warn anyone with a system that could be exposed to the same infection.

Laptop Computer Survival Kits

A selection of the essential components for computing while on the road, including the hardware to use various hotel phone sockets, can be purchased in traveler's kits.

Electronic Specialists in Natick, Massachusetts, markets one for $149.95 and can be reached at 800-225-4876.

However, a cheaper solution is pick out what you will need from the equipment described in this section and take the list along to your nearest Radio Shack or other electronics outlet.

Get the Facts—Fast!

Despite the fact that we live in the information age, many travelers still try to do business on the road without much of the basic information that can be so helpful in striking deals, making sales, and carrying out a host of other activities.

I have always found a few hours spent at the local Chamber of Commerce, library, museum, and a couple of realtors' offices a sound investment before starting operations in a new territory. These valuable sources of local information can usually all be found within walking distance of a city center hotel, and the exercise and lack of decision making involved in visiting them fit well into a jet lag recovery or stress reduction routine.

Even if no hard, immediately useful facts emerge from this research exercise, it helps enormously in acclimatizing oneself to a strange area and getting in tune with the clients, colleagues, and other business contacts with whom you will have to interact. Somehow you pick up the tempo and flavor of the local scene in a remarkable way that can make you far more effective in carrying out your mission than hitting the road running straight from the plane or catching a cab from the hotel to your first appointment without any acclimatization process.

I remember one very difficult mission in Spain I undertook for a multinational company. The temptation was to initiate a quick fix using conventional business wisdom. Instead I spent the first morning after my arrival wandering around town, visiting the library and museum, reading the local paper, and generally getting acclimatized. The time was well invested, as it soon became apparent that the quick fix would have been totally inappropriate for the local culture, and there was a far more cost-effective and satisfactory solution available.

If time is at a premium, there are various ways of getting local facts fast, especially if you use a computer. Subordinates, your local representatives, and others can prepare a background briefing for you, but unless you are in that kind of management position and they are really competent at this kind of research, you may not get the facts you require.

There are now several programs that will solve the problem. For example, the Economic Research Institute in California has put over four million key facts about life in more than three thousand U.S. and Canadian cities and suburbs just a few keystrokes away in its Geographic Assessor software.

Primarily developed to help companies to make salary and cost-of-living comparisons, the same information can be useful in many situations facing business travelers. Geographic Assessor costs $92 as a PC program on diskette or in hard-copy report format and is updated quarterly. Details from the Economic Research Institute, 901 Dove Street, Suite 155, Newport Beach, CA 92660.

The leading on-line databases provide a wealth of other information on specific areas in the United States and overseas. A well-constructed key word search will locate the data you need quickly, and it is really the only way to get the most current, comprehensive information on a locality.

Particularly useful for the international frequent flier is that rich mine of business and demographic data pro-

duced by *The Financial Times, The Economist,* and leading European specialist newsletters now on-line to American database subscribers.

For international information the quarterly reports on
165 countries produced by the *Economist* Intelligence
Unit are a unique resource of intelligently analyzed facts
and short-term forecasts. Some business travelers would
no more leave them behind than they would their toothbrush. Details are available from Business International's
office at 21 Park Avenue South, New York, NY 10003, 212
460 0600, or direct from the *Economist* Intelligence Unit,
40 Duke Street, London W1A, 1DW, United Kingdom,
01-493 6711.

A search of such sources as these before departure can
enhance the effectiveness of almost any business trip, but
comparatively few frequent fliers are yet taking full advantage of these invaluable information age tools.

TIPS ON BATTERIES

An important point about laptops and any other electronic
device using nickel-cadmium batteries is that they develop memories, and you need to run them right down
before recharging if they are to give the maximum life
next time. If you recharge when the batteries are only half
discharged, they will repeat that cycle and only last, say,
one hour instead of two, or even as little as ten minutes.

I tend to take several battery-powered devices with
me when I travel, and I have tried to standardize their
batteries as much as possible so that I can swap batteries
between them. So I usually travel just with AA NiCads,
which I boost with a small charging unit that plugs into
any standard wall socket.

Most of my equipment uses AA or AAA cells, and the
same charger takes both, with little converter modules for
the smaller AAA batteries. I can switch batteries between
my camera strobe light, my personal tape player, my

pocket memo recorder, flashlight, even the shaver and electric toothbrush.

ENTERTAINMENT ON THE ROAD

The personal tape player is a real boon to the frequent traveler, although I find lots of businesspeople still seem to associate these portable sound systems with teenagers and rock music and do not like to be seen walking around airports wearing earphones. That really is ridiculous, because the ability to use traveling time to listen to a wide range of recorded material makes good sense. Many business books are available now as audio cassettes you can either buy or borrow from a club or library. Traveling time can be used also to listen to instructional tapes— foreign language courses are an obvious example—music, or just a good book.

I usually stock up with a selection of audio tapes from the local library before a long business trip, but also often use the occasion to listen again to recordings I have made at conferences and similar occasions. The most convenient earphones I have found are those very small light ones that slip directly into the ear. They are certainly far less conspicuous than conventional headsets. I also make good use of a sleep mask with built-in earphones. If the travel situation is such that I want complete seclusion, cutting out both ambient light and sound, it enables me to slip into my own isolated environment. The mask and earphones hooked up to a tape of relaxing music can induce sleep otherwise disrupted by changing time zones or by noise.

It is most convenient to have a personal stereo player that also incorporates AM and FM radio reception. Ideally it will have a small built-in speaker so that you can use it in the hotel when it is not convenient to be hooked up to earphones, and even better if it can record as well as play

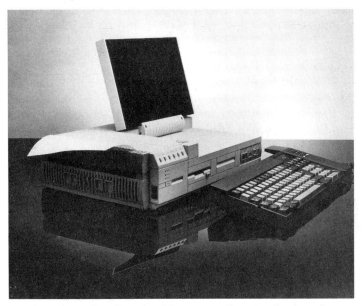

You *can* take it all with you!. Globe-trotting frequent flier Farad Azima
believes that the dominant trend toward making portable equipment
lighter and smaller could be counterproductive for some business
travelers. So the Persian-born Canadian has compressed technology in
the interests of portability only as far as can be done without compromising on performance.

This is the result—the world's first IBM PS/2 compatible portable
with built-in inkjet printer, up to 200MB hard disk, cellular phone with
integrated voice/data communications, bar code or magnetic card
scanning, gas plasma VGA monitor, and a wealth of other features not
usually found even in elaborate static office systems.

"The professional traveler should be able to take a comprehensive
productivity environment around with him," maintains Farad Azima.
In this case, it all goes in a black leather shoulder bag and carries a
price tag of between $10,000 and $20,000, depending on options.

The computer manufacturers catering for the business traveler who
needs technological sophistication in a portable package say that these
frequent fliers are not very sensitive about the price it costs to get the
best equipment to do the job. But a system like this that weighs close
to 20 pounds will probably have to be complemented on the road with
one of the new generation of pocketable computers.

Details of Farid Azima's Darius Proportable from 18303 8th Ave.
South, Seattle, WA 98148, 604-432-7727.

back. Then you can use it for note taking and other recording purposes and avoid the need to take along a separate machine for this.

If you do have a portable memo recorder that uses microcassettes but at times want to play back on a different, standard audio cassette system, say in the car, transfer the recording from one system to the other using a double-ended patch cord. One end of the cord goes into the earphone socket of the machine with the original recording, the other into the line input of the machine to which you are transferring the tape. An alternative is to make the transfer using one machine's loudspeaker and the recorder's microphone, placing them close together, but there is a loss of sound quality.

I was given a portable television set about the size of a pack of cigarettes as a travel gadget but found it to be of little use. However, if you are an avid TV viewer, they can while away waiting time at airports.

PORTABLE PHOTOCOPIER

Far more useful is a portable gadget that attracted a lot of attention when it was first marketed but never seems to have realized its potential. I have a portable photocopying machine that goes easily into my briefcase and gives quite clear copies on the same type of sensitized rolls of paper that some thermal printing calculators use. You run it over the text or visuals you want to copy in a painting motion. I find it particularly useful when researching in library reference sections and often bring it out during flights when I want to copy a section of text in a book or magazine I am reading. These miniature portable copiers have been discounted down to around $100 and they are a wonderful value at that kind of price. There are also more sophisticated portable fax copier and scanning combinations at substantially higher prices.

Many businesspeople who would not dream of leisure traveling without a camera seem rarely to take one with them on working trips. However, the new generation of compact 35mm automatics with built-in flash take up very little room, are tough, and enable you to get more from travel by being on the lookout for interesting picture opportunities. In addition, a camera can be a useful business tool for making visual records—I've often used mine to copy documents when a photocopier was not available. Fill the picture frame with the document, making sure that the text is in focus and brightly and evenly lit. Even cheap drugstore color prints should be easy to read with the aid of a magnifier.

PHOTOGRAPHY

If you want to take photographs through the window of the aircraft, these tips will make all the difference between success and failure.

Get as close to the window as possible without touching it. Too far away, and there will be undesirable reflections. If your camera touches the window, the vibrations will make the picture fuzzy.

Remove a polarizing filter, if one is fitted, because there can be strange effects resulting from light passing through both the window plastic and the filter. However, an ultraviolet (haze) filter will be beneficial.

Remember that fast films are much more easily fogged by x-ray machines than slow ones—and that all films are susceptible to the cumulative effects of x-ray examinations.

There is still a great deal of confusion about the vulnerability of film to the x-ray luggage-searching systems at airports. The theory and the practice do not always coincide. In theory, the dosage of x-rays used to examine baggage in the United States is not sufficiently strong to harm any but high-speed film rated over ASA 400. But the effects of the radiation are cumulative. While the same roll of undeveloped film may go through x-ray equipment five times or more without harm, it is a risky business. You easily lose track of the number of times a roll of film has been inspected, and especially in some foreign countries, the radiation dosage of the equipment can vary considerably.

Never check in cameras or film. I usually travel with spare film *and* a miniature camera loaded with film, all in a larger version of those special foil-lined protective bags sold at airport shops and photographic suppliers. I then pass my hand baggage through the x-ray scanner, and if the security attendant regards the package as suspicious, willingly open it up for visual inspection.

An alternative, especially if your camera is too large to fit easily into the foil bag, is to put film and camera together in one of those self-sealing plastic bags I mentioned earlier and have this readily accessible in your hand luggage. Remove it just before passing through the security point and request that it be examined separately.

In the United States you have the right to a separate visual inspection of hand baggage, but this is not the case in many foreign countries. Some security people even insist that a camera be opened to check if anything hostile is concealed inside. If you are traveling where security is likely to be particularly tight—Communist bloc and some Third World countries, for example—hassles at the checkpoint can be reduced by having the camera empty. Otherwise, to open it without fogging exposures you have already taken involves rewinding the film and probably wasting much of it.

You can rewind a partially exposed film and reuse it if you take note of the number of exposures and then rewind slowly and carefully with the camera to your ear. That way you hear the film being transported and should be able to pick up the moment when the end tongue comes off the take-up spool. Stop winding at that point, so that the tongue does not disappear into the cassette. Later reload the film in the usual way and run off the same number of exposures plus at least two extra frames with the lens cap on and covered with a dark cloth in case any light gets in. It's best to do this in subdued light. I've often got away with opening cameras with jammed film or some other problem in ordinary hotel rooms at night, crouched under the bedclothes with the curtains drawn. With slower films and sensible precautions you don't need a perfect darkroom. Indeed, many hotel bathrooms can be made sufficiently dark to process film and even make prints, although the techniques for that are not needed by the typical business traveler.

With fully automatic 35mm cameras, rewinding and reusing partially exposed film can be more difficult, even impossible. The Instamatic type of camera, which takes drop-in cartridges, has some advantages in this respect, but the quality of the pictures they take is not up to that of 35mm equipment. However, if you want to keep the weight and bulk to the minimum, it makes sense to take at least a cheap instant camera along on every business trip. If you are caught away from home with a need for a camera but did not bring one with you, the disposable ones sold ready loaded with film in chain and drugstores can produce surprisingly good results within their limitations. However, don't tuck one away in the corner of your carry-on bag and forget about it. Just a couple of trips can result in enough passes through x-ray security equipment to affect the film.

Putting film into checked, not carry-on, baggage may prevent it from being exposed to x-rays, but this is by no means certain at some airports, where items of checked luggage may be x-rayed as part of the overall security procedures. To be safe, always put film into foil bags.

TRAVEL GADGETS

At one time miniature alarm clocks were one of the most popular traveling gadgets, but they seem to have faded from the scene. However, you may need to be sure to be awakened to catch a flight or perhaps make an important meeting despite suffering from the disturbed sleep rhythms of jet lag. Wristwatches with built-in alarms are a possible solution—if the alarm is loud enough to wake a sound sleeper. I don't trust them anymore after oversleeping despite deliberately wearing the watch in bed because I thought that would make it more likely that its beep would penetrate my sleeping state. During the night I put my arm under the pillow and muffled the sound.

Now, if relying on an alarm watch, I put it on the bedside table, usually in an ashtray, which will help to amplify the sound a little. But I still back up the alarm watch with a request to the hotel switchboard for a wake-up call. They are are 90 percent reliable, but that other 10 percent can be crucial to you. If so, then a proper traveling alarm clock can still make sense.

Another gadget, useful to some travelers but unnecessary baggage to others, is an inflatable pillow. I find those miserable little pillows they provide on most airlines, certainly in economy class, to be of limited use in supporting my head, and unless my head is comfortable I find it difficult to sleep during flights. So I have an inflatable neck pillow shaped like the letter C that goes round my neck and props me up nicely, especially in window seats.

If you work with paper on planes, in airports, or at hotels, there always seems to be at least one moment on every trip when you need a paper clip, a stapler, scissors, or some other desk paraphernalia. To cope with this situation, I always carry one of those compact traveling stationery kits that you can now buy anywhere for less than $10. It has a stapler, tape measure, scissors, roll of adhesive tape, knife, and glue bottle in cut-out sections of the foam plastic interior, so that they keep in their respective places and are always accessible. There is a hinged compartment for pins, spare staples, paper clips, and eraser.

I augment this kit with the most useful writing instrument ever developed for the frequent flier—the combination ballpoint pen and highlighter, which together enable you to write notes and emphasize points in text. I try never to use an expensive pen or propelling pencil while actually traveling—the world's air routes are littered with gold-rolled Cross and Parker pens mislaid by travelers. Fountain pens are great to write with—anywhere but underwater and in the varying pressure of a jetliner. They are better left at home when flying, but if you really do prefer traditional nib and ink, use the cartridge fountain pen, which seems to be less susceptible to leakage during flights than the one with a rubber refillable ink sac.

If you need to write frequently when on trips, some form of clipboard can be useful, especially if your carry-on baggage does not include a rigid briefcase suitable for putting on your lap and using as a portable desk. A combined clipboard and document folder has many merits and need not be bulky. Plastic lap desks costing $12 to $15 combine a clipboard with a document container behind to form a box writing slope. They can be the most effective way to organize papers and writing materials within the confined space of an airplane, and the whole thing will slip into a carry-on bag.

While one needs a rigid, firm container for papers that have to be protected or to provide a working surface, most of the traveler's impedimenta and gadgets are best carried in soft containers that protect without being inflexible for convenient packaging. For example, my computer diskettes and my audio cassette tapes go into flexible fabric containers with individual pockets, not into rigid plastic boxes. Indeed, for a long trip during which I will need several audio tapes, I take them out of their cases and put them into the pockets of the flexible fabric case and save a lot of space and awkwardness without exposing them to excessive dust.

What other traveler's gadgets are worth considering? Not many, although you will find luggage stores loaded with all kinds of gimmicky hardware that appears superficially attractive but will not stand up to the harsh realities of frequent flying.

Portable irons and coffee and tea makers are a menace, taking up too much weight and space unless you really are prepared to make a convenience trade-off because you need to press your clothes or cannot survive without a hot drink whenever the urge strikes. Follow the advice in the section on packing, and your clothes should not get seriously wrinkled and require pressing. If they do, hanging them in a steamy bathroom can do wonders at removing creases from most fabrics. Or take a portable steamer in preference to a travel iron.

As for portable beverage heaters, they rarely earn their passage in these days when dispensing machines and room service can meet thirst needs in all kinds of hotels, from the cut-price motels to the big, expensive city center establishments. Even if you take along a plug-in immersion heater, you will still need a container in which to put it and the water. These heaters tend either to crack or to melt the glasses and plastic drinking utensils provided in a hotel room.

Traveler's clotheslines can be useful, but the self-rewinding types in special cases are heavier and bulkier without being much more efficient than a length of thin but strong nylon cord. I used to think that folding or inflatable clothes hangers were a waste of time also, but with so many hotels now having hangers you cannot remove from the wardrobe rail, it may make sense to take a folding or inflatable one with you for drip-dry garments that have to hang over the bath or in the shower cubicle.

Shoe cleaning materials also come packed in special travel kits some frequent fliers will find useful. However, if you plan carefully you should need only one color of polish and no more than one brush for the typical trip. I find the best solution is a small container of self-shining shoe polish with a built-in applicator. If my shoes get really dirty, I wipe them clean at night with water and tissues or lavatory paper, which even the worst hotel always supplies. By morning the shoes are dry and then just need wiping over with the self-shining polish to look smart again. Suede shoes can be great for traveling and do not need polishing, but you should take a small wire brush along to freshen them up.

A clothes brush takes up space and adds weight for little good reason when a foam plastic sponge will do most jobs as well, if not better. Pairs of men's hairbrushes in leather cases used to be popular gifts for travelers, but now most of us get by with light, small plastic brushes, which work just as well and can be washed and dried far more easily.

Some travel books still list pocketknives with all kinds of fold-out devices, typified by the classic Swiss Army knife, as being essential equipment. They may be if you are going on safari or need to get stones out of horses' hooves, but rarely on the typical business trip. Also, if you take a knife in your carry-on baggage, you will have problems at the security checks. I was with a business group traveling out of Tokyo once when even pairs of scissors caused a major incident at the airport. We had all been given these smart desk scissors as a gift at one of the Japanese factories we visited. Most of us were wise enough to stash them in our checked baggage, but several put them into their carry-on bags. These were picked up by the security people, who seemed to think for a time that our group included an organized gang planning a skyjacking. All the scissors were confiscated, traveled separately under the guard of the crew, and were returned at our destination. *Anything* with the potential to be an offensive weapon does not belong in carry-on luggage.

Portable hair driers and curling irons are listed in some travel books, but most men and women frequent fliers with short hair seem to manage well enough without them by a little careful planning of hairwashing time and engagements, coupled with some vigorous toweling. If you do take these or any other electric appliances overseas, allow for the varying voltages and cycles of electric current in different countries. Many inexperienced travelers buy electrical travel sets that contain combination plugs to cope with half a dozen or more different types of sockets but that do not convert the current to the 110–120-volt 60-cycle American standard.

Most of the world is now on 220–240-volt 50-cycle electrical power, so you need either dual-voltage equipment or a transformer. The cycles don't matter too much for most equipment except sensitive electronic gear, but you can fry your gadgets very quickly if they are meant for 110 volts and you run 240 through them. Small step-down transformers are available more easily in the United States than in most overseas locations, but make sure that they can cope with the maximum wattage and other requirements of anything you are going to run from them. Some will be fine with a small radio but not cope with a hair drier or immersion heater.

Most better hotels now have electric shaver sockets in the bathroom that will deliver 110–120-volt power for light equipment, so you may not need a transformer along at all. I use these sockets to run my little battery charger, and virtually everything electrical I take with me works on these batteries, so the line current variations are no problem.

In fact, the fewer gadgets you take with you when you travel, the fewer problems you are likely to have. To modify the traditional saying, he or she who travels lightest not only travels farthest but also has fewer hassles. Many gadgets sold for the traveler's convenience often add

Take your table with you. There is rarely a problem at any time for the traveler to find somewhere to sit down while on the road, but there never seems to be a suitable table around when you need one.

So Michael Whelan, a New Jersey frequent flier, came up with this simple folding table which is just the right size to support a portable computer on an aircraft, or to use as a lap desk for taking notes during conferences and meetings. It folds in half to carry like a document bag and has a flap pocket to hold papers.

The computer in the picture demonstrates an important point if you are buying a machine which will be used on an aircraft. The screen should hinge from around the middle of the computer, like this one, not from the back, or you cannot swivel the screen to a workable angle without fouling the back of the seat in front.

More details on the Lap-Xtender, which costs under $20, from Michael Whelan at 11 Atlantic Street, Hackensack, NJ 07601 (210-342-3443).

weight, bulk, and complications. There is a writer's maxim for good communications with the acronym KISS: Keep It Simple, Stupid. That's good advice for travelers also.

E-MAIL KEEPS YOU IN TOUCH

Electronic mail services are a very efficient way to
keep in touch while on the road, especially as the
main carriers make their services more
interconnecting. However, for maximum efficiency,
economy, and convenience, it can pay to plan
carefully.

Remember that the true cost of time on the
road is higher than that of workers back at the
office, so delegate if possible the sorting of your
electronic mail. A secretary, assistant, or colleague
can quickly compile an edited version of your
electronic equivalent of the in-tray, combining
E-mail with any other information that has reached
your desk on paper. You can access this electronic
in-tray off your own office computer via either your
portable or a computer in one of the business
centers springing up in the better hotels.

A massive amount of information can be
captured quickly, stored on diskette, and processed
by you without touching any paper. In the same
way, you can draft responses in your hotel room and
zap them back to the office for printing and
dispatching.

An important point where confidentiality is a
consideration is that E-mail and other computer-to-
computer links are essentially more secure than fax.
Industrial espionage is a growth business, and hotel
fax services can be compromised. An obvious
example is a major industry conference or trade
show attended by senior personnel from competing
companies. The conference hotel's fax facility would
be a prime target for industrial espionage—and you

> might never know that your competitors were
> reading your messages.

COST-EFFECTIVE ALTERNATIVES TO HOTEL AND OFFICE

Business and leisure travelers now have a number of alternatives to conventional hotels. Short-term rental of a furnished apartment, condominium, or house can be more practical and competitively priced. The choice is wide around the world. In London, for example, you can have a luxury fully furnished one-bedroom apartment near Buckingham Palace for about $500 a week, or similar accommodation behind your own front door in central Paris for a little less.

The choices range from fully serviced units in specialized buildings such as the Executive Suites operation in the United States down to individual owners offering short-term leases for their own properties. Information is available from good travel agents, from the classified columns of leading newspapers and magazines, and from specialized agencies listed in the Yellow Pages. Check carefully before parting with any money.

The office accommodation services now available in many major cities around the world can be very good. I had a prestige address, telephone answering service, and the use of other facilities such as telex and fax in central London for $150 a month, with a separate office or conference room and a secretary at reasonable hourly rates whenever I needed them. It proved an attractive alternative to working out of the hotel room and maintained continuity of a local contact address in between trips to the city. Indeed, I found out later that some of my British business contacts assumed that we had a full London branch office, not just an accommodation address.

Leisure Time

On business trips quality leisure is a crucial—and cost-effective— consideration.

Fun is the missing element in most business travel. Eighty-one percent of the frequent travelers in the Hyatt Travel Futures Project Report survey said they enjoyed the experience because they got to meet new people and see new places, while virtually all returned from a trip with a feeling of accomplishment. But these answers reflect the fact that our attitudes to the positive and negative aspects of any business travel are predominantly work-related; personal benefits rarely come into consideration.

Most of us mentally categorize business travel as a distinctly work-related activity, not a balanced blend of work and leisure, as life as a whole should be. This colors our attitudes considerably. Can you remember the last time a colleague waxed lyrical about having a great fun time while on the road on the company's time and expense?

Business travelers readily verbalize all the stresses, strains, and woes they are suffering in the interests of the corporation. It's just not the done thing to acknowledge that it could be an opportunity for fun as well. Although the concept of business entertainment of clients and contacts is well established, we too often either do not use business travel as an opportunity for quality leisure or feel guilty if we do enjoy ourselves. Yet this is costing us and our employers dearly in stress and consequent lowered productivity, quality of decision making, and other negative consequences.

The tax rules in many countries foster this attitude. An activity is approved as tax deductible if it can be directly related to productive work generating income, disallowed if it is primarily for leisure or enjoyment. Eagles, Family Tieds, Tightrope Walkers, and Road Warriors alike seem somewhat reluctant to admit even to themselves that they are being given fabulous opportunities for fun while on the road—opportunities that need not be expensive in either time or money and that complement rather than compete with their business mission. Perhaps it is apprehension about being thought to be exploiting an opportunity denied to office-bound colleagues.

SUBCONSCIOUS MOTIVATIONS

Certainly, with 80 percent of those surveyed feeling that business travel is important for their career advancement, there must be strong subconscious motivations for wanting to be seen by colleagues as treating travel as a very serious business even involving an element of martyrdom. It is difficult to relate the objective of career advancement with going off to Chicago, New York, Los Angeles, or London *to have fun*. The business environment still perpetuates traditional work ethics. You achieve recognition and rewards by being seen to be industrious, making personal sacrifices, working overtime—even accepting stress in the interests of the organization.

Consequently, it is easy to rationalize that the business traveler both *expects* and *accepts* stress as an integral part of business travel, reinforcing the belief that it is advancing his or her career. We used to be told that if aerobic exercise hurts, then it must be doing us good. But that has proved to be wrong, even dangerous advice.

Having fun on company time and money is still a somewhat alien concept to many of us with traditional work values. We find it difficult to believe that if business travel doesn't hurt, we are not exerting ourselves sufficiently to further our company's interests or obtain the career advantages that the Hyatt Travel Futures Project revealed so many of us see as the prime tangible benefit from the pain of business trips.

When I was in the movie business, I never completely got rid of the guilt feelings about going to exotic places at considerable expense and thoroughly enjoying myself watching the best of the newest productions.

Now I will admit that when I returned, I would play down to both colleagues at work and the family at home what a good time I had had. The overwhelming majority—83 percent—of married business travelers in the Hyatt report feel that business travel adversely affects their spouses; most also express concern about the negative consequences on their children. So there are subconscious motivations to avoid revealing at home as well as at the office just how self-indulgently pleasurable some business trips are.

Indeed, many spouses already resent the business travel of the partner. "The traveling spouse is viewed as being freer, as having a more exciting life," the researchers reported.

SELF-PERPETUATING SITUATION

We seem to have a complex self-perpetuating situation in which it is not felt appropriate to equate business travel with personal pleasure, so a mind set develops among many travelers that they are not going to have a good time and should not expect it.

The typical business trip is organized as strictly work-related, undertaken under significant pressures to perform well, with no expectation of enjoyment from it and with no serious consideration for opportunities to relax in the trip's planning or execution. The Hyatt research identified many examples of the considerable performance pressure—a specific and very damaging form of stress—on today's travelers as they embark on "a heightened, charged experience in which every pitfall is magnified and every small inconvenience is perceived as a threat—not just to the business at hand, but also to the traveler's sense of personal mastery."

There is a great deal at stake, particularly for individual career advancement, and complex self-imagery to be sustained, typified by the way that the respondents so readily fell into the categories of Eagle, Road Warrior, Tightrope Walker, and Family Tied. Each group is under a variety of pressures to tackle a business trip as a serious undertaking that demands concentration on the task at hand to the exclusion of self-gratification through leisure. Business travel is performance-, not fun-oriented—although the responses from many of those surveyed showed that it can yield enjoyable highs of excitement and achievement.

COMPLEX INFLUENCES

Many complex and subtle business and sociological factors influence our attitudes to business travel. For example, two primary shifts in American society affect the nature of business travel today, the Hyatt report points out. One is the changing nature of American business activity, and the other the aging of the Baby Boomers who now make up the majority of frequent business travelers.

"American business in the early 1980s began a shift from hierarchy towards decentralization, from stability to flux, from 'management by decree' to 'management by learning,'" the Hyatt report says. "As middle management ranks thin out and business transactions become more interactive, less a matter of routine, travel in the 1980s has become a highly visible vehicle for promotion, a swift leg up on the corporate ladder.

"But there is a downside in this. The less regimented, flexible corporate workplace means there is increased per-

Printing on the road. Printers were left behind in the development of computing portability. The little battery-powered Diconix was, for a long time, the most practical choice. Now it has some rivals, but has itself improved vastly in performance since Kodak took over the company. The frequent flier now has the ability anywhere to print text or graphics by ink jet on plain paper to near letter quality. The unit is about the size of a book and weighs 3.75 pounds with its batteries.

formance pressure on today's traveler. The rewards are higher, but so are the risks—there is more at stake than ever before.

"The baby boom generation's personal life has changed as well. They are no longer free agents, but are becoming householders with families, living regular, patterned lives. They are now husbands and wives, fathers and mothers.

"In some ways, the heightened experience of travel, the sense of adventure, excitement and self-fulfillment it can provide, harkens back to the earlier values of the 60s. When the business trip works, it confers upon the traveler not just a sense of work-related accomplishment, but also positive redefinition of the self as an individual.

"Taken together, then, the emphasis on individual initiative in business meshes with the earlier 60s-70s values of the baby-boom generation. Autonomy, the search for the self—these were the ideas that galvanized this generation. In sum, business travel is then both a high pressure path towards achievement and career advancement as well as an experience wherein the individual can recapture and reestablish feelings of excitement, enjoyment and fulfillment."

We *can* get feelings of excitement, enjoyment, and fulfillment from business travel—but *do* we? And must these positive returns only be work-related? Although the Travel Futures Project research team found evidence that the sense of freedom, lures of adventure, excitement, sophistication, and opportunities for temporary escape from the more routine worlds of work and family are important elements of contemporary business travel, the high levels of stress felt on business trips indicate that it is not the all-round enriching and fulfilling experience that it could be.

TRAUMATIC CHANGE PRODUCES STRESS

There is another reason why we are not obtaining more positive benefits from business travel, in addition to the work-related performance pressures. Travel involves change, often quite dramatic changes in environment, pace, the method of working, the people around you, the meals you eat, and so on. A wealth of emerging evidence indicates that stress is an excessive physiological and psychological response to change. Complex homeostatic balancing mechanisms strive to maintain equilibrium in the chemical and electrical reactions going on all the time within the brain, central nervous system and other body functions. When those balances are upset, various forms of stress occur.

The rush to the airport, the pretakeoff tension, just the anticipation of things going wrong at any stage of a journey, are changes in routine that can affect hormone levels and have significant effects on the body's endogenous opioid and adrenocorticotrophic (ACTH) systems, which are directly linked to stress reactions. What is the best antidote? How can you try to swing the balance back toward normal again to ease business travel–related stress? The answer is delightfully simple—and very attractive. Enjoy yourself!

PLEASURE—THE BEST ANTISTRESS PILL

Businesspeople are flocking to lectures by brain researcher and Nobel Prize nominee Dr. Mark Gillman. He explains how reward and pleasure stimulate the endorphin system to counter the effects of stress. Author Norman Cousins wrote a bestseller on how he literally laughed himself out of a potentially fatal disease. The depressed and mentally ill have shown remarkable benefits from the pleasure to be derived from interacting with pets. Runners get pleasurable highs from endorphin reactions, which also boost their performance; music stimulates the same pleasure-sensitive systems to inspire and change mood.

At my last medical checkup, I asked my doctor for guidance on the best precautions to take as a middle-aged, overweight frequent flier with a family history of heart disease. I got the usual litany about diet, exercise, and not smoking—plus the latest high-tech medical advice on alleviating stress.

"Above all, *minimize stress by enjoying yourself*," he emphasized. "Have a good sex life, pay a lot more attention to quality leisure time, and generally have fun. Evidence of the positive benefits to be obtained from stimulating the endorphin system, the body's natural narcotics, by pleasurable inputs is now overwhelming. Happy people get far fewer heart attacks."

TAKE A DOSE OF PLEASURE

Dr. Gillman agrees. "You can alleviate travel and other forms of stress by deliberately giving yourself a strong dose of pleasure to stimulate the endorphins in a way that is both legal and healthful. Exercise is good, but recent research proves that too much, especially to the point of pain and discomfort, does not create beneficial endorphin reactions and may even damage the immune system. The best highs come from exercise that is pleasurable. There are beneficial endorphin reactions from listening to music, although some types of music can be stressful, especially if played excessively loudly, and will stimulate the ACTH system rather than the endorphins and actually induce stress.

"Leisure, pleasure, fun, relaxation, enjoyment—whatever you call it—is an essential element in coping with travel stress. A stressed business traveler cannot perform to his or her true potential, so it is in both the interests of the individual and of the employer that leisure and pleasure be an element of any business trip. You can justify it in business terms by seeing it as a cost-effective strategy. To physicians and their patients it just makes good sense."

He and other medical specialists I consulted added a warning that such advice should not be taken too far. Be careful about approaching the leisure element in the same performance-driven way that we do the work aspect of business trips; otherwise you only create high-stress leisure. In contemporary society we often carry work-related concepts over into our play times and get involved in still more competitive, time-critical, and demanding leisure activities. The business traveler needs regular stress-relieving doses of true leisure, which Webster's defines as "freedom from occupation or business; idle time; time free from employment during which a person may indulge in rest, recreation, etc."

The missing element for many performance-pressured business travelers is *creative, enjoyable leisure time*, which I hope you are convinced by now is not to be equated with wasted time, from either the traveler's or the employer's viewpoint.

BUSINESS DISGUISED AS LEISURE

We do not build leisure into our schedules because we do not acknowledge it to be an integral part of the business travel experience. If it is there, it is usually work-related socializing, such as dining out or playing golf or tennis with contacts, associates, or clients.

For example, a business trip to Japan can easily become overloaded with scheduled "leisure," which many Western businesspeople find adds to the travel stress instead of reducing it. Lots of Japanese admit this privately as well. The elaborate business etiquette associated with the ludicrously overpriced expense account bars, the artificial social interchanges that take place in them, and the elaborate dinners culminating in amplified solo singing performances that often embarrass as much as they amuse are a well-orchestrated extension of the elaborate business interchanges that took place during working hours. Once novelty of this culture shock phenomenon has worn off, it does not constitute quality leisure, which refreshes, stimulates, invigorates, and expands one's mental or physical capabilities.

If you approach a business trip to Japan with your personal leisure needs in mind, you can add enjoyment—and probably save money too—by breaking away from the Western-style hotels and restaurants for at least a night. In Japan, for example, be pampered in a traditional ryokan inn with a personal maid, the fun of a communal bath, or just the opportunity to relax. I have been to Japan on several business trips on which I worked very hard and came back with a great sense of business achievement. But ask me for the single most abiding memory, the experience there that enriched me more than any other, and without hestitation I will recall a quiet half-hour looking through the screens from my room in a Kyoto ryokan at a simple waterfall in the tiny garden outside. It was a moment of exquisitely peaceful leisure providing me with an insight into Japanese culture that I am sure exerted a direct and positive influence on my work performance during the rest of that trip. If there had been a fee levied on it, I would have had no hesitation putting it on my expense report as a legitimate charge. Of course, the IRS might not agree, but an enlightened employer investing in my acquisition of knowledge to pursue its interests in the Orient should do so without hesitation.

LEISURE IS COST-EFFECTIVE

The first step in adding quality leisure to business travel is to recognize that it plays a valid, cost-effective role in enhancing work efficiency. There is now undeniable evidence that the work efficiency of many business travelers is adversely affected by negative aspects of their psychological and emotional states while on the road. The Eagle and Road Warrior types defined in the Hyatt report, just as much as Family Tieds and Tightrope Walkers, display symptoms not usually associated with conventional stress but just as counterproductive. These symptoms may be alleviated by quality leisure.

The sense of being harried and tense because of the

frustrations of dealing with airlines, hotels, and other travel-related services is compounded frequently by loneliness and loss of control. As we noted in the section on jet lag, long flights have physiological consequences that result in depression and other adverse symptoms, and appropriate leisure activities can help to alleviate them. In such circumstances passive leisure—dozing off in front of the television, for example—may worsen the situation, but exercise nearly always brings benefits.

PLEASURABLE EXERCISE

The fitness enthusiasts who schedule opportunities to pursue their routines while away undeniably benefit by maintaining their work efficiency—as well as by prolonging their productive lives. There is now no problem in selecting hotels that either have in-house exercise facilities or can arrange guest membership in a health center nearby. The better ones will even put a rowing or cycling machine in your room if you prefer to exercise in private, although this is not a good practice when suffering from jet lag. Social contact and daylight are important in helping circadian rhythms to adjust to a new time zone.

Some hotels provide maps indicating recommended walks or jogging runs in the vicinity—the best way of relaxing, getting to know the new environment, and exercising all at the same time. A brisk walk or jog through the neighborhood is a great way to counter jet lag symptoms but may not always be practical—or safe, especially for women, in some cities. Instead many frequent fliers choose to work out or play games like racquetball at clubs that have reciprocal membership arrangements with those back home. YMCAs and YWCAs are particularly plentiful, although often not conveniently located near downtown and airport hotels.

PURSUE HOBBIES

Hobbies and other interests can be pursued in new places very effectively, adding a relaxing leisure enjoyment dimension to business trips. Collectors can allocate time to visit specialty shops and markets; photographers and artists are presented with infinitely varied opportunities to expand their hobbies; new museums and exhibitions can be visited and sporting events attended. The list of current events held by the hall porter or concierge or included in the free literature in the room usually only focuses on highlights and has a strong tourist slant. If you have particular interests, the local newspaper and library may be a better source to find out what special groups are up to. It is an unusual organization of any kind that will not welcome out-of-town visitors to its meetings if they share the enthusiasms of the local members.

Sometimes on a business trip I go on a theater and concert binge, especially if there is a good cut-price ticket bureau in town. In Washington, New York, San Francisco, London, and other big cities I obtain great leisure pleasure ending a working day with a stroll to the discount theater ticket office and selecting a show from those on offer. These discount ticket facilities seem mainly to be patronized by tourists, with most business travelers missing out on the bargains and fun evenings to be had.

FINDING COMPANIONS

Not knowing anyone in town can be depressing if you don't like going out on your own or are apprehensive about security. If you are not a yuppie snob, you can have some great evenings by joining group tours of the night spots, but check with the hotel staff or somebody with local knowledge on the tour operator's reliability and whether the places to be visited really will appeal to you.

Faced with a lonely birthday in New York, I once joined a
tour around Manhattan night spots that was cheap and
fun. A friendly group of tourists that included a women's
bowling team adopted me when they heard it was my
birthday and turned it into a memorable occasion. In Sydney, Athens, Paris, Rome, Istanbul, Tokyo, and many
other diverse cities, I have found the group tour of entertainment spots a convenient, hassle-free way of spending a
free evening and much better than a meal alone or sitting
in the hotel room watching television, although both activities can provide valuable leisure time if appropriate to
your mood and needs.

More expensive, but favored by some business travelers, is to make use of professional escort services, which
can provide compatible male or female companions. Of
course, you need to be able to distinguish between those
providing sexual services and those offering intellectual
companionship.

A free treat in lots of cities, especially if you are suffering from jet lag, wake early and cannot get back to sleep,
is an early morning walk. It is fascinating to see a city
wake up and start the day, something that in a normal
work and sleep routine you might never consider doing.
Especially interesting are early morning markets, which
may sell anything from meat, fish, flowers, or produce to
antiques and collectibles, and are full of colorful charac-
ters and lots of action.

BOLT-ON PACKAGES

Determined seekers after active leisure on business trips
now have many opportunities with the wide range of
"bolt-on" packages available. Leave a few days early, or
stay on a few days extra, or plan your trip with an initial
jet lag recovery period, and take advantage of various leisure packages that can economically be added to either

scheduled or discounted air fares. Particularly attractive propositions for the active business traveler alone is to join one of the enormous variety of short adventure or cultural holidays on offer. Even with only a few days available, you can walk among lions and elephants in Africa, go white-water rafting in Canada, scuba dive in the Mediterranean, attend a music master's class in a British castle, sample gourmet food and wine in France—the list of fascinating bolt-ons to business trips is endless.

To make the best deals it may be necessary to book and pay at the same time as you do the business travel bookings, but if you find or create free time during a business trip, you can usually make last-minute arrangements to have some weekend fun.

FREE FUN

You don't even need a free weekend to take advantage of many of the remarkable add-on deals offered by the airlines, especially on international trips. Just as an example, British Airways and Visa USA got together on a Showstopper promotion, which added on to a round-trip ticket to London charged to your Visa card a theater ticket and a free evening of dining and Tudor high jinks at an Elizabethan restaurant, together with a chauffeur-driven car to or from the airport. Many of these special promotional offers are compatible with business travel schedules, and they provide additional fun at little or no extra cost to an otherwise routine trip.

Another frequently offered airline promotional deal is a heavily discounted ticket for a companion, which can build in a leisure dimension to a business trip and ease some of the strains that frequent absences may impose on a relationship. Also, of course, you can use your frequent-flier bonuses to take along a friend or spouse.

This is just a sampling of ways in which business trips

can be enriched by constructive exploitation of the leisure opportunities that they offer. The opportunities are there for the taking without compromising the main working purpose of the journey and probably enhance your work performance while on the road. Even if there is much stress and frustration in business travel, there is no reason why we should not add some fun to it without feeling guilty.

SEEK SANCTUARY IN A CHURCH

Even the smallest, most remote place where the business traveler is likely to end up provides a readily accessible, free place where one can sit and relax, perhaps meditate for a few quiet moments to ease away travel or work stress.

This universal sanctuary for the stressed traveler is, of course, one of the local churches. In cold climates it is usually warmed, in hot places it offers cool relief from the sun; everywhere it will protect from rain, noise, and crowds. You don't need to be religious to benefit from a church. If a service or some other activity is going on, there is the opportunity to become gently attuned to the local community. If there is a priest around to talk to, then the traveler can even start networking into a fountain of local knowledge that often produces useful business information.

EVEN THE CLUB MED IS USEFUL FOR BUSINESS TRAVELERS

Typifing the major changes going on around the world to open up primarily holiday destinations to the business traveler is the way that several of the Club Mediterranee's

132 villages now offer quite sophisticated facilities. These and other resorts have become practical venues for sales conferences, seminars, and other projects, with the opportunities to do financially attractive out-of-season deals while remaining great places to relax.

Keep Up-To-Date with the Expenses

Keeping a record of business and other out-of-pocket expenses while on the road is a hassle, but trying to remember them all after you get back can be a nightmare.

Expense claim forms differ widely, but most require expenditures to be itemized on a daily basis. The easiest way to keep track is to put the receipts collected each day into a separate envelope and record details of the expenditures incurred that day on the outside of the envelope—before you go to bed and forget them.

You may find the daily expense summary on page 287 helpful. If you have a photocopier that will copy onto #10 envelopes, copy the summary directly onto enough envelopes for the trip; otherwise run off copies on plain paper and staple or stick them to envelopes. Keep the envelopes with the summaries—and the enclosed receipts if you do not have to submit them—to verify your travel expenses for your employers, your accountant, or the IRS.

COMPUTERIZE YOUR FREQUENT FLIER LOG AND LOOK FOR BONUS MILES

One way to ensure that you get the most out of frequent flier programs is to plan and record your trips on computer. *The Frequent Flier Log*, for example, calculates the precise number of miles to be credited to your account when you enter the three-letter alphabetic codes for the departure and arrival airports. One version, costing $25 to run with Excel software on the Macintosh, covers major airports in North America and for $10 more lists leading airports overseas also.

Daily Expense Summary

Day _____ Date _____ Place _____

Hotel

Taxis

Fares

Car rental

Car mileage start

Car mileage finish

Gas etc.

Parking and tolls

Phone and postage

Breakfast

Lunch

Dinner

Entertainment

Laundry

Tips

Services

Supplies

Misc. expenses

Daily total

Daily allowance

You can extend the value of these logs into comprehensive travel planning and record databases so that you keep accurate track of all flights, their purpose, and tax deductibility, mileage, bonus miles, and other factors.

Other microcomputer programs can be invaluable for independent fliers with their own or the use of company planes. There are comprehensive programs that make preparing a flight plan much quicker and easier, automatically calculating altitudes and routes to achieve the best time or fuel use and maintaining a comprehensive log of each flight. The directories cover all airports in the United States with at least one paved runway and some overseas territories as well.

Other microcomputer programs calculate plane ownership costs. For example, there is one for only $9 called *Cruise Cost Calculator* for use with Excel or Works on the Mac or PC and clones that predict how many dollars you can save in a year with various cruising power settings.

The Female Factor

The Woman Business Traveler

Businesswomen who travel now demand—and get—a much better deal than a few years ago. Using their $25-billion-a-year travel buying clout, women are making hotels and airlines pay overdue attention to the legitimate grievances that went unheard when women formed a very small part of the business travel community. Now female entrepreneurs are responsible for the majority of new start-ups and, together with their increasing numbers in the professions and corporate management, they are becoming important frequent fliers, comprising about a third of all business travelers in the United States, although still only around 10 percent in Britain and Europe.

Times have changed dramatically since the 1960s, when United could run one of the most successful airline advertising campaigns ever, encouraging women to write "take me along" messages to husbands traveling on business as the only effective way of generating more female patronage. Now the airlines and hotels campaign aggressively for the steadily increasing purchasing power that the businesswoman deploys in her own right, but still the promise in the advertisements too frequently fails to be delivered.

When Britain's Businesswoman's Travel Club surveyed two hundred members, the major complaints were

- *Poor service from waiters in hotel bars and restaurants, who tend to treat men with more respect*
- *Equally poor service from flight attendants, who concentrate on men passengers while ignoring women*
- *Inconsiderate seating on planes, with women on business trips put near noisy children, while male travelers are grouped together in quiet sections*

- *The failure of many hotels to consider the security of women guests, particularly in not offering safe transport to and from airports or ensuring that their car parking areas are well-lit and secure*
- *Receptionists who divulge the room numbers of women traveling alone without considering the possible consequences*
- *Hotel hairdressers catering only to women who are free during the daytime by closing out of normal office hours*

If that British survey is extended internationally, similar problems are found all over the world. Some countries score very badly, even those like the United States and much of Europe, where there is extensive legislation to combat sexual discrimination. Many of the problems facing the businesswoman on the road result from insensitivity, bad attitude, and sheer incompetence, none of which is readily susceptible to change by legislation.

A *Harvard Magazine* survey in the early 1980s revealed that many women ranked having to eat alone in a restaurant as more traumatic than asking for a loan or having a gynecological examination. Like some other statistics from surveys, such as that most people fear public speaking more than dying, that kind of apprehension seems inconceivable until you think seriously about it.

"I know women who lock themselves in a hotel room and order room service when they're on a business trip because they're afraid to venture out by themselves," wrote Susan R. Pollack of the Gannet News Service.

"Hotel corridors, especially in the Big American hotels, tend to be long, deserted alleyways—they may have fancy wallpaper and fitted carpet, but a woman walking alone down one at night is just as vulnerable as going into a deserted alleyway in New York or Los Angeles," says California jewelry designer Kate Drew-Wilkinson. "Hotels must pay greater attention to the security needs of women traveling alone, and one small step would be not putting them in remote rooms a long way from the elevators and higher-traffic areas.

"Young attractive women traveling alone on business are particularly vulnerable. Clothes are a big problem. A man does not put himself at risk when he selects something to wear, but a woman's clothing sends out all kinds of messages—and she can never be sure how men will interpret them. You dress to look attractive and it may be interpreted as a come-on, but if you dress down or very severely to disguise your femininity, you neither look nor feel your best, and that can be a major psychological disadvantage in business dealings.

"You put on a business suit with pencil skirt and high heels to present yourself to good advantage—and then you can't even run for cover very fast if you need to! There is a lot of stress for women traveling on business that men just are not aware of. I feel particularly sympathetic towards the many young women now out on the road having to cope with sexism issues on top of all the other emotional and physical strains inherent in business travel."

Those young women are the Tightrope Walkers discovered in the Hyatt Travel Futures project, under thirty-five years of age and inexperienced in travel. When they are on the road, they feel enhanced personal power mixed with negative sensations of harassment and tenseness.

Two-thirds of the young women surveyed described traveling as very or somewhat stressful, but only 44 percent of the young men did so. The research found striking differences in how men and women coped with travel-related problems, with women far more likely to find it very difficult to deal with bad service from airlines, hotels, or rental car companies.

Almost twice as many women as men—23 percent compared with 13 percent—found it very difficult to cope with the lack of control over one's schedule that it is inherent in business travel. A third of the women, but only a fourth of the men, felt strongly that they were under more stress when traveling to an unfamiliar city. Very few—a mere 8 percent of the young women Tightrope Walkers—found the physical stress of travel not at all difficult to deal with, compared with more than twice that number of women generally (17 percent) and 25 percent of the men questioned. The physical stresses for a woman business traveler can be a major problem, reducing her performance and damaging her attitude to the whole travel experience.

"Pity the poor woman sales representative, who is generally young and pretty and has to cope with more personal luggage than a man and carry her samples along as well," says Kate Drew-Wilkinson. "Not only does she have bulk and weight to carry around, but also aggravated security problems. When I was younger and made my first jewelry sales trip to New York, it was one of the most frightening and exhausting experiences of my life. I had to carry thousands of dollars' worth of samples, and the weight and worry of being mugged made it really traumatic, far more than would have been the case for a man.

"When you are traveling on business, you have to find creative ways of tackling the problems that inevitably arise, and there are more of these for women than for men. In that particular instance, I bought a large inconspicuous cloth shoulder bag and hid all my jewelry sample boxes inside. It was the only way I could physically carry my business needs around in comparative safety, but it was still exhausting and very stressful trying to maintain an attractive businesslike appearance while coping with the combination of physical and emotional stress."

About half of the travelers questioned in the Hyatt project felt harried, hassled, and pressured, but these feelings were significantly more prevalent in women than in men. They seemed to become less of a problem with age and greater travel experience. Two-thirds of the young women felt harried or hassled, this proportion falling steadily with age until the oldest group of women, aged forty-five or more, were almost identical to men in the same age group, only 38 percent of whom usually had these negative feelings when away on business.

So women travelers of all ages generally feel more pressured than men but cope with it considerably better as they get older, while the proportion of men who feel pressure does not vary significantly by age. As such negative feelings as being harried, hassled, and pressured are excellent indicators of stress, we can see that the young women Tightrope Walkers are a very vulnerable group, made even more so by their apparent inability to cope as well with being away from home and family as single men do. Only 15 percent of the unmarried women questioned found it not at all difficult, compared with 31 percent of unmarried men.

The same gender difference was not apparent among married travelers, for whom the critical issue is the presence and ages of children in their household. Women of all ages who try to combine a career with marriage and child rearing face particular problems, but it seems from the Hyatt Travel Futures Project's initial results that women as a whole who make the decision to be frequent travelers do not feel any more strongly than men about the conflict between their careers and their family lives.

Because on average women seem to find it more difficult to cope with business travel stress, those who choose to engage in work which requires frequent travel tend to be more motivated. Sixty percent of the women questioned felt strongly that business travel is important to their career advancement, a view shared by only 45 percent of men. This self-selection element—a typical woman frequent flier has more problems to overcome than a man and so is more strongly motivated about travel—shows up in the significantly larger number of women who say they feel excited about being on the road. The researchers concluded that frequent business travel is a more intense experience for women, especially younger women, both the anxieties and the exhilaration being more pronounced.

This could be an important element in the comparative efficiency of men and women business travelers, especially when they have been on the road for several days. The survey produced clear evidence that those who see travel as a positive aspect of their job, who get a feeling of accomplishment from business trips, and who view travel as a challenge maintain their efficiency away from base longer. Women who travel frequently tend to have such positive feelings more than men.

They certainly need them! Married businesswomen who travel, especially those with young children, have more complex pre- and post-trip home arrangements to make as a consequence of their journey and will be more likely to try to maintain close involvement with parental and home management tasks while they are away. The mothers I spoke to all make a practice of phoning home daily, many in the morning before the children leave for school and again in the evening. This helps to ease the loneliness of being away from home, which both men and women business travelers feel to a greater extent than is usually recognized, but it seems to expose the women to additional stress in often having to come up at long range with solutions to minor family crises which husbands and children dump on them down the telephone. Some sociologists also believe that businesswomen tend to experience more anxiety and put more effort into pre-trip preparations and get greater post-travel backlash. The greater highs that women experience from the positive aspects of travel are counterbalanced by the blues that both sexes often feel when they return to the reality of home and office.

The most frequently cited tips for coping with these situations involve having slick organization at home and work, particularly the effective delegation or sharing of tasks with spouse and colleagues so that the woman traveler does not get into an overload situation either before or after a trip.

While on the road, veteran women travelers recommend, with the more stringent baggage carry-on regulations, that checked luggage be limited to one large, stiff-sided suitcase with wheels, while briefcase and soft shoulder bag are carried into the cabin. For short trips the ubiquitous garment bag is still favored if it avoids the need to check in any other luggage but can be heavy and awkward. Experienced women travelers—particularly flight attendants—make particularly good use of collapsible luggage carts. (If you are above average height, make sure that the handle extends enough to be comfortable.)

The women in the Hyatt Travel Futures Project survey voted strongly for hotels and airlines to coordinate their customer services and get baggage transferred directly from the plane to the hotel. As women tend to have more luggage—and more difficulty in handling it—their stress on business trips could be reduced considerably by selecting the hotels that are the most efficient at these tasks and that have airport transfers.

On the important security issues, there is a lot to be said for the special VIP or concierge floors, which half of the female frequent fliers surveyed said they use. The surcharge may not be very great, but the added security and better facilities of these rooms are particularly appreciated by women. A number of other things can make a woman's hotel stay safer and more enjoyable. At the check-in desk, passing over a business card establishes credibility without proclaiming who you are to everyone within earshot. It makes security sense for a woman's business card to contain only her work address details.

Really hold out for a room in an easily accessible, well-lit, secure section of the hotel, not in an annex or tucked away down a long corridor far from the elevator. Keep the room number to yourself and take care not to leave your key lying around where the number can be noted or the key stolen.

When you get to the room, especially if arriving at night, the bellhop should check it for you, making sure that the wardrobe and the bathroom do not conceal an intruder. If you return to the hotel late at night, it is reasonable to ask the porter to arrange for you to be escorted to the room.

Leaving the radio or television playing quietly and a do not disturb sign on the door when you are not in the room are deterrents to anyone who may be tempted to try to get in. Once inside, lock the door securely and fasten the chain. Some women frequent fliers carry small wedges that slip under the door and prevent it from being forced open. There is an electronic kind that will sound an alarm if an attempt is made to force the door.

Some of the more enlightened hotels go out of their way to make women comfortable in the dining rooms. Others tend to put a single woman in the most awkward place, perhaps tucked away in a gloomy corner next to the kitchens. Some train their staff specially to understand the new business environment in which women merit equal status. An indication of this may be the subtlety with which the check is presented. A sensitive waiter will usually tune in to the fact that the woman is playing the host, and if there is any doubt, will position the check on the table so that either of the parties can pick it up.

All hotels these days should make special efforts to cater for the special needs of women travelers, and if one or a chain is not coming up to scratch in this respect, avoid it and patronize another. That can be difficult when companies have done special deals to get lower corporate rates or room upgrades, but if the company's choice gives grounds for legitimate complaints from its women employees, it makes sense to review the situation or for management to give permission to use more suitable accommodation.

Men still dominate as hotel patrons, but women are becoming more important customers and have every right to insist on appropriate facilities and service. But however hard the hotels themselves try, there is a limit to what they can do to control the behavior of their guests. One London hotel, the Reeves Private Hotel in Shepherds Bush Green, tries to do that by keeping men guests away as much as it can without contravening Britain's sex discrimination laws. It concentrates on catering for women only, with special security procedures for its female clientele.

There are hotels catering specifically for businesswomen in other European cities also.

Frequent Flying Tips of Particular Interest to Women Travelers

You can rent a room for a fraction of a day—even just an hour or two—at some airport hotels to rest, change, and freshen up. A few major airports have showers and sleeping cabins.

Need a quiet, secure place between flights or when delayed? Some airports have chapels, which can be great refuges.

Check with airline personnel or airport information for special facilities for children. Some international airports have nurseries or play areas.

Don't forget your favorite skin moisturizer—dry climates and excessive air conditioning, coupled with hard water, can make skin excessively dry. Cleansing lotions and creams are practical and convenient for men as well as women, although most men don't seem to know it. Even if you do not use eyedrops normally, they can be a boon when traveling to freshen dry, tired eyes.

Travel with cosmetics packed in tubes when possible—they're convenient, lighter, and more leakproof than tubs or bottles. Petroleum jelly—Vaseline—in a tube is a great multipurpose traveler's standby.

Check the effect of your makeup coloring, especially lipstick, under the often widely varying lighting away from home.

Pack a head scarf for emergency warmth, protection against rain or wind, and to avoid offense if you are visiting churches in the many countries where women are still expected to have their heads covered in places of worship.

Be careful what you trust to the laundry in countries where clothes washing is still equated with very hot, even boiling, water. If you plan to do some overnight washing yourself, you can decant small quantities of your favorite detergent into sandwich bags to take with you, buy detergent in sachets, or use shampoo in an emergency.

A fast fix for wrinkled clothes is to hang them over a bathtub filled with steaming hot water or in the bathroom while showering.

Keep to your diet and stretch your budget by avoiding the hotel restaurant and eating at health food or vegetarian restaurants, now to be found in every city.

Nervous about going out alone at night? Many cities offer guided tours of night spots, enabling you to join a group and usually save a lot of money.

Want to take gifts for hosts overseas? Duty-free scotch or bourbon, or American cigarettes or cigars are much appreciated by drinkers and smokers in countries like Japan and England, where these items are heavily taxed. American magazines and novel costume jewelry also make inexpensive but appreciated gifts that are easy to pack.

Ask to see your room before checking in at a hotel to make sure it is secure and satisfactory in other respects.

Prepare to have your hand kissed when introduced to men, especially on formal occasions, in some European countries. It is no longer commonplace but may still happen. The proper etiquette is for his lips not to touch your skin—if they do, he's trying to come on! In Japan bow slightly as you present your visiting card, which should have a Japanese translation on the reverse if you are doing serious business there.

PREGNANT FLIERS

The physical and mental stress associated with flying is likely to cause more discomfort to women when they are pregnant, but there is little specific danger to mother or child.

Nausea may be a problem in the early weeks of pregnancy, and the stressors of travel may slightly increase the risk of premature birth in the later stages, but there are no accurate statistics on this. Airlines are reluctant to carry expectant mothers in the ninth month, and a letter from the obstetrician saying that it is all right for the woman to fly is a useful precaution from the seventh month onward. If nothing else it may save arguments at the check-in desk.

Many of the problems of sitting down for long periods in an aircraft are worse during pregnancy, particularly swelling and impeded blood circulation in the legs. So regular exercise during a long flight, wearing loose clothing, attention to diet, and other measures should be followed.

Take along written details of key facts about the pregnancy in the event that medical treatment is needed. This should include the predicted date for the birth, any complications expected, blood pressure and blood type, medication being taken, and emergency contact numbers for both doctor and nearest relative.

If the seat belt will not fasten comfortably, the flight attendant will be able to supply an extension. It is safer for both mother and child to buckle up, even in the later stages of pregnancy, than to go unbelted.

Occasionally babies are born on commercial flights, but contrary to popular belief, the odds against are so long that flight attendants do not get any special training on how to cope with emergency births.

When Things Go Wrong

If They Hassle You Hassle Them
How to complain and get your rights—
and more

One consequence of airline deregulation is that travelers now have to fight most of their own battles when things go wrong. You can lose your temper, phone the Department of Transportation's hot line, threaten legal action, or run to the nearest Better Business Bureau. None of those actions will do you much good unless you know your rights and act promptly and appropriately to get satisfaction.

How well you will fare if things go wrong can depend on routine actions taken well before the trip begins. For example, it is becoming a golden rule of frequent business or leisure travel to avoid paying cash whenever you can. The best tactic is to use a credit card, the next to charge or write a check so that you at least have the threat of withholding payment money to support your complaint.

CREDIT CARDS

Paying with plastic gives you all kinds of legal rights and protection—and it gives you access to a skilled and powerful team at the issuing bank or card company who may fight your legitimate battles for you at no charge.

Often your possibilities of recourse if you have paid for a flight by credit card go beyond the basic written rules. These stipulate that you can get a refund for any ticket you buy with a credit card within seven days of the purchase. This in theory excludes heavily discounted and other fares described specifically as being nonrefundable. However, that rule gets bent frequently if the card company backs up a customer with a legitimate grievance.

Indeed, the credit card company should prove your ally at any stage of travel in which you get bad or dishonest service or if you feel there has been a breach in the actual or implied contract between yourself and the travel service supplier. Notify the company immediately about the problem, supplying copies of all documentation, and respond again in writing if or when the relevant charge crops up on your monthly statement.

PASSENGERS' RIGHTS

The ticket issued when you book your flight is a contract between the airline and you and should state on it any major restrictions. However, since deregulation it is routine for the ticket to refer to the individual airline's rule book, or *Conditions of Contract of Carriage*. These are bulky documents full of all kinds of obscure policies that most airlines' staff are not familiar with—or may even be unable to find if you try to exercise your right as a passenger to see a copy.

The only way to negotiate this maze if you have a problem is to know that some basic passenger rights are still protected by federal legislation. In other cases the airline personnel have considerable flexibility to interpret or bend the rules, and there are some insider tips to increase your chances of getting what you want if you adopt the appropriate strategy.

Refunds

Suppose problems arise before departure. You seek a refund on a nonrefundable ticket and the credit card refund procedure is not available to you. Still do not despair. Many travel agents are able to juggle with reservations and void tickets they have sold, even nonrefundable ones. They are not supposed to in most cases, but it obviously makes good business sense for an agent to make that kind of effort for a good customer, especially an executive able to influence a major corporate travel account.

However, the agents do risk retribution from the airlines if they are found out, and an agent may not be able to void a nonrefundable ticket if the system has already charged the cost to the agent's account. Remember also that some agents are trading in seats for which they have made block bookings—they are effectively reselling seats they own—and this should give them greater flexibility if pressured to alter travel plans.

Even nonrefundable tickets can usually be changed or a refund made in the event of exceptional medical or compassionate grounds. Some doctors are very flexible about issuing medical notes to patients, even to the point of conspiring to defraud the airlines. That is not a praiseworthy practice, but it happens. The rules about refunds on medical grounds vary a lot between airlines. Even if a request is turned down at the first attempt in strict accordance with the rule book, it may be worth persisting with alternative ways of putting pressure on the carrier. We look at them in more detail later.

You are entitled to a refund—even on a nonrefundable ticket—if your flight is canceled, because that is a clear breach of the contract that the airline has made with you. Adverse weather conditions, mechanical problems with the plane, and a crew not being available are the few main reasons why a carrier is legally entitled to cancel, not because there are too few passengers to make the flight an economically viable proposition. Passengers may speculate that this is a frequent reason for cancellation, but such suspicions are almost impossible to prove. Anyway, it would not make much sense for an airline to engage in this practice frequently because aircraft are such capital-intensive equipment that flights are scheduled in a complex, interlinking way to make the best use of them every hour of the day and night. To save operating costs by frequently canceling uneconomic flights would result in a chaotic chain reaction throughout a fleet.

The airline is not obliged to get you another flight if it does cancel the one for which you have a confirmed booking, but may according to its individual rules and policies make a refund instead.

The refund must be made within seven days if you paid by credit card. You may have to wait a month if you have paid by cash or check. Usually the airline will try to get you on its next flight to your destination, but if that is not convenient for you, insist on being switched to the first available flight by any other carrier. The airline personnel may resist, but it can pay to be insistent.

Bumping

In cancellations, overbooking, and any similar situation in which there is a face-off and apparent impasse between a passenger and the airline staff, it may pay to move away from the confusion around the departure gate. Go to the nearest phone and get directly on to the airline or your travel agent, tell them the problem and get them working immediately to find you a solution. If you have planned ahead and know already what alternative flights are available to you from competing airlines if your original schedule is disrupted, go straight to one of those competitors and make a booking. (That is the kind of situation in which the *PC Flight Guide* computer program on a laptop can be invaluable—see page 383 for details.)

Such tactics should give you the edge over other passengers who also want to switch flights. However, if delays in your trip are not critical for you, then a cancellation or being bumped can be a bonus.

Airlines routinely overbook because a significant proportion of passengers with refundable tickets do not show to take up their reservations. Some frequent fliers who are uncertain which flight they will be able to catch place multiple reservations. This makes flying a lottery, and on any trip you may become one of the nearly one million passengers who are bumped in the United States every year.

Annoying as that may be, if your number comes up in the lottery, you can ride with the situation and be as much as $1,000 better off, or use the system to get satisfactory compensation. However, to win in this game you must follow the basic rules, the most important of which is to get to the airport within the stipulated check-in time. If you are late for the check-in, you may get bumped without compensation. If you miss the flight altogether, you may be penalized, although airline policies differ greatly. Some will not punish you if there are exceptional provable reasons for your delay, such as heavy traffic or a breakdown on the way to the airport.

If the flight is overbooked, the usual first course for the airline is to ask for volunteers to give up their seats. The incentives offered vary between airlines and circumstances, together with the differing degrees of discretion exercised by the airline staff on the spot. If the initial response is not sufficient, they may up the ante to give further encouragement. For example, the first offer may be for travel vouchers of $300. If that does not generate sufficient volunteers, the compensation may go up to $500. It can top $1,000 in exceptional circumstances on intercontinental flights.

If you volunteer and the incentive is increased before your voucher is issued and ticket changed, insist on getting the greater amount. Any incentive should be over and above—and not a substitute for—the cost of getting you to your destination as soon as possible. Some airlines will give bumped volunteers—or the victims of a canceled flight—a free ticket anywhere on their system, plus meals, hotel accommodation, compensation for telephone calls, and other benefits. Sometimes getting the best deal is a real horse-trading situation and battle of wits. Don't be overly tempted in your bargaining by the offer of being placed on the standby list for any flight; it's not worth much. Be wary also of compensation in cash or kind that will be whittled away by the real cost to you of being delayed.

If there are not sufficient volunteers to be bumped, the airline personnel will make their own selection and may only give compensation according to the minimum federal scale. The airline is obliged to give you a written statement describing your rights, together with an explanation of how they selected who should fly and who was bumped. Again, the ways airlines make these choices vary considerably. Usually children and handicapped passengers are given priority, or those who pay the higher fares are selected. Often the first passengers to get bumped are those who checked in last.

If the airline can still get you to your destination—and that includes onward connections—within an hour of the scheduled time, then you are not entitled to any compensation. If you are going to be delayed by more than one hour but less than two on domestic flights, or less than four hours on international flights, then you are entitled to at least an amount equal to the one-way fare, or $200, whichever is less.

A delay of over two hours on domestic flights in reaching your destination, or over four hours on international routes, entitles you to double the compensation—the lesser of twice the one-way fare or $400. Remember, this is *compensation*, over and above the value of your original ticket, which you either transfer to another flight or get refunded.

The airlines have some escape clauses in the federal regulations. They may avoid bumping compensation if charter flights are overbooked, if a smaller plane is substituted for the one scheduled and not all the passengers will fit on, or if the plane involved holds sixty or fewer passengers. Passengers also lose their rights if they miss the deadlines for either the issue of the ticket or the actual physical check-in.

The motto is to get to the airport early, in good time

to collect your ticket if it is being issued there *and* to pass through the actual check-in procedure. Some airlines and some flights stipulate that the check-in is actually at the boarding gate, so you need to allow time to get through the ticketing, baggage check-in, and security procedures. In these days of concern about terrorism and airport congestion, you may need thirty minutes or more after arrival at the gate to get to the actual boarding area and so qualify as having checked in timeously. Even if you do get there on time, your chances of being bumped are increased by being among the last to arrive. Like the early bird getting the worm, it is the early passenger who stands the best chance of catching the plane.

If you are bumped without volunteering and are only offered free flight vouchers or other compensation in kind, you can still opt for the legal cash compensation. Usually the airline's offer will have a face value of more than the legal compensation figure, but it may not be worth more to you. If you prefer a check and the right to use your ticket or get a refund, insist on being compensated accordingly. You can hold on to the check—usually for thirty days—and try to improve the deal by taking the airline to court or negotiating with its complaints department.

Once you have cashed the airline's check or accepted vouchers, free tickets, or other compensation, you probably have lost your rights to go after the airline for any more.

Although the highly competitive field of air travel is making generous compensation for being bumped more widespread, you must be prepared to press for an attractive deal. Overseas, including on flights bound for the United States, procedures vary greatly and may not be as satisfactory as those for U.S. domestic flights. While the majority of European airlines offer similar compensation to passengers when they are bumped and pay actual out-of-pocket expenses incurred by cancellations or overbooking, there are few standardized practices.

Nowhere in the world are you likely to get more than free meals or accommodation for delays caused by technical problems, labor disputes, or the weather—and you may have to hassle for them. There is no obligation on the part of any airline to compensate for delayed arrivals if takeoff was on time, even if that delay means you miss a connection for another flight with the same carrier. But air travel is a highly competitive service business; passengers who protest and demand quality treatment usually get at least some satisfaction. That compensation when things go wrong is much easier to get in kind than in cash. The on-the-spot airline personnel have considerably greater flexibility—more than they may reveal—to give away free tickets or provide meals and accommodation than to offer actual cash in compensation.

You certainly stand no chance of getting a cash payment for consequential losses caused by a canceled, delayed, or overbooked flight—even if you missed the deal of the century. Of course, there is always the option to sue the airline for breach of contract or some other offense, but they fight tooth and nail not to let any legal precedents be set for their responsibility to get you either off the ground or to your destination on time.

That is understandable because with all the modern technology of the aviation industry, airline timekeeping is still pathetic. In a typical month, at least one in four of the domestic flights operated by the twelve largest American airlines fails to arrive within fifteen minutes of its scheduled time, and those Department of Transportation figures do not include delays caused by mechanical problems.

Complaining

The proportion of passengers who complain varies as widely between airlines as do the policies they apply in dealing with those complaints and their actual performance from month to month in the quality of service they provide. DoT figures for April 1989 showed that Pan Am received 7.58 complaints for every 100,000 passengers, the worst among the major airlines, but a year previously Continental was at the bottom of the list with 14.94 complaints per 100,000 passengers.

So it is impossible to recommend which airlines are likely to give you least cause for complaint at any given time. Taken on average over an extended period, they are all very much as good—or as bad, depending on your viewpoint—as each other. But there are consistencies on *how* to complain to all of them, the main constant being to insist on receiving quality and vigorously pursue your demand for compensation if that quality is not delivered.

If you do not get satisfaction from the airline staff face to face, then a detailed letter—especially under a corporate letter heading—should bring results. Address your complaint to the consumer affairs or customer service department, or to the frequent flier program if you are a member, with the full details of your flight and ticket numbers, the date, and so on, together with copies—not originals—of all the relevant documentation. Give a daytime telephone number because most airlines are sufficiently customer-oriented to want to follow up legitimate complaints promptly. Irrational, hysterical, or petty moans are unlikely to be treated so well.

"Don't clutter up your complaint with petty gripes that can obscure what you're really angry about," advises the DoT in its useful *Fly-Rights, A Guide to Air Travel in the U.S.* "No matter how angry you might be, keep your letter businesslike in tone and don't exaggerate what happened."

The DoT recommends being specific about what you expect the carrier to do to make amends for any inconvenience. If you want an apology from a rude flight attendant, compensation for a hotel room, a refund, or a free flight voucher, spell it out, as long as it is a fair reaction to what you have suffered.

NEARLY THREE MILLION PARTS

Next time your jumbo jet is delayed because of mechanical problems, rather than getting angry, marvel at the technological skills that enable a device with over 2.5 million components to function efficiently for the great majority of the time.

Other facts about the Boeing 747: The first one entered service in 1970, and more than eight hundred have been built since. There are various versions, some stretching the normal capacity of about five hundred passengers, extending the range of seven thousand miles or supplying special military or freight-carrying needs.

"Be reasonable," advises DoT. "If your demands are way out of line, your letter might earn you a polite apology and a place in the airline's crank files."

If you do not get any satisfaction from the airline—or from the airport if its service, facilities, or personnel are the cause of your complaint—you can get advice from the DoT's Office of Community and Consumer Affairs. They will at least investigate if your complaint was properly handled. It is best to telephone—202 366-2220—but if you prefer to write, give a daytime telephone number for a faster response. The address is 400 7th Street, S.W., Room 1045, Washington, DC 20590.

Complaints about airline safety should be sent to the Community and Consumer Liaison Division of the Federal Aviation Administration, 800 Independence Avenue, S.W., Washington DC 20591, 202 267-3481.

If all else fails it may pay to take the matter up with your state or city office for consumer problems. Airlines

BUMPED FOR BEING TOO FAT!

Being overweight can add to the discomfort of flying; it might even get you bumped from a flight.

Just that happened to twelve passengers on an Olympic Airways Boeing 737 flight from the island of Samos to Athens in 1989. The weight ratio of passengers to fuel and luggage was too high, an Olympic Airways spokesman told Reuters to explain the two-hour delay in takeoff.

There was a vigorous argument among the passengers and the crew until agreement was reached on the twelve passengers who were most overweight and should wait for the next flight to Athens.

---

are also sensitive to complaints that generate publicity, so the radio, telephone, and newspaper consumer reporters often get results when other attempts fail.

Complaining about poor service or more serious problems with other travel-related businesses can be more difficult because they are less closely regulated than the airlines. The bigger and better hotel groups generally respond well to complaints addressed to the consumer relations department at head office. City and state consumer affairs offices can also play a role—often with legal clout because hotels are subject to a wide variety of local and state ordinances. One little-known aspect of this situation is that in most states, hotels and inns may be held liable for property stolen from rooms, despite all their disclaimers to the contrary.

The large car rental groups handle complaints in much the same ways as hotels. There is no independent government or volunteer agency you can go to, but their head offices will try to resolve problems, and if you are not satisfied with their response, you can pursue the matter through consumer groups.

The ultimate sanction for the dissatisfied frequent flier is to stay at home. That was the advice given by Patrick K. Stewart of ConAgra Inc., Santa Clara, California, in a letter to *The Wall Street Journal* complaining about the problems of air travel.

"The critical issue for the traveler is the loss of productivity when faced with delays, lousy service, and overcrowding," wrote Mr. Stewart. "What I as a business traveler and manager of manufacturing company intend to do is find alternative systems to replace the necessity for business travel, and get these systems in place as quickly as possible.

"Teleconferencing equipment, fax machines, conferencing computers and express mail are bringing into play systems that replace the traditional customer call or company meeting. And we are only a step away from truly significant breakthroughs in television conferencing.

"The airlines lost control when they determined that price was the key factor in their business. The fact is that schedule reliability and hassle-free service are the dominant requirements."

TRAPPED ON THE GROUND

One of the most frustrating, high-stress elements of flying occurs on the ground, when passengers are trapped inside a plane during a delayed takeoff.

This situation can result from many factors—mechanical problems, the weather (such as a windshear warning), security scare, traffic congestion. The sense of loss of control, such a stress factor in flying, is aggravated when the flight crew fail to explain the reason for the delay and refuse permission to disembark—even when the plane is still at the gate with the door open.

Passengers have been confined in planes without air conditioning or access to the toilets for hours on end—it is akin to being hijacked. Some have rebelled against instructions to remain on board and left to seek alternative flights. Such action may aggravate the problem for other passengers and cause further delays, particularly over the identification of baggage in these security-conscious times.

The legal position is unclear and seems to depend entirely on individual circumstances. An airline may not be held liable for keeping someone on board against their will except in such extreme cases as illness. On the other hand, it would be difficult for an airline to take action against passengers who refused to be confined unreasonably. Passengers who left a plane kept on the ground for more than three hours in New York sued for damages and received an out-of-court settlement in their favor.

In other instances passengers who insisted on being treated in a more considerate manner at least received an explanation for the delay and in some instances were taken off the plane and compensated with food, accommodation, and alternative flights, while their more tolerant fellow passengers continued to suffer.

As on-the-ground delays are a fact of frequent flying, it may be worth taking precautionary measures, including packing snacks, especially when traveling with young children. The failure to supply food and drink during these delays is partly poor service by the airlines but also a consequence of the regulations preventing planes from taking off before the impedimenta of catering are collected and safely stowed. It may aggravate the delay if drinks and snacks are served to several hundred passengers and everything is cleared away before clearance for takeoff is given.

Denying passengers permission to disembark during intermediate or refueling stops can happen for a number of valid reasons, particularly on international flights. In some cases this hinges entirely on local health and agricultural restrictions designed to reduce the risk of introducing infections to a country. If this is the case, the flight crew should explain.

In the event of mechanical malfunction, it may be impossible for the captain, when making a decision about disembarking, to know how long it will take to diagnose and fix a problem. He may wrongly guess this against the time taken to unload and reload several hundred passengers. At least the crew should go out of their way to relay messages to families and business contacts for passengers who have critical schedules that are being affected by delays.

There are also various practical and technical reasons why it may not be possible to show a movie, feed, or otherwise entertain the frustrated passengers during the delay. You really are trapped when you are grounded in this way, so an essential technique of defensive flying is to be prepared both emotionally and functionally.

You have lost control and there is probably nothing you can do about the situation, so proper acceptance of that fact can help to reduce the anger, frustration, and associated stress. Having a snack, or at least something to suck, will help any hunger or thirst pangs that cannot be satisfied—and perhaps ease the craving of smokers who are prevented from lighting up. Really addicted smokers who fly frequently may use nicotine gum to reduce the craving.

The in-flight exercises in this book will help to ease the main physical problems of being confined for an extended period. A good printed or recorded book, or some work that you can get on with, will prevent the delay from being regarded as time wasted.

Best of all, if you have come prepared with strategies designed to make all the time spent traveling quality time, then the delay may even seem to be a bonus!

In his syndicated newspaper column on achieving corporate excellence, author and business consultant Tom Peters advocated that we use our traveling time—including the delays—for original thinking. Time used in this way is never wasted.

WHEN ALL ELSE FAILS

The best way to resolve complaints is in direct negotiation with the offending company on the spot. When that fails, contact the head office, and if that does not bring satisfaction, there may be a trade association or third-party organization prepared to help resolve disputes. The addresses of some that can play these roles are listed below.

The easiest and cheapest way to complain to a company is to call its 800 number if it has one. To find the number, AT&T offers 800 directory assistance on 800 555-1212.

If you need to write, call the company's 800 number for the address and preferably the name of the president. Complaints sent by name to the top person seem on average to bring better results. Or your local library should be able to find the relevant address details from the Consumer's Resource Handbook or one of the directories of organizations, corporations, trademark owners, and advertisers.

There are about 170 Better Business Bureaus in the United States, and your local one may be able to help— even to provide binding arbitration to resolve your complaint.

Many federal agencies settle complaints, and those most relevant to the traveler are listed below as well. Readily accessible sources of assistance are the state, county, and city government consumer offices. Most of them require complaints to be made in writing, but will explain over the telephone the procedure to follow.

Sample complaint letter.

(Your Address)
(Your City, State, ZIP Code)
(Date)

(Name of Contact Person)
(Title)
(Company Name)
(Street Address)
(City, State, ZIP Code)

Describe your purchase

Name of product, serial numbers,

Include date and location of purchase

Ask for specific action

Enclose copies of documents

Dear (Contact Person):

Last week I purchased (or had repaired) a (name of the product with serial or model number or service performed). I made this purchase at (location, date, and other important details of the transaction).

Unfortunately, your product (or service) has not performed satisfactorily (or the service was inadequate) because (state the problem).

Therefore, to solve the problem, I would appreciate your (state the specific action you want). Enclosed are copies (copies — NOT originals) of my records (receipts, guarantees, warranties, canceled checks, contracts, model and serial numbers, and any other documents).

I am looking forward to your reply and resolution of my problem, and will wait (set time limit) before seeking third-party assistance. Contact me at the above address or by phone at (home and office numbers — with area codes).

Sincerely,

(Your name)
(Your account number, if appropriate)

State the problem

Give the history

Allow time for action or response

Include how you can be reached

Keep copies of your letter and all related documents and information

When making a written complaint, the U.S. Office of Consumer Affairs recommends being brief and to the point but giving full details. Their recommended sample complaint letter for all consumer problems is reproduced on page 319.

The following are addresses of some of the more useful national organizations that may be able to help as last resorts.

Department of Transportation

Airline Passenger Complaints
Office of Intergovernmental and Consumer Affairs
Department of Transportation
Washington, DC 20690
202 366-2850

Air Safety
Federal Aviation Administration
Community and Consumer Liaison Division
Department of Transportation
Washington, DC 20690
800 FAA-SURE

Railroads
Federal Railroad Administration
Department of Transportation
Washington, DC 20690
202 366-0522

U.S. Customs Service

Department of the Treasury
1301 Constitution Avenue, N.W.
Washington, DC 20229
202 287-4097

Federal Maritime Commission

Office of Informal Inquiries & Complaints
1100 L Street N.W.
Washington, DC 20573
202 523-5807

Department of State

Overseas Citizen Services
Department of State
Washington, DC 20520
202 647-3666

Passport Services
1425 K Street, N.W.
Washington, DC 20520
202 523-1355

Visa Services
Department of State
Washington, DC 20520
202 663-1972

Other Agencies

International Airline Passengers Association
P.O. Box 660074
Dallas, TX 75266
214 520-1070

Airline Passengers of America
4424 King Street
Alexandria, VA 22302
703 824-0505

American Hotel and Motel Association
888 Seventh Avenue
New York, NY 10106

American Automobile Association
811 Gatehouse Road
Falls Church, VA 22047
703 222-6446

American Society of Travel Agents
PO Box 23992
Washington, DC 20026
703 739-2782

Automotive Consumer Action Program
8400 Westpark Drive
McLean, VA 22209
703 276-0100

Insurance Information Institute
110 William Street
New York, NY 10038
212 669-9200 or 800 221-4954

The International Association of Travel Research and Marketing Professionals
c/o Travel and Tourism Research Association
P.O. Box 8066, Foothill Station
Salt Lake City, UT 84108

Council of Better Business Bureaus
845 Third Avenue
New York, NY 10022
212 754-1320

U.S. Tour Operators Association
211 East 51st Street
New York, NY 10022
212 944-5727

The travel editor of your local paper or your favorite magazine may seem a promising last resort of complaint. However, much travel writing is influenced by the advertising muscle of the airlines and other providers of travel-related services—plus the practice of providing all kinds of attractive incentives to both staff and free-lance journalists who cover the travel scene. These incentives may fall short of payola, but they are a very real factor in distorting media coverage of the travel scene and inhibiting investigatory zeal in pursuing readers' complaints.

So you may make more progress by directing your complaint to journalists specializing in consumer affairs rather than to those on the travel beat.

The Future

Many of the less desirable aspects of business travel may well get worse before they get better, but the long-term prognosis is for more relaxed, convenient, safer and less stressful business travel. The future for the frequent flier is exciting. Technology will bring important benefits in comfort and convenience, ranging from larger and faster aircraft to completely new forms of in-flight entertainment. Airports and hotels are changing to meet the needs of the business traveler in particular, but demographic trends make the leisure traveler another increasingly important influence.

Some change is being accelerated by critical concerns about air safety. The terrorist threat demands better security, particularly in the monitoring of baggage. If the whole system is not to seize up, that tighter security must be accompanied by more efficient ways of dealing with baggage—which should as a by-product reduce losses and delays.

The spate of mechanical failures in aging commercial jet aircraft in 1989 prompted a drastic reappraisal by the airlines of their fleet replacement policies. As passengers showed the first tendencies to make their travel choices based on such safety factors as an airline's maintenance reputation and the age of its planes, there has been a dramatic increase in the orders for new aircraft. This in turn will stimulate the more rapid introduction of new technology—but must also increase the pressure to raise airfares, which are already on a sharply upward trend.

The Hyatt Travel Futures Project team asked the hundreds of respondents what developments they would like to see take place. A popular and achievable suggestion is to be able to go directly to a preassigned hotel room without having to check in at the front desk—just as credit cards have made it possible to leave without the frustration of waiting in a long line at the desk because every guest wants to arrive or check out at about the same peak time.

Frequent business travelers, especially women, voted strongly for a way to have their baggage transferred directly from their plane to their hotel room. This would avoid the time-wasting and physical and mental stress at present associated with collecting your own bags from the baggage claim, humping them out of the terminal to the ground transportation, and all the other hassles.

Bar coding of all bags to track them from the moment of check-in will probably become a univerally adopted luggage-handling technology, if only for security reasons. Bar codes are capable of conveying a great deal of information, so it will become conceivable for hotels and airlines to coordinate their baggage services, at least in getting bags directly from planes to hotels. Taking over this chore from the passenger in the reverse direction could prove more difficult because of security considerations, but that is not an insuperable problem and would be an important benefit for the individual business traveler which holiday makers on group package tours often enjoy already.

The business travelers surveyed also voted strongly for better office facilities at hotels. Those who displayed the greatest enthusiasm for this development were male travelers who reported high levels of travel-related stress. So expect easier access to fax and photocopying machines and personal computers in hotels in the future as a direct reaction to this need of the Family Tieds, Tightrope Walkers, Eagles, and Road Warriors alike.

There are lots of other exciting developments on the horizon. Let's take an imaginary business trip in the future to learn what we can anticipate for the next couple of decades.

We decide to make the trip at the last minute to tackle firsthand a crisis at a distant branch office. But that presents no problem. A few keystrokes on the desktop PC connect us to a database and the recommended most convenient available flights at the most competitive fares.

We click the button on the mouse—or just dictate our instructions if we have voice recognition hardware—to specify our flight decisions. We get immediate confirmation of the airline, departure and arrival times, and seat allocation. There are no smoking or nonsmoking choices these days—all smoking on U.S. domestic flights was banned in the early 1990s. But we are able to choose our meals a la carte in advance from the colored graphic display menu, and the computer gives us an immediate calorie count as it confirms the order.

We are business class frequent fliers, and the database has already checked and confirmed that our preferred aisle seats are available and that our favorite cocktails will be ready and waiting when we board. The laser printer by the desk prints out our ticket and bar-coded baggage tags. At the same time, the cost of the fares is deducted from the corporate travel account and our frequent flier programs provisionally credited with the correct mileage.

The computer prompts us to decide about a hotel booking and car hire. We key in the hotel reservation—and get a further automatic frequent flier program credit. The computer's speaker emits the familiar jangle of a slot machine scoring a jackpot. We have reached a bonus point level that qualifies us for an automatic room upgrade. The hotel is running a promotion and is offering a second night at half price if we want to stay over. This is scheduled to be quick turnaround trip, so we decline.

There is no need to alter the database records of our preferences for a nonsmoking room, Perrier water, tomato juice and vodka in the icebox, and dark rather than milk chocolate for a snack. The room air conditioning will be set to our preferred level and our favorite daily newspaper will be delivered the following morning. The hotel has special preview cassettes of three new movies not released to the theaters yet, and we pick one we particularly want to see. The cassette will be waiting in the room so that we can screen it at any time. Freedom of choice is a key element of both business and leisure travel in the future.

The room upgrade is good news because that class of room provides a personal computer with modem. There will be no need to take the laptop with us on this trip. Any messages to our electronic mailbox will automatically be forwarded so as to be accessible from the hotel room for the duration of our stay. Urgent ones will set off a flashing light by the bed and be available for instant display on the monitor or for printing out.

A few minutes after making our travel arrangements, another beep from the office desktop announces that the airport shuttle coach will be arriving at the street intersection by the corner of our building in about thirty minutes. Do we want it to stop for us?

The timing is right for our flight, as the shuttle dispatcher's computer knew it would be as soon as the air reservation's computer informed him of our flight booking. We confirm and get together the papers we will need for the trip. Fortunately we have an emergency overnight bag already in the office, although even without it there would be no need to go home to pack as disposable socks, underwear, and a shirt from the hotel shop could tide us over on this short journey.

However, we need to take a case of samples as well, so we decide to check in both bags and attach a bar coded label to each of them. Although the labels were printed by the office laser, the code and the routing details, like those on our ticket, were generated by the airline's mainframe computer and contain all the information required to handle our baggage from the moment we put it on board the airboard shuttle in the street below to the time when the bellhop delivers it to our hotel bedroom.

The computer beeps again. The shuttle will arrive in ten minutes, so we collect everything and head for the street.

The shuttle bus gets held up by a red light, so it is a minute or so late, but soon our bags are in its luggage compartment and we are on board. The driver is already pulling away from the curb as the optical scanner reads our plane ticket. The video display in front of the driver changes to record the fact that he has other passengers to drop off at International Air's departure area in terminal three. The computer on board the bus also notes that our corporate account is to be charged for two fares from the city center to the terminal, information that will be transferred to the central database when the bus returns to its depot at the end of the driver's shift.

The video screen directs the driver to two more pickups in the center of the city, then displays the fastest route to the airport according to prevailing traffic conditions. The seats on the small bus are very comfortable, each with a telephone extension so that we can make a couple of calls that we did not have time to complete before leaving the office. The video monitor overhead is alternating the cable news headlines with the stock market closing prices, and we are able to listen to the audio by leaning back in our seats so that our head triggers a micro-switch and turns on a speaker concealed in the seat headrest.

When we reach the airport terminal, we walk straight from the bus to the departure gate, confidently leaving our luggage to be unloaded, put on the conveyors, and delivered directly to the plane. It will not be loaded on board until the scanners at the departure gate have read the bar code on our ticket, verified our identity from the central database files of our voice and hand prints, and confirmed that we actually board the plane. As we walk through the departure terminal, we have to clear a number of security checks—some automated metal detectors and vapor sniffers, others staffed by security personnel. No major alert is in progress today, and the atmosphere is relaxed and well under control.

A notice board near the gate displays a formal announcement that bomb threats have been made against all International Air's flights this month, but the passengers hardly give it a second glance. The notice was a mandatory legal procedure following a California court case a couple of years previously, but as so many hoaxes and false alarms are being made, it is virtually impossible to find a plane that is not the subject of some kind of threat. The security technology and procedures have become so much better than they were in the 1980s that we passengers feel more confident trusting our safety to the airport and airline experts.

We no longer need boarding passes, as our ticket contains all the essential information to enable airlines to control their passenger inventories far more efficiently than any of the old manual or computerized systems of the past. In fact, the ticket produced by the laser printer in our office becomes a kind of smart card; its magnetic strip will acquire information and store data needed during our trip by the airlines, hotels, and other providers of travel-related services.

This technology advanced particularly rapidly because of the need to tackle the security problems that arose from terrorism and threats of sabotage in the 1980s, but it has brought lots of other benefits. The stress levels of the business trip in the future are much less, and substantial time is saved, because even when traveling at a peak period, we encounter very few delays and virtually no queues at any of the points where passengers used to get held up. Our smart ticket interacts with computerized machines very rapidly, although airport and airline staff are still around in substantial numbers for supplementary security and to provide any human assistance required.

Our plane is a new-generation stretch jumbo, carrying 850 passengers at subsonic speeds. From the outside it looks very similar to those of the 1980s, which are still flying, many having been updated to share important cabin features with this new model. The seats are the most obvious development, especially in business and first class. They are a real tribute to evolutionary design, actually taking up less space than the older versions but offering significantly more room for the passengers and far more comfortable.

A really welcome improvement is the control panel, which enables us to customize the seat to our individual requirements by lengthening the seat squab and moving the head and arm rests in several planes. We can increase the degree of lumbar support for our lower back and make very precise adjustments around the area of our head and neck, thanks to small inflatable sections built into the seat.

The drop-down table is also a cleverly designed console, incorporating a small color video screen for a selection of in-flight movies, music videos, business and children's programs, a continually updated display of the flight status with such details as ground speed and estimated time of arrival, and a view of the ground below from a video camera mounted in the nose of the plane. That camera gives really sensational pictures of takeoffs and landings.

One armrest can be opened up to reveal a joystick with buttons to control a selection of video games, including some new releases the producers supply to the airlines ahead of their full market release in an enterprising product promotion program.

Passengers who have work to do can ask the flight attendant for a small keyboard and portable disk drive, which plug into sockets in the console and turn the video into the display monitor for a personal computer terminal. You can load and store data on diskettes supplied by the airline, which are compatible with all the most popular computers back home or in the office.

There is, of course, a cellular telephone extension concealed in one of the seat's armrests on which we can receive as well as make calls. Some planes even have a fax machine on board, although most people really operating under pressure take and receive encoded documents via the computer terminals, modems, and telephones in their individual seat consoles.

The consoles in the coach section of the plane contain only the video and audio entertainment facilities, but have the same crisp, clear five-inch liquid crystal screens of the more expensive seats. This technology first appeared in smaller prototypes tested by Northwest, Qantas, and British Airways in 1988 and 1989. The passengers loved it because of the freedom of choice it offered, not only for those selecting a program to watch but for other passengers who prefer to read or look out of the window. The LCD screens are so efficient that there is no need to lower the window shades or dim the cabin lights to see the picture clearly.

The range of programs on some flights is enormous because the plane of the future can pick up national and international broadcast television services by tuning in to their satellite signals. In areas of poor reception, there is always a good selection of video programs carried on board from which to select.

The same unit displays details of the in-flight menu and items available from the cabin bar service, so you can leisurely select your meals and drinks and send the order through to the flight attendants just by highlighting your choice and pressing a button. One channel on international flights takes you on an audiovisual tour of the duty-free shops at the airport you are heading toward. You can compare prices and select attractive items, then radio ahead your shopping choices so that they are waiting for you as you disembark.

This is not only convenient for passengers, but it saves the aviation industry a great deal of money in fuel costs every year. We now look back with amazement at the ridiculous situation of the 1980s and early 1990s, when at any given time, thousands of tons of liquor and other duty-free goods were being flown wastefully round the world. In those bad old days you might, for example, buy a bottle of Johnnie Walker Red Label Scotch whisky in the free shop at JFK Airport in New York and lug it with you into the cabin for its second expensive Trans-Atlantic crossing to Scotland, just because of quirks in international pricing practices and revenue taxes and duties. Not only did all those duty-free goods being flown needlessly around the world consume fuel, they also caused inconvenience and cluttered up the cabins to the point of being dangerous in an emergency. The airlines like this new system for purchasing duty-free goods, as now they only need to carry on board the liquor they serve for actual consumption in flight. Passengers who want to buy duty-free bottles to take with them order these via the video shopping service and collect them when they disembark. The airline automatically gets credited with a sales commission.

Of course, the channels on the entertainment console built into the seats enable you to change your onward flights, buy tickets, make hotel and theater reservations, book rental cars, and connect with other travel services.

While the seating in coach class is less luxurious than business or first class, it is still far more comfortable than the equivalent of even a few years ago. Some flights even have versions of special bunk seats in all their fare classes, stacked three high in coach, doubled up in business class and in the form of luxurious singles fully convertible from seats into bunks for first class passengers.

It was found that on long overnight flights, a significant number of frequent travelers, particularly businesspeople, wanted more than anything else to lie down and spend most of the trip reading or sleeping. They gladly gave up full meals and other cabin services that required them to be seated, opting for snacks and convenience foods from vending machines that they could nibble on while lying down. Reading, listening to the audio programs, or watching the little LCD screen could be done just as well lying down in a plane as in bed back home.

So first as an experiment and then as a regular feature, airlines offered bunk sleepers on long night flights. Coach passengers booking bunks must lie down all the time, while the seats in business and first class are easily changed from seats to loungers to fully flat beds as the passengers wish.

At first some airlines resisted the entertainment consoles and the new seat designs because they added between five and ten pounds to the weight of each seat, but the use of new carbon fiber and other plastics subsequently eliminated the weight penalty. In the latest designs, these very sophisticated seats with all their electronic features actually weigh less than the old traditional designs.

Weight saving has been a prime objective of the airlines in recent years, and as we look around this plane on which we are taking a flight into the future, we can see why it has been such a concern. Much of the need to save weight to accommodate new equipment has stemmed from passenger demands for better and more flexible inflight catering. Our flight is quite a long one, so we do not have as many of the food and beverage vending machines that are now familiar features on short hauls, but our plane is equipped with some automatic vendors as well as refrigerators for fresh fruit and other perishable foods. It has also larger quantities of higher-quality drinking water than used to be carried on flights and much more efficient air conditioning to meet passengers' demands for better ventilation.

Much of the refrigeration and cooling on this new plane is achieved by passive cooling, an important avionics development of the 1990s that saves a lot of weight and energy consumption over the active mechanized cooling systems of the 1980s. It is also simpler and consequently more reliable.

The overhead bins are bigger than on the older jets because even the improved airport systems for handling checked bags failed to discourage a large proportion of passengers from wanting to keep as much luggage as they could with them in the cabin.

Some travelers are disappointed that supersonic planes have not become more widely available yet, but they probably never will prove practical for other than intercontinental or other very long distances. We are still lumbering along on this trip under seven hundred miles an hour, although Boeing is well advanced with its hypersonic jets for Pacific and Atlantic long-distance routes. Scheduled for service by 2005, they will cruise at two thousand miles an hour, with later versions already under development capable of five times the speed of sound and going from New York to Tokyo in under three hours instead of the fourteen taken by subsonic planes.

These new supersonic planes overcome the major handicaps of the Concorde by being more fuel-efficient, carrying better payloads, and meeting environmental concerns. They hold 450 passengers and climb quickly to their 100,000-feet cruising altitude, a height at which they can travel supersonically over land without causing unacceptable noise below. When they reach their cruising altitude, the engines switch from conventional jet fuel to a special methane mixture that will not cause undue damage to the ozone layer and that is more environmentally acceptable in other respects also.

About five hundred of these internationally designed and built supersonic planes will be completed by the year 2015. They are seen as a major factor in the continuing travel boom among the Pacific Rim nations. On the shorter routes, particularly between cities in Europe and within the United States, the new thousand-seat subsonic planes are beginning to dominate, bringing down fares and enabling the volume of leisure travel to rise to double that of the 1980s. Most of this growth has come as a result of demographic changes, particularly the explosion in numbers of elderly people with both the time and the money to travel frequently for pleasure.

WILL PASSENGERS EVER BE CONTAINERIZED?

Futurologists, science fiction writers—even aerospace scientists—periodically speculate that future air travelers may be encapsulated in modules.

The concept of containerizing passengers, just as their baggage is handled more efficiently in this way, seems at first to have many attractions, especially for long intercontinental flights. You would check straight into a pod, module, or container—whatever it is called—along with your baggage. Each module might contain twenty-five, fifty, or a hundred passengers going to the same destination. They would be handled mechanically in bulk right from departure to arrival terminals.

VIP super–first class passengers could invest in their own personal air travel modules, just as wealthy travelers used to have their own railroad cars. A film star could have a module with recreational, sleeping, and other facilities for herself and her retinue. A company president would have one with sophisticated communications and business equipment.

Another important demographic development has been the enormous increase in women business travelers, who now outnumber men.

There are more children traveling also in these days in the not-too-distant future. Hotels and airlines have introduced a number of plans with incentives for business travelers to bring their families with them, especially to func-

FLIGHTS TO NOWHERE

Congestion at established airports is getting so bad that in the not-too-distant future we may increasingly travel to remote rural places with no significance except as wayport hubs.

Over half the passengers using the major airports in the United States do not actually want to be there at all—they are passing through, changing flights to somewhere else. The hub-and-spoke pattern of air routing is unlikely to change, but as existing airports in and near urban areas are difficult and expensive to expand, their role as transfer hubs may have to be taken over by wayports. Located on cheap land in rural areas, these have only one function—to transfer passengers from one flight to another on their way to and from the main urban airports.

These wayports are only about a third as expensive as a new airport in a conventional location near a big city. They will cost about a billion dollars each, but the land for them is cheap, and many underused or redundant military airfields could provide the basis for these new transfer wayports. The main savings come from the fact that passengers arrive and leave again quickly, only by air, so there is no need for expensive access roads, car parking, and other arrival and departure services provided at the conventional terminals.

The concept has been proved very effective by Federal Express and other freight and mail handlers. Modeling the efficient movement of passengers on the experience in expressing parcels from one side of the country to the other could prove the most effective solution to airport congestion in the future.

According to the Air Transport Association, since airlines became deregulated, Chicago O'Hare has become the busiest airport in the United States, handling 57.5 million passengers in 1988, nearly 10 million more than second-place Atlanta with 47.6 million. Next come Los Angeles with 44.9 million and Dallas/Ft. Worth at 41.9 million, up dramatically from only 19.9 million since 1978, largely because of its growth as a hub. Denver handles 32.4 million, John F. Kennedy, 30.2 million, San Francisco, 29.8 million, New York's La Guardia 25.2 million, Miami 24 million, and Newark 23.5 million, a nearly threefold increase over the ten years.

Dallas/Ft. Worth, open since 1974, is the last major airport built in the United States, demonstrating the difficulty of financing and overcoming the logistical problems of such a major development near a big city. The Transportation Research Board of the National Academy of Sciences believes that as many as twenty remote wayport hubs may be necessary.

tions in resort areas. Changes in the school and college curricula and the much greater use of computerized systems for educational purposes have made it easier for youngsters to take frequent short breaks and spread the traveling more evenly throughout the year than was the case when so much family leisure travel had to be concentrated in a single summer vacation.

Although there is a lot of stormy weather about, we

have no real concern on this trip that our flight will be delayed. It seems inconceivable that in 1989 some of the biggest airlines had nearly 30 percent of their flights arriving fifteen minutes or more after scheduled time—and that does not include the delays caused by mechanical problems. Now, in this near future, the Microwave Landing System has become universal, guiding aircraft in and out of airports safely and efficiently even in very bad weather. Other technological advances in air traffic control and the use of more remote rural hubs to reduce air traffic congestion around the airports serving urban centers have eliminated most causes of delays.

When we arrive at our destination, our disembarkation is as quick and smooth as was our boarding, especially as we have no need even to think about our checked baggage, which will be conveyed directly from the plane to the hotel room. We planned in advance to use a ground shuttle from the air terminal to the hotel, and our smart ticket carries all the details necessary for the pickup to be arranged as soon as the ticket is read by an optical scanner near the exit. No need to make a phone call.

If we had booked a hire car, it would be ready and waiting with no documentation to fill in. And if we want to make last-minute changes, the smart ticket, our credit cards, and the computerized services with which they communicate can rapidly cancel one arrangement and substitute another—all in obedience to instructions we keyboarded in from our seat on the plane.

Now that we have seen the future, maybe we can be more optimistic that the travel hassles of the present will largely be overcome, and so tolerate them more readily. All the developments outlined in this scenario are based on technology that exists already or is close to reality. Some developments are being tested already, and you may encounter them on trips in the early 1990s. Others may not arrive until a decade or so into the twenty-first century. But they are all achievable and will contribute to the survival of the frequent flier.

The ultimate travel experience—through time—may still seem a fantasy. But in the wonderful, magical world of travel, do not dismiss any possibilities. Three distinguished astrophysicists from the California Institute of Technology and the University of Wisconsin have suggested that the laws of physics may not prohibit travel through time and space. They speculated in the prestigious scientific journal *Physical Review Letters* that travelers in a more advanced civilization will pass through tunnels in both space and time. That concept would mean that there are literally no boundaries to travel in the future.

Appendix—Frequent Flier Fast Facts

Catch an anti–jet lag flight to help adjust more easily to different time zones. The pioneer program was in first and business classes on Continental flights to Tokyo. The seats of participating passengers are tagged, and they get special protein- and carbohydrate-balanced meals served at particular times, in-flight video exercise programs, and social interaction, light management and other activities to help adjust their circadian rhythyms. Details: 800 231-0856.

Cheap can be expensive if the ticket costs you dearly because it is so loaded with restrictions that you get no refund if you need to change the reservation—or miss the flight through no fault of your own. Double-check the restrictions on bargain fares. Don't buy them unless you are certain the restrictions will not affect you. Consider cancellation insurance from a company such as The Travelers, 800 243-3174, or Access America, 800 851-2800.

Get there early to minimize stress, because arriving at the airport in good time is voted by frequent fliers as one of the best ways to reduce travel tension. It may also prevent you from being bumped from an overbooked flight—airlines usually first bump the last to arrive.

Beware of standby compensation by not being too ready to accept an offer of a standby seat on the next flight. This is often part of the compensation for passengers who volunteer or who are forcibly bumped from an overbooked flight. But it may be worthless, leaving you grounded for hours, always near the back of the queue for succeeding flights. If you are bumped, hold out for a confirmed seat—perhaps on another airline—unless the compensation package is really too good to turn down.

When animals fly, book well in advance and select an airline with rules that fit your needs. Some will not accept pets at all, others impose a variety of restrictions. Also, check for interstate and international health requirements and arrive early for the flight in case of problems.

When traveling to underdeveloped countries, get expert advice on particular health risks and vaccination requirements. Take prophylactic medication for malaria and so on, and your own sterile pack of hypodermic syringes with spare needles, together with a note from your doctor explaining why you have them.

When returning from underdeveloped countries, give your doctor details of your overseas trip if you develop any unusual medical symptoms, or seek advice from a specialist in viral or tropical infections. Insist on such a specialist's second opinion if your problem does not get better.

When traveling with an infant, notify the airline when booking and check airline policy over fares, allowing car safety seats, and other concerns. Pick an off-peak travel time to increase your chances of getting the use of a vacant seat without paying extra. Take diapers, premixed formula, wet wipes—all the things you are likely to need. Don't rely on the airline for anything. Get the baby to suck a bottle during ascent and descent to minimize the risk of earache from pressure changes.

If you do NOT want to travel next to an infant, avoid the bulkhead seats, where the bassinets can be fixed and so are most likely to contain passengers with babies.

When going by train, book a sleeper as far in advance as possible, as they are much in demand and the penalties are not usually too severe if you have to cancel.

To minimize heartburn and acid indigestion, reduce—preferably stop—intake of alcohol, coffee, and tobacco. Switching to decaffeinated coffee will not help. Eat moderately and avoid chocolate and fatty foods.

To reduce that bloated feeling on the plane, do not drink beer or carbonated drinks.

When taking a photograph from the plane, do not rest the lens against the window, as it will pick up vibrations that make your picture fuzzy. Remove any polarizing filter, as it interacts with the plastic of the plane window to affect the light.

When taking computers, cameras, and other valuables overseas, insure for replacement value—probably most cheaply by extending your homeowner's policy. Take a photograph of everything you pack, including accessories, and record serial numbers in case you need to make a claim. Register equipment with customs as you leave to avoid hassles when you get back. To reduce customs hassles overseas, get a Temporary Admission Carnet for valuable equipment from the U.S. Council for International Business at 212-354-4480 in New York or 415-956-3356 in San Francisco. Some countries place limits on the number of cameras and rolls of film a visitor may bring in—check with the consulate concerned.

When film has to pass through security x-ray machines, do *not* put it in checked baggage. Protect it in a special shielded pouch. Remember the cumulative effect—the chances of fogging increase with each exposure to x-rays. Fast films of ASA 400 and higher are much more vulnerable to fogging than slower films. Ask for a hand visual inspection (but you may be refused outside the United States).

If you want the best fare deals, travel at off-peak times; you will find also that planes and airports are less crowded and stressful.

Who travels on business? More than 70 percent of the 35.3 million business travelers in the United States every year are aged under forty-five, with 32 percent aged twenty-five to thirty-four years. Thirty-eight percent are women, and 57 percent are professionals, managers, or self-employed. Salespeople, the archetypal business travelers, make up less than 15 percent. *(Statistics from a survey in 1987 for the U.S. Travel Data Center.)*

How air traffic has grown. After the first ten years of deregulation in the United States, the annual number of commercial airline passengers grew from 278 million to 450 million. The average cost of flying dropped by 13 percent (allowing for inflation) and nine out of ten passengers flew on discounted fares. The number of passenger planes and the intensity with which they are operated rose to a takeoff in the United States every five seconds.

Traveling on holiday may not be good for you, especially at peak holiday times. Vacation travel has most of the negative elements of frequent business flying, and the change of routine can be particularly stressful to the person not used to traveling much. Symptoms such as upset stomach and headaches, anxiety attacks, behavioral disturbances, and so on can result. If your prime objective is to relax and counter work stress, it can be more healthful to stay at home and make more relaxed day trips.

The ultimate traveler is a member of the Traveler's Century Club and has visited every one of their 308 separate country and territory destinations.

Data on delays: Every day, delays at U.S. airports waste about two thousand hours of aircraft operating time. The annual cost to the airlines is about $2 billion.

Don't sue the airline unless you have a very strong case. The small print on the ticket and in the airline rule books greatly restricts your rights, especially for negligence claims for personal injury and loss.

The most unusual case that proves the point is that of a passenger who said his sex life was ruined when a flight attendant spilled hot coffee on his lap. The litigation took more than five years and was last seen heading on appeal to the Supreme Court as the airlines strove to prevent a dangerous precedent being set. The latest trend in litigation against airlines is to sue for "mental terror," impacts on the emotions that can come from almost any emergency situation.

For comfortable, easier trips, both on the ground and in the air, consider using a city's less popular airport—Oakland instead of San Francisco International, Baltimore-Washington instead of National or Dulles, Burbank or Long Beach instead of Los Angeles, for example. Your commute, parking, and other factors may be enhanced by creative use of alternative airports and by routing to avoid busy hubs such as Chicago and Atlanta, where delays are frequent. Some airports are used just because they may have unusually attractive facilities, like the Tattered Cover bookstore with over 100,000 titles only 15 minutes from Denver's airport.

If you really travel a lot, consider using a fashion, image, or color consultant to go through your wardrobe and pick the most effective color-coordinated outfits or to send you off on a shopping spree for a fresh start putting together practical and stylish travel gear.

The world's largest airline is the Soviets' Aeroflot, which flies about 137 billion paying passenger miles a year, almost double that of second place United. British Airways ranks first in international traffic, with over 35 billion revenue passenger miles a year on services to eighty countries.

Fares and fuel costs are closely linked, so expect fares to go up and perhaps book ahead at a confirmed price if the oil price is expected to rise. A 1 percent increase in fuel price can cost an airline $5 million in lost profits.

If you want the best service and maybe the highest maintenance standards also, choose an airline with a good employee profit sharing or co-ownership program. It's never been publicly quantified, but the incentive of employee participation usually works to improve standards. For example, after 94 percent of British Airways employees received an ownership stake and participated in profit sharing, passenger satisfaction soared. One measure of this is that a business class passenger traveling between London and New York now gets sixteen personalized contacts from the flight attendants—called "touches" in the business—to represent each occasion when the attendant comes into direct contact to render service to the passenger.

If you don't want to blow your electrical appliances when operating them overseas on different voltages, remember to use the appropriate *type* as well as size of converter. The transformer for appliances rated up to 50 watts and the solid-state kind for loads up to 1,600 watts should be used with different types of electrical equipment as well as to cater to variations in load, measured in wattage.

Transformers supply the steady converted 120-volt electricity required by all American motorized appliances and those containing electronic circuitry on their own internal transformers. Examples include contact lens disinfectors, oral hygiene devices, battery chargers, tape recorders, and radios. They need the true electrical sine wave that this transformer type of converter produces.

The solid-state travel converters have electronic semiconductor switches that interrupt foreign 240-volt electric-

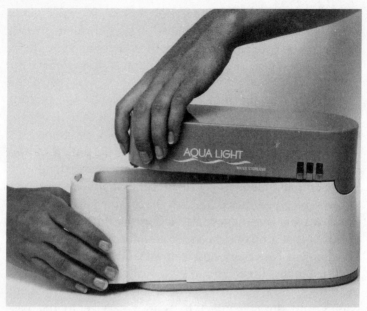

Combat traveler's diarrhea caused by water-borne bacteria and viruses by taking an ultraviolet water purifier with you.

It is often difficult to boil water when traveling; purification chemicals can result in an unpleasant taste; filtering devices need careful use if they are to be effective in removing bacteria. The traveler's version of the ultraviolet treatment used by hospitals and food and beverage manufacturers overcomes those snags.

This device was invented by financial consultant Theodore Merriam after he contracted traveler's diarrhea on a trip to Mexico. It weighs a couple of pounds and runs on batteries or an adapter. Fill it with tap water, and in two minutes ultraviolet light kills many of the organisms responsible for travelers' health problems, including infectious hepatitis, cholera, and typhoid. The manufacturer is Hybernetics Inc. The unit retails throughout the United States for around $99.

ity several times a second, enabling American heating appliances such as steamers, curlers, hair driers, and so on to function as if on 120 volts. But the converters do not produce the sufficiently pure current for electronic and motorized appliances.

If you want your airline to deliver on its frequent flier promises, watch out for little-publicized changes in the program rules. The airlines have got a tiger by the tail with their frequent-flier programs and bonus plans. If they have to meet all their commitments, the cost will be enormous—disastrous for some carriers. So they are trying to reduce their liability in the hope that many passengers entitled to free trips will not collect.

Restrictions that limit both the eligibility of passengers and availability of free seats are quietly being imposed. The trend is to increase the number of miles needed to win an award, sometimes by 60 percent or more. The days on which awards can be used are being reduced by blacking out sections of the calendar, sometimes with very little notice.

Cutoff dates are being imposed as well, so you may find that there was a time limit by which you must have used your coupons for a particular flight.

Another dodge is to impose severe limits on the number of seats available to award holders on certain flights. You may qualify for the trip to Europe or Australia for which you have been piling up the miles but not be able to go because the airline has arbitrarily limited the number of seats available for frequent-flier awards.

Some domestic airlines are ending or making substantial changes in their frequent-flier program arrangements with foreign carriers, so the overseas trip for which you were accumulating miles may no longer be available at all.

As this book goes to press, some class-action suits against the airlines over frequent-flier programs are pending, and Better Business Bureaus and other consumer interest groups are becoming increasingly concerned over the airlines' tactics.

To protect your interests, read all the information that you receive as a participant in a frequent-flier program, looking out for notice of changes or additional restrictions that affect you. In theory, the airlines have great freedom to do what they like with frequent-flier programs, but there is a practical limitation imposed by the need not to upset the business travelers the programs were created to attract in the first place. So if you think you are getting a raw deal, complain strongly.

If you want to join the Mile-High Club, a mythical group of those who have made love in the air, or if you want privacy for other reasons, then rent a stateroom on MGM Grand Air. The airline runs a service between New York and Los Angeles with usually fewer than thirty passengers on specially converted Boeing 727s. The space is designed for nearly four times that number.

The fare is similar to that for the normal first class coast-to-coast ticket, but the facilities are far superior. The staterooms at the rear hold as many as four people, and the seats are convertible into double beds.

If you lose things frequently, consider having duplicate credit card accounts. If you lose one set of cards, they can be canceled immediately and the reserve set brought into use.

If pressure earache is a problem for you, try pinching your nostrils and *gently* blowing your nose to equalize the pressure in your middle ear. Yawning, chewing gum, and sucking a sweet are other methods.

If you wear contact lenses, a squeeze bottle of lens lubricant will help to combat the problems caused by low cabin humidity.

To speed up travel time to the airport, look at a city's transit services. Often there is a subway or fast train that will get you quickly and cheaply from a city center to within a short cab or bus ride of the airport. For example, the subway beats the Manhattan traffic jams to get you to a bus stop near La Guardia; the London Underground has direct service to Heathrow; and the suburban train is by far the fastest way to get to Gatwick.

Trains are particularly advantageous if you have to get to or from an airport in rush hour or when the weather is bad and road traffic subject to delays. Subways and trains are usually cheaper than either special airport buses or cabs.

Keeping in touch when traveling has become much easier as a result of satellite paging. The CUE service covers 90 percent of the American population in nearly 150 metropolitan areas and the air space over them. It lets you receive messages on the ground and in the air via a four-ounce pocket pager with a message memory and digital display. It is a highly cost-effective alternative to the cellular telephone, with some practical advantages despite only receiving messages. Details from CUE Paging at 800 824-9755, Sky Page at 800-456-3333, or other paging services—but verify that they cover the areas to which you travel.

Other services transmit stock, commodity, and currency market figures direct to personal receivers, helping travelers keep in touch. Quotrek, 800 367-4670, broadcasts real-time market quotes in seventeen U.S. cities, and the Reuter Pocketwatch service is available in New York, Chicago, Toronto, London, Tokyo, and Hong Kong.

Rent a portable telephone by the day if you have an occasional specific need to keep in touch. The facility is widely available; Mutual of Omaha supplies it at its business service centers at several U.S. airports.

Secretarial services are available at some airports and good hotels. You can dictate letters or other documents and have them typed up before you leave. If you are in a rush, you can dictate the letter and have it typed and dispatched after you have left.

It's a great way of giving fast confirmation of the details of a deal or recording what took place at a meeting. If you do not have the opportunity to check the transcript before it is sent, insert a protective phrase stating that it is dictated and subject to later confirmation.

For fast, secure document transmission, around two thousand hotels and airports offer special fax services for travelers. A self-service fax booth is more secure than the normal hotel fax or any other service if you cannot directly supervise the transmission or reception.

If you do a lot of computing on the move, take along a spare battery, or a 12-volt converter if you will have access to a car cigar lighter socket. On a long flight, you may be able to plug your charger into one of the plane's 110- or 240-volt outlets, but don't bank on it. Some trains have 110-volt outlets under the seats, but the voltage can be unstable and should be used only with a converter or battery charger to protect your laptop against power surges.

Cut your computer baggage by using integrated software, in which one program provides several functions, such as word processor, spreadsheet, modem communications control, and other functions. PFS:First Choice is particularly easy to use.

Save money calling home from overseas by using AT&T's US DIRECT service. It enables you to charge international calls and so reduce many hotel surcharges. There are other cost-cutting deals, and you can eliminate the hassles often associated with foreign telephone services by getting through to an American operator quickly. Details from 800 426-8700.

Beware of attention-distracting tricks used by airport thieves and pickpocket gangs on the streets, which include throwing money behind you and saying that you dropped it, asking for the time or for directions, and spilling or squirting something on your clothing. If any of these things happens to you, suspect trouble imediately. The distraction trick may well be performed by an attractive woman or an innocent-looking child.

Car rental regulations are changing to protect the consumer from sharp practices. Collision damage waivers and some other charges are banned in a number of states, while more car owners' insurance policies cover rented cars. In some states policies are required to provide this coverage. Before renting a car where the waiver fee still applies, check if you have coverage already from your own insurance or pay with a credit card that provides this coverage automatically.

Airline clubs can be good value if you spend a lot of time at airports. Membership comes with some frequent-flier programs or for a fee, which may be around $75 a year but will save more than that in airport snacks and drinks alone. Usual services are a comfortable lounge with a hostess to serve refreshments and to provide flight information and check-in assistance. Some clubs have private meeting rooms, and virtually all of them provide desks and telephones so that you can conduct business. The club restrooms are also more private and better equipped than the airport's public restrooms, enabling you to freshen up after arrival before your first meeting.

You do not have to take the first cab in the line or the one summoned by the hotel doorman if it is dirty or has no air conditioning on a hot day, if the driver cannot understand you, or if you have any other reason for not wanting it. If the driver only wants a long trip, for example to the airport, and hassles you over accepting a short ride, move on to the next cab in line. The second driver

FAST FACTS FOR FREQUENT FLIERS

The myths about the help that U.S. consular officers can provide for Americans abroad give a false sense of security to overseas travelers. The State Department emphasizes that U.S. consular officers abroad can

- *Ensure insofar as possible that the detainee's rights under local law are fully observed and that humane treatment is accorded under internationally accepted standards*
- *Visit the U.S. citizen as soon as possible after the foreign government has notified the U.S. embassy or consulate of the arrest*
- *Provide the detainee with a list of local attorneys from which to select defense counsel*
- *Contact family and/or friends for financial or medical aid and food, if requested to do so by the detainee*

U.S. consular officers abroad <u>cannot</u>

- *Demand a U.S. citizen's release*
- *Represent the detainee at trial, give legal counsel, or pay legal fees or other related expenses with U.S. government funds*
- *Intervene in a foreign country's court system or judicial process to obtain special treatment*

will either be glad of the fare or will help to enforce the unwritten rule of the cab line, which is that the driver at the front has to take whatever comes his way.

Beware of luggage cart hustlers at airports that charge rentals for carts. Some hustlers simply retrieve abandoned

MEDICAL DETAILS

Name . . . .
Address . . . .
. . . .
. . . .
. . . . Tel. # . . . .

Blood type . . . .
Allergies . . . .
Medical problems . . . .
. . . .
. . . .
. . . .

Medication Prescribed

Trade Name   *Generic Name*

Emergency contact
(Next of kin, friend or relative) . . . .
. . . . Tel. # . . . .
Physician's name . . . .
. . . . Tel. # . . . .

Physician's signature and stamp

Your Medical Checklist. It's better to be safe than sorry when traveling, so always carry essential medical information about yourself. Copy and get your doctor to complete this form.

Leading modern hotels like the Sheraton New Orleans now get most of their revenue from business travelers and so make a big effort to provide special services. This Sheraton has an Executive Business Center open seven days a week with staff and equipment to complete most projects. You can rent personal computers and software, purchase office supplies, hire a secretary, make presentation slides, and so on. Video checkout is a new development in which your bill appears on the bedroom TV screen, where you can check and approve it, then collect a printed copy on your way out, for a fast getaway.

carts to collect the return fee. Others try to make more by renting them direct to passengers. Some hustlers go further, wearing official-looking clothing and using the carts to push porterage services, which may be linked to other scams. Be particularly careful of any unofficial porters, who may knock your bags off the trolley or hide them when loading the car so that they can be picked up by accomplices. At times there have been hundreds of luggage cart hustlers working Kennedy Airport in New York, many supporting drug habits, and numerous violent incidents have occurred.

Flight delays caused by the weather are most likely early in the morning, sometimes at dusk, and particularly at airports affected by fog. So avoid those times for arrivals as well as departures, especially in winter.

Save time as well as money by using off-airport parking and car-hire facilities. You can sometimes get to and from terminals faster and more conveniently on the free minibus shuttle operated by off-airport parking and rental companies. You may also avoid long queues at rental desks and the exits from busy airport parking garages, as well as the delay looking for a space to put your car and the stress of driving youself through a busy and unfamiliar airport.

When renting a car in an unfamiliar city, pick a company that offers computerized route guides. These will give you written directions all the way from the terminal to the street address you need to reach.

Share a cab or a limo for fast and economical trips to and from airports. Arrangements can be made with other passengers on the plane, at the baggage claim, or at the curbside, particularly in the queue waiting for a bus that is delayed.

Airport shuttle bus services are getting better all the time. Frequent fliers find that taking a bus from the office or home is the most economical and least stressful way of getting to the terminal. The shuttle is especially economical when going on an extended trip, when the saving on parking can be substantial. Some services now provide through baggage check-in, seat assignments, and ticket services.

Even if you do not use the airport bus, it can pay to follow one to the airport after it has made its pickups. The drivers know the best routes at different times of the day to avoid traffic congestion.

Conferences at the airport can be cost-effective when senior management, consultants, or specialists are passing through a terminal and can meet with local staff between flights. It may pay to bring staff into a convenient hub, do a day's business, and all depart again without leaving the terminal.

The rates for hiring conference rooms by the hour vary widely—$40 for the first hour in San Francisco and Detroit, for example, but only $7 in Minneapolis-St. Paul, where you can also rent a two-person office for a bargain $5 an hour.

Most airport business center conference rooms hold up to eight people, and the rate comes down substantially if you take one for a full day. Nine people can use a conference room at O'Hare International's business center for only $90 a day. Presentation equipment such as overhead projectors and video players can usually be hired, but these and the rooms should be booked a week or more ahead if possible. Typical rate for an overhead projector is $35 a day, and personal computers usually go for about $20 the first hour and $10 for each successive hour.

For the 25 million handicapped Americans, the Airport Operators Council recommends making reservations well in advance and telling the airline what assistance or special arrangements you will need. This will ensure that such critical information as whether you are bringing your own wheelchair or will require one, if you have a guide dog or need portable oxygen equipment, will get fed into the system in good time.

Check in earlier than normal so that your special needs can more easily be met and you can more readily be preboarded. The AOC produces a comprehensive guide to facilities for the handicapped at more than five hundred airport terminals in sixty-two countries. You can get free copies by writing to Access America, Washington, DC 20202, or the Consumer Information Center, Pueblo, CO 81009. The Air Transport Association's survey of regulations covering the handicapped is obtainable from the ATA Public Information Office, 1709 New York Avenue N.W., Washington, DC 20006. Enclose a stamped self-addressed envelope.

Cost saving overseas can be achieved by getting the special advisory booklets that many national tourist offices are producing in these travel cost–conscious times. Travel agents may not have them—or even know about them— so you may have to get a copy from the nearest office of the tourist agency for the country you are visiting. The local consulate is probably the easiest source for the address and may have copies itself.

One of the best of these cost-saving books is from the Japan National Tourist Organization. It describes how a bus and train link from Narita Airport to downtown Tokyo costs only $11 compared to $125 for a taxi.

Staying at a home when away from home is an excellent way to get to know a strange country and to start networking; it can save money as well. Most countries have plans to enable foreigners to stay with, or visit, local people. Details from national tourist offices.

Check your ticket as soon as you get it, because it is your contract to fly and must be correctly filled out. Ensure that the status box says OK; otherwise you do not have a confirmed reservation.

Your reservations may be canceled if you do not reconfirm at least seventy-two hours before an international flight. It pays to reconfirm domestic flights also in case the schedules have been changed.

If you want a nonsmoking seat, all U.S. air carriers are obliged to provide you with one, even if it requires expanding the nonsmoking section. However, you must comply with seat assignment deadlines and have a confirmed reservation. Standby passengers do not have a right to a nonsmoking seat, and the rules are different on foreign airlines.

Cigar and pipe smoking are banned on American commercial aircraft, and no smoking at all is permitted on planes seating fewer than thirty passengers.

Seat belts should be worn all the time when in the air and when the plane is still moving on the ground. Passengers who stood up to get their belongings together while the plane was still taxiing have been injured in sharp turns and sudden stops. The commonsense rule for planes is the same as for cars—wear your seat belt all the time while the vehicle is moving and you dramatically reduce your risk of injury.

Oxygen masks, seat belts, and exits can differ considerably between planes. Belts fasten and unfasten in various ways. Oxygen masks and exits are located in different places. Ensure that you are familiar with the location and functioning of these basic lifesavers before every flight takes off. No other single action more effectively reduces personal risk.

Ask to see the airline's troubleshooter if you have a problem that other staff are not able to resolve. The Customer Service Representatives on duty at airports have considerable discretionary power in dealing with passengers, and they offer the easiest, fastest way of getting on-the-spot help.

Fly the night before a business meeting to minimize stress and the consequences of delays.

If you have to make connections, allow a minimum of one hour between flights and try to stay with the same airline for the entire trip. The distance between arrival and departure gates used by the same airline is usually less than if you have to change carriers, and the chances of your baggage being lost are reduced considerably if the same carrier handles them all the way through. Also, an airline may hold up a flight if one of its own connecting flights is delayed. A nonstop flight is the surest way to get to your destination on time.

Adequate insurance is vital for all aspects of travel. For example, do not get trip cancellation insurance that merely covers the cost of a discounted air fare. In an emergency you may have to cancel a nontransferable ticket and buy one that costs two or three times as much for the same trip at a different time. Scheduled flights, charters, and package tours are hedged around with conditions that disclaim responsibility for injuries, accidents, delays, and other problems. The fine print may not limit your rights to compensation as much as it appears to do, but claiming and litigation can be very slow and difficult. It is best to have your own adequate insurance tailored to fill the gaps in your regular homeowner's, medical, auto, and other policies that leave you exposed to risks when traveling.

Self-sealing plastic bags are invaluable travel aids. They separate and protect all the small items in your baggage, yet keep them visible so that you can locate things easily. Squeeze out the air before sealing a bag so that it takes up less space.

When going to a cold place cover your head, ears, and neck. Up to a third of lost body heat can leave through those areas.

The best first step in getting health information can be the National Health Information Center, sponsored by the Federal Office of Disease Prevention and Health Promotion, PO Box 1133, Washington DC 20013-1133. 1-800-336-4797 (or 301-565-4167 in DC or Maryland)

To find an English-speaking doctor abroad, contact the nearest office of the International Association for Medical Assistance to Travelers. The headquarters are at 417 Center Street, Lewiston, NY 14092, 716 754-4883.

Narcotics are not the same the world over and in some countries, such as Saudi Arabia, may include alcohol, barbiturates, amphetamines, codeine, and many substances not regarded as narcotics in the United States or Europe.

Travelers taking medication containing narcotics abroad should carry a doctor's certificate, keep the medicines in their original labeled containers, and before leaving consult the embassies of countries they are visiting where problems might arise.

The countries accounting for most drug-related arrests of Americans are Mexico, Jamaica, the Bahamas, the Dominican Republic, and the Federal Republic of Germany. Those with the toughest laws include Singapore, the Communist bloc nations, and the Arab states. Every year about three thousand Americans are arrested on drug offenses in some sixty countries; more than 40 percent are detained—often in primitive prisons—for possessing as little as a third of an ounce of marijuana.

If you suffer from motion sickness, select a seat over the wing, where the motion is less; recline the seat; and keep your head still. Do not read; instead, close your eyes or look at the horizon, if possible.

Comfortable feet can make all the difference when traveling, So always wear well broken in shoes that you know to be comfortable for long periods. They should not be too tight, as feet swell on an air trip.

Backache on planes can result from unsuspected causes. Two of the most common are the after-effects of carrying heavy shoulder bags around the terminal and objects in your pockets that press on nerves. Ease the pain by sitting upright with pillows in the small of your back—and check your back pockets!

First class passengers fall into two categories, according to research by British Airways. There are the self-made *achievers*, status-conscious conspicious consumers who want to be recognized as winners, and the *patricians* with established wealth who do not seek pampering but just automatically buy the highest-quality goods and services.

The typical first class passenger is a male top business executive in his late forties, but the number of women business travelers is growing rapidly, and more of them are moving into first class. An increasing category is frequent fliers cashing in their bonus miles to find out what it is like to be an achiever or a patrician!

Frequent-flier mileage can be boosted by the many other travel-related service providers who have tied in with the airlines, but to get credit for miles may mean paying more than the best available rates. Hotel mileage credits, for example, are usually tied to standard or corporate rates, when often there are better deals to be had.

Save money by avoiding airport shops; they pay high rents and other overhead for the privilege of having access to a captive market of travelers who spend an average of ninety often boring minutes in terminals. Even with the duty-free concessions, electronic goods and liquor in some airport shops tend to be more expensive than at discount stores. Branded luxury goods may be more expensive than even in the quality stores. The prices on candies and snacks are loaded as well.

When lightning strikes your aircraft, there is little cause for alarm. The plane itself is unlikely to be damaged, although the flight control computer systems are vulnerable to excessive electrical energy. Research by NASA indicates that three out of every four instances of aircraft being struck by lightning are caused by the planes themselves. The movement of the plane through the air creates an electrical field that attracts lightning.

State Department Travel Advisories can be obtained by calling the Citizens Emergency Center, 202 647-5225. Using a touchtone phone gives you faster access to advisories on specific countries. The center also arranges the transfer of emergency funds to destitute Americans overseas. Money can be wired by Western Union to the State Department, which will notify an overseas consulate to release the funds to the traveler in trouble.

To complain about safety violations by airlines, call the Federal Aviation Agency hotline, 800 255-1111.

Don't get fleeced by restaurants that display low-price fixed menus or specials and then pad the bill, especially for drinks. Check all prices before you order and don't hesitate to ask for the menu again to verify your final bill. To avoid unpleasantness, give the waiter the opportunity to correct an "innocent mistake" rather than backing him into a corner with accusations of dishonesty. If you are really being ripped off, ask for the manager or proprietor. In many countries the consequences for a restaurant or hotel fleecing tourists can be serious.

Beware of very attractive exchange rates quoted by money changers, who may add on charges that make their rate less attractive than that offered by banks. Hotels and some of the changers at airports are notorious for doing so. Better deals may be obtained by paying for goods in foreign currency and getting the store to give you change in local notes.

Changing money on the black market can yield the best exchange rates in some countries —usually those where the penalties for being caught doing so are very stiff. Black market and street money changers are most likely to shortchange you by trying to exploit a traveler's lack of familiarity with the denominations of local currency notes. Often the design of banknotes has changed, so you may encounter new, physically smaller notes that appear less impressive than old large notes actually worth much less. Beware also of counterfeits passed by black market money changers and of calculators and adding machines that have been "fixed." Check the conversion on your own calculator in suspect situations.

How much are you worth if you die in an air crash? Well under $400,000 is the average payout to the families of victims. A study by the Rand Corporation found that awards—averaging $363,000 per victim in the twenty-five worst American air accidents between 1970 and 1984— represented less than half of the economic loss the victim's family actually sustained. If you are concerned about the risk and the possible consequences for your dependents, additional travel insurance is worth investigating.

A friend in need may be found at tourist organizations that provide some form of traveler's ombudsman service. They may intervene in disputes with hotels, airlines, taxis, restaurants, and other travel-related services and provide help in a variety of problem situations that visitors encounter.

Beware of the block, a universally popular technique used by pickpockets. The victim is jostled in front and behind, often in a very apologetic way, while pockets are picked and the straps of cameras and bags cut. Reduce the risk by getting against a wall, which is also an easier position to protect if you have to wait with your luggage in a crowded airport or railway or bus station.

Filling the bathtub with water is a classic veteran traveler's tactic favored by foreign correspondents used to covering wars, riots, and other civil commotions. Radio broadcasts, the telephone, and the water and electricity supplies all seem to be prime targets during such situations, and water is the only one you can do much to counter.

Public transport is the best bargain in virtually every city in the world if you do what the locals do and purchase a book of tickets or a special unlimited daily or weekly travel voucher. For example, about $3 a day will take you anywhere on the Paris Metro, suburban trains, and bus services. London Transport has similar packages, as do most American cities.

Organizations with employees who travel abroad can alert them to dangers and precautions by showing the State Department's twelve-minute videotape *Traveling Abroad More Safely*. The VHS and Beta versions cost only $9 and the three-quarter-inch tape, $12.50 Send payment plus a $3 handling charge to Video Transfer Inc., 5710 Arundel Avenue, Rockville, MD 20552, 301-881-0270.

When to bribe is a perennial problem for travelers to countries where baksheesh is expected. The best solution is to be advised by trusted locals and use them as go-betweens so that the petty bribery is handled by someone who knows the form and the going rates.

Be particularly careful about bribing officials; it can get you into serious trouble. Veteran travelers leave a currency note or two folded within the pages of a passport or international driving permit and say nothing. When the document is examined, the official can either remove the money or leave it there.

Cigarettes and liquor are more acceptable than money for greasing the wheels in some Third World or Eastern-bloc countries; trendy T-shirts work particularly well in some places.

Great gateways in and out of the United States exist in surprising places. As some of the main international terminals, such as New York's JFK and LAX in Los Angeles, get more crowded and the immigration and customs queues lengthen, consider some alternatives. Charlotte, North Carolina, is better than most for fast immigration clearance and baggage reclaim when arriving from Europe. It's easy to get away from again, with nearly four hundred flights daily to seventy-six U.S. cities. More than half of the American population is within an hour's flying time of Charlotte.

Passports should be applied for well in advance, as delays are usual, especially in the peak period, January to August. You need a completed DSP-11 application form and proof of U.S. citizenship, usually a birth certificate. You must apply in person for a first passport, either at one of the passport agencies in major cities or at an authorized post office or federal or state court. Renewals by mail are possible.

Ask for a forty-eight-page passport if you intend to travel overseas a great deal.

Some countries require a visa, a passport with at least six months' validity remaining, a return air ticket, and proof of sufficient funds. Some, including Mexico, have special regulations about children traveling with only one parent. This is aimed at combating international child abduction.

For information about passports, contact your local agency or authorized post office or court. The agencies have twenty-four-hour telephone recording services that give general information and telephone numbers for specific questions.

Addresses of Passport Field Agencies and Geographic Coverage

Boston Passport Agency
(Maine, Massachusetts, New Hampshire, Rhode Island, and Vermont)
John F. Kennedy Bldg.
Government Center
Boston, Massachusetts 02203

Chicago Passport Agency (Illinois, Indiana, Iowa, Michigan, and Wisconsin)
Suite 380, Kluczynski Federal Bldg.
230 South Dearborn Street
Chicago, Illinois 60604

Honolulu Passport Agency
(Hawaii, Wake Island, Midway Island, Johnston Island, and The Trust Territory of the Pacific Islands and American Samoa)
Room C-106, New Federal Bldg.,
300 Ala Moana Boulevard
Honolulu, Hawaii 96850

Houston Passport Agency
(Texas and New Mexico)
One Allen Center
500 Dallas Street
Houston, Texas 77002

Los Angeles Passport Agency
(California [all counties south of and including San Luis Obispo, Kern, and San Bernadino] and Nevada [only Clark County])
13th Floor, Hawthorne Federal Bldg.,
11000 Wilshire Boulevard
Los Angeles, California 90024

Miami Passport Agency (Florida, Georgia, South Carolina, Puerto Rico, and U.S. Virgin Islands)
16th Floor, Federal Office Bldg.
51 Southwest First Avenue
Miami, Florida 33130

New Orleans Passport Agency (Alabama, Missouri, Kentucky, Arkansas, Kansas, Louisiana, Mississippi, Oklahoma, and Tennessee)
Postal Services Bldg.
701 Loyola Avenue
New Orleans, Louisiana 70130

New York Passport Agency (New York City [walk-in traffic only])
Rockefeller Center,
630 Fifth Avenue
New York, New York 10111

Northeast Passport Processing Center (not open to the public) (New York City and all N.Y. counties except Dutchess, Orange, Putnam, Rockland, Sullivan, Ulster, and Westchester)
Federal Bldg.,
Room 1108
201 Varick Street
New York, New York 10014-4898

Philadelphia Passport Agency (Delaware, Pennsylvania, and New Jersey)
Federal Bldg.,
600 Arch Street
Philadelphia, Pennsylvania 19106

San Francisco Passport Agency (California [all counties north of and including Monterey, Kings, Inyo, and Tulare], Arizona, Nevada except Clark County, and Utah)
525 Market Street
San Francisco, California 94105

Seattle Passport Agency (Alaska, Colorado, Idaho, Minnesota, Montana, Nebraska, North Dakota, Oregon, South Dakota, Washington, Wyoming, and Guam)
Federal Bldg.,
915 Second Avenue
Seattle, Washington 98174

Stamford Passport Agency (Connecticut and New York counties of Dutchess, Orange, Putnam, Rockland, Sullivan, Ulster, and Westchester)
One Landmark Square
Broad and Atlantic Streets
Stamford, Connecticut 06901

Washington Passport Agency (Virginia, Maryland, North Carolina, Washington, D.C., Ohio, and West Virginia)
1425 K Street, N.W.,
Washington, D.C. 20524

Buy before you leave to save money on car rental, special train passes, hotel and entertainment packages, and other overseas deals. Many of these special incentives are available only to foreign travelers, so they must be purchased outside the country in which they are to be used.

Although intended to encourage tourism, the business traveler can exploit these packages to good advantage— even if not all the benefits are fully used. For example, many American businesspeople are traveling extensively between European cities in preparation for 1992 and the full integration of the European Economic Community. You can do that efficiently, comfortably, and very cheaply with a Eurailpass, which at the time of writing costs only $320 for unlimited first class travel for fifteen days *if* purchased in the United States.

When the dollar is weakening, you can protect your budget by buying these deals ahead and booking travel, hotels, and rental cars at guaranteed exchange rates.

Beware of excessive phone charges from airports, hotels, hospitals, university campuses, convention centers, and others who use alternative phone operator services. Calls that you bill to your phone card can cost three— even five—times as much as they should because they have been routed via an alternative service operator, not the AT&T operator, as you thought. The owner of the phone facility you use gets a cut of the exorbitant charge.

Although many states are acting against the most exploitive of the OAS companies, make sure before you put calls through the operator that you know with whom you are dealing and what the charges are likely to be.

Before traveling on flights operated by developing nations, check on the age and quality of the aircraft. African airlines have over a hundred planes that are not permitted to fly in Europe, and many of the carriers are in such financial straits that they cannot afford to buy replacements. Some have even had their planes seized for not paying maintenance bills.

Indeed, the average International Air Transport Association (IATA) airlines can find from their profits only about 1 percent of the cash they need to replace their aging planes. Often the airports in developing countries are in a bad way also, with runways in poor repair and unreliable air traffic control, firefighting, and other equipment. If an airport previously used by the major international carriers is now being boycotted by one of them for safety reasons, that is a very clear warning.

Want to take your bike on a plane? Cycling is one of the fastest-growing leisure activities as well as a great way of getting around, so more travelers are taking their bikes on trips.

Usually a bike can go as part of the checked baggage allowance, but some carriers impose special charges and require the bike to be packed in a carton. Swissair has great cheap plastic bags. Some air carriers require the wheels and handlebars to be removed. Trains almost everywhere in the world will accept bikes free of charge or for a nominal fee and with very few restrictions.

You can hire a cycle almost anywhere these days, in Europe and Scandinavia at many of the train stations for as little as $3 a day.

Check the package deals to save a lot of money. Not all travel packages are applicable only to vacationers. Some travel plus hotel deals are very practical for business travelers. In addition to accommodation, they may include at at little or no extra cost meals, airport transfers, discount vouchers, and other benefits that save a lot on your subsistence expenses. Some airlines block-book seats for popular shows you might not be able to get into otherwise.

The seasons can reverse in a few hours when you are traveling. If you have allergy problems caused by the weather, high pollen counts, dust, and so on, prepare for a flare-up and take your medication with you.

Don't overrun your credit card limit, as Americans have been arrested in some countries on fraud charges for accidentally exceeding their credit limit. Before a long trip, pay the monthly account in advance and perhaps reduce the total owing to give you more credit while away. Determine if giving your credit card number for a hotel or car rental deposit blocks some of your available credit.

Trauma as a result of accident is the major cause of serious disability and loss of life when traveling overseas. Infections are a problem for many thousands of travelers every year, so before an international trip, get the latest version of the government's comprehensive *Health Information for International Travel*. It costs only $4.75 from the Superintendent of Documents, U.S. Printing Office, Washington, DC 20402, 202 783-3238.

AIDS testing is required in about 30 countries, particularly for students and long-term visitors. Travelers may wish to check the latest position with the relevant embassy or consulate before leaving. Results from HIV tests from the United States are not acceptable everywhere. Most travelers may be able to get extensions on arrival, so that they do not have to be tested locally before they leave the country.

Don't always believe foreign salespeople when they tell you that the warranty they offer will be valid back home or that special arrangements have been made with U.S. Customs for you to import your purchases without paying duties. Both are old tricks to clinch a deal.

Beware of "international guarantees" that are badly

printed, have inferior English text, are entirely in a foreign language, are photocopies, or give no American or European addresses for service. Counterfeit goods usually come in counterfeit packaging with fake documentation. Telling customers that their purchases will be tax-exempt in the United States is a regular dodge to clinch a sale— and will not get you much sympathy from the customs officer back home if it proves untrue.

Don't get your visa too far in advance. Some are issued for only a limited period and may expire before you can complete your stay.

Declarations to Department of Agriculture inspectors on food, plants, and animal products you bring into the country are very serious. Every month some 1,250 travelers who fail to declare prohibited items or make false declarations are fined on the spot and may suffer more serious consequences. A sausage contaminated with foot-and-mouth disease virus could cost American farmers billions of dollars.

The USDA uses beagles and special x-rays to find hidden fruits and meats. To be safe, declare everything. You are permitted to bring in some fruits, vegetables, and plants if they are found to be free of pests. Certain plants for growing require an advance permit. Endangered plant species require a permit from the country of origin as well as from the U.S. Fish and Wildlife Service.

Generally meat products are prohibited unless the inspector can determine that commercially canned meat was sufficiently cooked in the can to remain stable without refrigeration. Hides and hunting trophies are tightly restricted and require special permission.

Certification, permits, inspection, and quarantine apply in varying degree to live animals and birds. Biological materials of all kinds require permits. The only soil, earth, or sand you can bring into the country is an ounce or less of decorative beach sand, although rocks, minerals, and shells can be imported if they are clean.

Further information can be obtained from the Import/Export and Emergency Planning Staff of USDA-APHIS, VS, 6505 Belcrest Road, Hyattsville, MD 20782; the U.S. Customs Service, PO Box 7474, Washington, DC 20044; and the Federal Wildlife Permit Office, U.S. Fish and Wildlife Service, Washington, DC 20240.

Tipping practices vary widely, so it is wise to check on registering at your hotel if a service charge is included, what tips it does not cover, and what are the going rates for different gratuities.

Starting from the front door when you arrive, the *doorman* should not expect anything unless he has rendered particular service other than simply opening the taxi door for you. *Bellhops* get about a dollar a bag, more if the luggage is very heavy or awkward. Room service usually includes a service surcharge, but *waiters* still expect a couple of dollars. The *chambermaids* in many hotels do not expect tips anymore but should be rewarded if they give more than the basic service. Two or three dollars per day of stay is usual. You can put it in an envelope and arrange with the clerk on checking out for it to be given to your maid.

How much you tip *concierges* depends on what they do for you. The superior kind tend to expect superior tips and will not be impressed by anything less than $5, substantially more if they really deploy their skills and contacts to help you. The same goes for *majordomos* and *headwaiters* in restuarants, while the waiters themselves expect 10 percent to 15 percent of the bill in most places except where a specific service charge is added.

Receptionists and other staff should not be tipped unless they do something really exceptional for you, and then only with discretion. If you will need special handling of telephone, telex, and fax messages, it pays to tip the responsible personnel in advance, when you explain your needs.

Plane tickets and boarding passes can be issued in hotel lobbies through a new and expanding fax service. Details at 800 322-4448.

The safest place if fire breaks out in a hotel may well be your hotel room. Before opening the door, feel it and the surrounding frame for heat, look at the bottom and through the peephole for smoke, and go outside only if it seems safe to leave. Head straight for the nearest fire exit, which like the exits on an aircraft, you have memorized on arrival. Crawl along the floor if there is a lot of smoke.

Use the stairs, not the elevator. In a fire or other emergency, the elevator may jam or take you closer to the fire, not farther from it. Hotel staircases should be substantially fire- and smoke-resistant and enable you to walk down to an exit.

If it is not safe to leave the room, telephone to let the staff know where you are and to get instructions. If unable to get through, signal from the window for help, but do not break glass, which may fall and injure people below. Also, breaking glass or opening the window may let in more air to feed the flames.

Smoke is your biggest danger, so do everything possible to keep it out. Fill the bath with water and soak towels and bed sheets, which you use to block vents and gaps around the door and to cover your nose and mouth. Shut off the air conditioning. At night check for a candle and matches in the room in case the electricity fails and there is no emergency lighting.

The Insurance Information Institute produces a free leaflet called *Be Fire Smart: Tips for Travelers*. You can get it by calling 800 221-4954.

   A **corporate travel manager** could be a good investment for your organization. Travel and entertainment make up the third largest area of expense that companies can control by efficient management. (The first two are salaries and data processing costs.) An American Express Travel Management Services survey of sixteen hundred companies, governments, and educational organizations found that 30 percent of them added a travel manager to the staff in 1988. Many more are doing so now, as American business is expected to spend over $115 billion on travel and entertainment in 1990 and is looking for the best ways of getting maximum value for money spent.

   The hot line for flight delays and weather updates is 800 USA-2FLY. Operated by the Airline Passengers of America, it provides much information for travelers. Call from a touchtone phone. Key in your membership number if you belong to APA and pay 55 cents a minute, or use your credit card number and pay 75 cents a minute. You must key in the three-letter code for the airport you are inquiring about.

   Telemarketing fraud is a serious problem that has generated a consumer warning from the Federal Trade Commission. The FTC says that the scams take many forms, misrepresent the deal over the phone compared with the fine print of any written follow-up material you may receive, and use high-pressure and time-pressure selling tactics.
   The best defenses:
   • *Beware of great deals that offer too much for too little.*
   • *Resist being pressured into making immediate buying decisions.*
   • *Ask detailed questions about exact costs, extras, cancellations and refunds. Evasive responses are a clear warning of a scam.*

- *Double-check with hotels and airlines in the package.*
- *Do not agree to any deal without acceptable written confirmation.*
- *Do not give your credit card number to unsolicited callers.*
- *Do not send money or give money to a messenger. If the offer checks out as being all right, you still have more rights under the Fair Credit Billing Act if you pay with a credit card.*
- *Check with your local FTC office or Better Business Bureau that no complaints have been lodged against the company making the offer.*
- *If in any doubt, pass the deal by and hang up.*

The basic rule for buying cut-price air tickets from discounters is that as the price gets lower, the chances of problems arising go up. The discounters are consolidators who buy blocks of excess airline capacity and then resell seats below airline rates. While they can offer tickets substantially below the scheduled fares, there are usually many restrictions, and reservations are difficult if not impossible to cancel for a refund. The carrier used may be little known, the consolidator may go out of business, or you may be a victim of bait-and-switch.

Check out any bargain fares carefully and buy by credit card, or if paying by cash or check, hold back a substantial proportion of the cost until you get a confirmed ticket. Some consolidators work entirely through travel agents. They act as wholesalers and the agents as retailers. You should be safe when dealing with an established, reputable travel agent, but the discounted ticket will probably still have many restrictions that may make it not such a bargain after all.

Corporate jets are becoming more popular and have a particular advantage for top executives who are vulnerable to terrorist attack. There are about thirty-five hundred business jet aircraft in the United States. Companies tend to play them low-key for security reasons and in case they are perceived by employees and shareholders as an unjustified management perk. In fact, they can be a good investment. Some have been appreciating in value at 30 percent a year recently. Budget at least $200,000 a year for maintenance, fuel, and aircrew for a corporate jet, but it could still be a bargain in convenience, time saved, security, and confidentiality if used efficiently by key personnel.

An attractive option is for a company to have part ownership of a plane, a form of time-sharing.

Upgrading from coach to business or first class in some frequent-flier programs may be free and automatic on certain flights. If you have to pay, the cost can be considerably less if upgrading is done in advance by phone rather than at check-in.

Leased apartments are saving many companies a great deal of money. Apartments in cities employees have to visit frequently can achieve savings of $70 a day or more over the cost of using hotels and restaurants.

Some of your credit will be frozen immediately when you use your credit card on check-in to guarantee a hotel bill. Even if you settle the bill in cash or by check, it may take two or three days for the frozen amount to be credited to your card account. This may create problems if you are close to your credit limit, and you may have to call the card's issuing bank to sort things out faster.

Hidden cities are a way to cut travel costs if you can exploit a low-price ticket offer to a destination routed with an intermediate stop at the hidden city to which you want to go. Some of these anomalies occur because of hub-and-spoke routing, with which fares do not always correlate to the distance actually covered. You can travel only with carry-on luggage, and the practice is likely to be monitored more carefully because of the need for greater security.

Savings may also be made by taking advantage of special fares to places reasonably close to your desired destination and hiring a car to drive the rest of the way. This technique works best when you want to go somewhere with an airport too small to attract promotional discounts but close to a large center where cheap fares are offered.

One of the cheapest ways to fly is as an air courier. The courier company lets you use a ticket for a fraction of the normal fare and sends its packages with you as accompanied baggage. There are lots of snags, such as lack of flexibility and the fact that you can take only limited carry-on baggage. Many of the courier companies have more volunteers than they need, but by phoning around you may find one that has assignments that fit in with your travel plans. They are listed in the Yellow Pages under Air Courier Services. Some agencies exist to bring volunteers and courier companies together, and some educational centers offer classes in how to be a courier.

Save by going around the world and stopping off in the right sequence at places you want to visit for business or pleasure. There are some great around-the-world fare bargains on offer. The secret is to pick one that offers the stopovers you want. Generally, you can stop over without extra cost as long as you keep traveling in the same direction. Some of the best deals confine your route to one hemisphere or the other.

It is possible to combine the cheap flight with an airline's special deals with hotels on the route.

Airlines are not all the same, and shopping for the differences can add new dimensions to routine trips. For example, in case you are interested in food and movies, some of the national airlines compete most strongly on the gastronomic variety of their in-flight catering and entertainment. Often the national carrier gets the best facilities at terminals in its own country.

Keep all your boarding passes as proof of travel if there are disputes over your frequent-flier mileage credits.

When cashing in your mileage awards, look out for special deals for off-peak times when load factors are low. You may qualify for the trip you want with many thousands of fewer miles.

To find acceptable hotels that are ready to negotiate discounts, look through the brochures of leading tour operators. They will have checked out the hotels in their packages, and although as an independent traveler you will not be able to get their group rates, the chances are that you can negotiate a discount.

You may not find out about frequent-flier special offers—or changes to programs—if you do not remain an active member. You can become inactive if you do not fly for as little as a month. Once you are relegated to inactive status, you may not have a new mileage credit added to your account. In any case, the number of complaints from frequent fliers indicates that there is a high error rate in processing the accounts of program members. Remain inactive for too long in some programs, and you may cease to be a member altogether.

The moral is to keep your own records of mileage flown and credits and bonuses achieved, to challenge any discrepancies promptly, and to keep informed of developments in the programs in which you have a vested interest. One way of keeping up-to-date is to subscribe to a frequent-flier newsletter such as *Frequent,* 800 333-5937, or *The Business Flier,* 203 782-2155.

Add bonus miles by using affinity cards. These credit cards are linked to frequent-flier programs, and they give you mileage credits for every purchase you make. Boost miles also by joining hotel chain frequent-guest programs. Make sure that the benefits to your frequent-flier account are not outweighed by sacrificing value for money in your qualifying purchases.

Be careful when wearing socks or slippers without proper soles if you go to the restroom during a long flight. The floor may well be wet!

Portable office in a bag. Another approach to the portable office packaging problem is to get a specialist company to customize the outfit you need into one fully integrated system. A typical bag contains a choice of laptop computer, ink jet printer, a fully featured cellular phone, and a modem for computing and voice and data transmission. Each component can operate independently, or they are integrated for "one touch" activation. (Details from DS Business Systems, 800 262-2720.)

Eye relief for travelers. The small blinking cursor and type on the typical portable computer screen are not easy to read when working in poorly lit places, such as aircraft, or when the available light strikes the screen at the wrong angle and you are unable to move to a better position. Ken Skier of Massachusetts developed two programs which can help business travelers overcome those difficulties, especially those with vision handicaps already. His No-Squint Laptop Cursor is a utility that enlarges the cursor. His Eye Relief software is the first word processing program that enables you to magnify the type by up to 300%.

There is a bonus for business travelers needing to give presentations. The large type works great as speaker's notes, either printed out or read straight off the screen. In fact, you can use your laptop as a teleprompter.

(Eye Relief costs $295 and you can order or get more details from Ken Skier at Skisoft Publishing Corporation 1644 Massachusetts Avenue, Suite 79, Lexington, Massachusetts 02173, 617-863-1876.)

Keep records to claim travel and entertainment deductions. IRS attitudes as well as the latest regulations make it essential to keep detailed records of travel and entertainment expenses if anywhere near the theoretical deductions are to be achieved. There is a whole new motivation for keeping a comprehensive Traveler's Diary!

One of the best quick references is *The Guide to Travel and Entertainment Deductions* which the Research Institute of America, Inc. produces for its clients. Details from 800-431-2057 or 800-782-8242 in New York State.

How to find out 250,000 different ways to get from Boston to Los Angeles. With no need for a modem, or payment of on-line charges, you can have at your fingertips details of *every* flight option between any of over 200 leading North American cities. For example, on any Monday in 1989, PC Flight Guide software found over 200 practical ways to fly from Boston to Los Angeles—and 250,000 choices if you were prepared to make two stops!

If you travel with a laptop computer, you can use this database to efficiently cope with delays or changes in your travel plans at any time—even stuck in a holding pattern at 30,000 feet.

PC Flight Guide also provides details of aircraft seating, airport parking, business hotels and popular resort and convention hotels in the U.S., Canada, Mexico, and the Carribean; toll-free and local telephone numbers of airlines, car rental and other ground transportation services; visa and passport requirements for every country; 3000 places to have a great business lunch, and much more.

PC Flight Guide was created by Edward J. Kligman, of Irvine, California, who has been a senior computer systems analyst and consultant to most of the major U.S. airlines. The program was created, just like this book, to give frequent fliers practical, unbiased information.

The full PC Flight Guide program is contained on nine standard 5-¼" or five 3-½" diskettes and is updated by mail, monthly from a single diskette. A hard disk and 640-k RAM PC or compatible computer is required. Details from PC Flight Guide, 5 Argent Circle, Irvine, CA 92714, 714 651-9405.

Tether your computer. There are two main theft risks while working on the road—theft of your confidential information or your valuable hardware. One negative effect of better laptop screens is that the data on them can be seen more clearly by other passengers as well as the user. Some frequent fliers who handle particularly delicate information say they have drastically curtailed using their computers in flight and in other public places for that very reason.

One precaution against the physical theft of valuable portable equipment is to tether it to the nearest secure point, e.g., by tieing a laptop to a table. The end of the tether is stuck to the computer with bonding agent similar to that used to glue parts of aircraft together—so it should be strong enough to deter a thief!

An important point to remember with hard disk laptops is that you risk losing data worth more than the machine if you do not keep a separate backup of your files in the event of either theft of the machine, or failure of the hard disk from such routine travel hazards as dropping the computer when rushing to catch a flight. (The portable equipment security kit costs $99 from Traveling Software, 800-343-8080.)

Desk for the car. Using a portable computer in a car is almost as difficult as on an aircraft. One solution to that problem is a desk or workstation base that fastens to the front passenger seat to provide both a working surface and a way of restraining the expensive computer and accessories in sudden stops. The platform swivels to the most comfortable position for operating and both the computer and printer have their own safety belts. (The workstation costs $99 and the printer platform $34.95 from Traveling Software 800-343-8080.)

Turn your hotel room into a window on the world. Frequent fliers who use laptops have found that there is a great way of turning lonely hotel rooms into a window on the world. They use their computers and modems to call up the Laptops Roundtable, a special interest group among the 150,000 subscribers to the GENIE on-line information service. It is run by that doyen of traveling laptop users, Dave Thomas. There are groups also for lawyers, small business owners and other special interests.

GENIE also has the Official Airline Guides, a Travel menu with a Travelers' Information Roundtable, an online travel newsletter, EAASY Sabre's airline and weather database and the Adventure Atlas. This last is an unusual feature enabling you to punch in the criteria for the next trip that you want to take and the program comes back with suggestions.

So, if you are reading this book in a hotel or motel somewhere and feeling really fed up and lonely, get out your computer and modem and call 800-638-8369.

When the connection is made, type **HHH**, which should generate the response **U#=**.

Then enter **XTX99694**, **GENIE**, press RETURN and have your credit card or checking account number ready to sign up.

Or call 800-638-9636 from anywhere in the U.S. or Canada for more information. There are now thousands of databases, bulletin boards, or other on-line facilities. The traveler with a laptop and modem need never be alone!

Get the risks into proportion. When any kind of risk is subject to extensive publicity, it can make us overly anxious about it. That is happening with all the publicity in recent years about aging aircraft, poor maintenance, terrorism, windshear, and other dangers.

In fact, if you took a scheduled air service every day for the thousands of years since we have first dreamed of flying, your risk of being injured or killed in an accident is still infinitesimal—far less than of being the victim of a violent crime or involved in a road accident. The *majority* of the population can now expect to experience those hazards, but only a very small *minority* of us will ever be injured in aircraft—however frequently we fly. The Federal Aviation Authority estimated in 1989 that a passenger boarding a commercial flight has only a one-in-a-billion chance of being killed in a crash.

Index